THE AMERICAN
FIREHOUSE

Country Fire House.

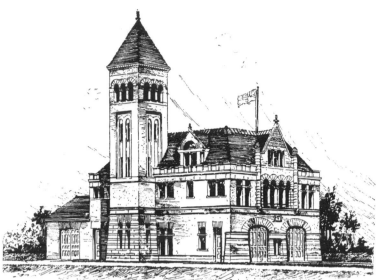

City Engine House.

City Hook and Ladder House.

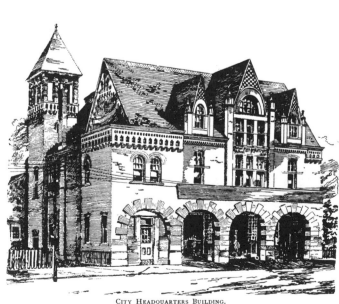

City Headquarters Building.

Types of Modern American Fire Houses.

THE AMERICAN
FIREHOUSE

An Architectural and Social History

by Rebecca Zurier
with Photographs by A. Pierce Bounds

ABBEVILLE PRESS • PUBLISHERS • NEW YORK

FOR OUR FAMILIES

I. Frontispiece: *From* Fire and Water Engineering, *May 1893 (see Chapter Five). In the 1880s, architects first designed different types of fire stations for different neighborhoods. The "City Engine House" is Engine 5 in Columbus, Ohio (see fig. 67), the "Headquarters" is in Fort Wayne, Indiana (Wing & Mahurin, architects), and the "Country Fire House" once stood outside Detroit.*

This book is based on research made possible by a Youthgrant from the National Endowment for the Humanities in 1978. All of that research is now part of an archive at the Library of Congress. Indexed by city and architect, the archive includes photographs and original negatives of about 300 fire stations and documentation for a few hundred more. Readers interested in finding out more about the archive or ordering photographs should contact the Curator of Architectural Collections, Division of Prints and Photographs, Library of Congress, Washington, D.C. 20540. A grant from the National Endowment for the Arts provided funds for new photography and completion of the manuscript in 1981.

EDITOR: *Walton Rawls*

Library of Congress Catalog Card Number: 82-073304

ISBN: 0-89659-314-2   First Edition

Contents

II

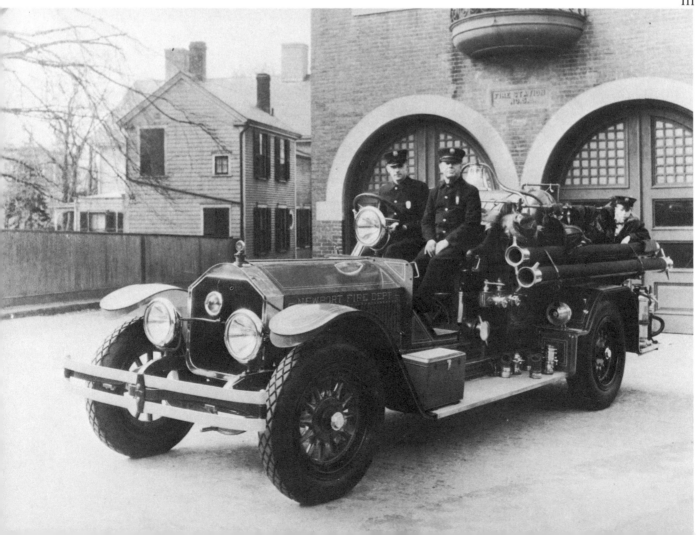

III

Acknowledgments

Over the course of four years and 17,000 miles (twice) one makes a lot of friends. So many people helped with this project that we can never thank them all adequately. Nevertheless, begging forgiveness for omissions, we will begin the list by acknowledging the contributions of Theresa Beyer—trusty driver and steady friend—who participated equally in the original research and travel. Her photographs form the bulk of the archive at the Library of Congress. We both should thank the Beyer family (immediate and extended), all of whom enthusiastically got caught up in the project, including Jeff.

The firemen and fire chiefs in every city we visited (and Pierce revisited) deserve thanks not only for their cooperation but their hospitality. We especially note the help of Chiefs John C. Gerard of Los Angeles, Frank Hanson of Seattle, Elliott Peterkin of East Orange, NJ, and Robert A. Rathman of Cincinnati; Lieutenant Gerald Edwards of Portland, OR, and Captains Richard Blackmon of New Orleans and Jack Hopper of Palm Springs. John McCarthy of the Boston Fire Department offered ideas and encouragement from the beginning. Firefighters Dennis DeLoach (Shreveport), Bob Hesse (Cincinnati), John King (Oakland), Sam Januzelli and Ducky Bonner (Conshohocken), James Staatz (Chicago), and Lee Barringer (Albany) all provided insights and good company, as did the crews at Engine 1 in New Orleans, Engine 18 in Shreveport (including Dee the dalmatian), Fire Stations 14 and 15 in Atlanta, and 30 in Kansas City. The entire Atlanta Fire Department, especially Captain H.

L. Berry, deserves thanks for showing three Yankees the true meaning of Southern hospitality. Retired Chief Steve B. Campbell of Atlanta shared a lifetime's collection of memories and memorabilia. In Denver, Secretary of Fire John Frasco and Chief Myrle K. Wise gave valuable advice and opinions. Richard Sylvia of *Fire Engineering* also shared his expertise.

Glenn Goldwyn, director of Community Development in Cortland, NY, took the time to discuss the politics of preservation on several occasions. We also thank Buffalo's City Architect Ed Linsey, G. R. Bianchi of Washington, D.C., Edward Lewis of the Seattle Buildings Department, and Greg Lathan of Harborview Medical Center in Seattle. Stu Huffman, editor of the *Republic*, offered insights into the untold history of architectural patronage in Columbus, IN.

Inventories compiled by state and local Historic Preservation offices around the country formed the backbone of our original research. Among the preservationists who went out of their way to help were Dan Becker (Sidney, OH), Mary Davis (Albuquerque), Antoinette Downing (Providence), Mark Edwards (Annapolis), John Ferguson (New Orleans), Richard Gipstein (New London, CT), Steve Gordon (Cincinnati), Betty Gould (Mobile), Tom Hanchett and Phil Neuberg (Salt Lake City), Larry Hancks (Kansas City, KS), Roger Hatheway (Los Angeles), John Hearn (Chicago), Terry Karschner (Trenton), John Merritt (Sacramento), Ronald and Cynthia Neely (Georgetown, CO), Sherry Piland (Kansas City, MO), Wally Sedovic and Mark Junge (Cheyenne, WY), Jackson Stell (Montgomery), Hilary Sternberg (Buffalo), Earle Shettleworth (Augusta, ME), John Turnbull (Seattle), and Judith Waldhorn, a kindred spirit in San Francisco.

Many historians in local historical societies and fire museums also provided valuable information, including George K. Bradley (Fort Wayne), Norm Brewer and George Morris (Los Angeles), Ranulph Bye (Doylestown, PA), Caldwell Delaney (Mobile), Lorena

---

II. *Hose Company 8, Newport, Rhode Island, c1890.*
III. *Engine Company 5, Newport, Rhode Island, c1925. In the thirty or so years between these photographs, the fire department of Newport went from horsepower to gasoline power for their vehicles (photographs courtesy of George Pennachi).*

IV. *Fireman Gargoyle. Fire Station 9 (now Prescott Neighborhood Center), Kansas City, Kansas, 1910. William E. Harris, architect. (See also figs. 255–257.) Over the years, architects have felt freer to indulge in whimsy when designing firehouses than any other building type.*

Orvañanos Donohue (Littleton, CO), John Green (Yarmouth, ME), Stephen Heaver, Jr. (Fire Museum of Maryland), Shirley Heppel (Cortland, NY), Byron Johnson (Albuquerque), Catherine Killelea, curator at the Firefighting Museum of the Home Insurance Company, New York, Ken Kroll (South Orange, NJ), Doris Foley Larsen (Nevada City, CA), Steve Plattner and Mary Jane Neely (Cincinnati), Douglas Preston (Utica), Andy Richards (Mobile), T. J. Robinson—senior and junior—in Richmond, VA, Tom Tye at Fireman's Hall in Philadelphia, and Carol Wotowicz of the Mutual Assurance Company in Philadelphia.

For permission to reproduce vintage illustrations we thank the Boston Public Library, the Chicago Historical Society, the Harvard University Libraries, the University of Missouri at Kansas City, the Library of Congress, the National Institute for Architectural Education, the Museum of the City of New York, the Picture Collection and the Research Library at the New York Public Library, the Historical Society of Pennsylvania, the Library Company of Philadelphia, the Insurance Company of North America, the Historical Society of Seattle and King County, the J. B. Speed Art Museum, and the Historical Society of York County.

Librarians were dependably helpful; we especially thank Kenneth La Budde and Gary Moore at the University of Missouri, Kansas City, Dennis Andersen at the University of Washington, Donald W. Fisher, Jr., of Columbus, IN, Adolph Placzek at the Avery Library, Columbia University, the staff of the Louisiana Division at the New Orleans Public Library, and the staff at the New York Public Library.

No worthwhile project could get very far without good meals, warm beds, and good friends to talk with, such as the Blackburn family, Bob and Mildred Bailey, Charly Berger and Sally Brockway, Rick Diamond (our West Coast editor), the Dowben family, Bill Drake and Lyle, Frank Earle, Valerie and Andy Edwards, Chuck Eldridge and Betsy Hodgson, the Frey family, the Gevers, Bob Gardner, Caroline and Lanny Giorgi, Jim McGalliard, Brendan, Curt, and Lesie Greer, J. W. Harrington and the house in Seattle, Joan Marie Hart, the Hermans, Kathleen James, Susan and Palmer and Ana Morrel-Samuels, Vince Patterson, Cousins Nat and Abe Percelay, the Poskanzer family (they earned it), B. J. and Turko Semmes, Betty and Bob Senescu, Diane Sherlock, Judy and Ed Stopke, Barb Tindall, Stephanie and Reese Toothman, Beth and Jack Westney, Judd Williams and Janet McDonnel, Barb and Stuart Williams, Jean and Frank Wetzel, Julie Wortman, all the California Zuriers, and Juli Davidson, who sang for Pierce in Manhattan.

Architects and designers William Burks, Alex Camayd, William Hidell, Ed Milam, Morris Nathanson, Robert Oringdulph, Austin Siegfried, and Forrest Upshaw patiently submitted to interviews; Robert Venturi was especially generous with time and ideas. We also thank the people now living in fire stations who kindly allowed us to poke around: Mark Adams and Beth Van Hoesen, Jim Croak, Charles Dermenjian and Timothy Johnson, Derek Gordon and Sharon Hoffeld at the Arts and Humanities Council of Baton Rouge, Ray K. Metzker, Philip Murthe at the Portland Community Music Center, John, Lynn, and Hillary Schackai, the Shohet family, and Mike Vogel. We all have especially fond memories of Jo Ann Elliott and Rosemary Andriesevic, grandmothers away from home at the Prescott Neighborhood Center.

Historians who kindly answered questions and made their research available included Howard Blyth, Warren Goldstein, Ken Little, Ron Mattes, Robert McCarl, George Pennachi, George Proper, Jr., T. C. Somerville—a most loyal correspondent—and Jim Stevenson. Stan Lokting, Neil Levine, John Stubbs, and the late Bainbridge Bunting suggested useful leads. Teachers, friends, and experts read portions of the text: Jon Roberts, Eleni Constantine, Brendan Greer, Susan Kaplan, Barbara Levine, Paul Lyons, George Proper, and Vincent Scully were thorough and thoughtful crit-

8

IV

ics. To John Coolidge go many thanks for all his tough questions and sound advice.

C. Ford Peatross and Mary Ison have been responsible for seeing the project through the Library of Congress in the best possible humor. Glenn Marcus gets credit for making the Humanities Endowment a good deal more human; Diane Maddex, Judy Sobol, Bob Cavenaugh, Dick Nale, and Tom Sheehan for many kindnesses along the way; and thanks to Ira Bartfield and the photo services staff at the National Gallery. Grace-Ann and Eliot Kone brought the manuscript into order and Walton Rawls edited the book with unfailing good judgment and patience.

The final acknowledgment goes to Cynthia Field, who taught me to look at buildings and who has been a treasured friend, critic, mentor, and role model ever since. Her confidence and high standards have kept this project going through some difficult times. Getting Cynthia to like fire stations has been a worthy challenge.

R.Z.

And thanks to Donna, my wife, who while I was away had to deal with all the hassles of buying our first house, and who spent many hours in the darkroom helping me print the photographs. Unlike Rebecca, I did my 13,000 miles alone, and my calls home from places far away and very different from Carlisle kept me going. Donna was always on my mind.

A.P.B.

V

VI

Introduction

This project began with two buildings and a couple of questions. The buildings stand a few blocks away from each other on North Main Street in Providence, Rhode Island. One is a small, blocky structure of red brick, trimmed in brown and yellow stone with wooden brackets under the roof. With its arched windows and squat tower, it looks like a stumpy Victorian version of a medieval castle. Few people notice the helmet, the number, and the date—1866 —carved into the keystone over the front door, which indicate that this building was once a fire station. Its tower was where the men of Niagara Engine Company 2 used to hang hoses up to dry. The building down the street is also a fire station, built to replace the older one in 1952. Long and low, built of brick without any ornament, Engine 2 / Ladder 7 serves many of the same functions its neighbor once did but in a very different style. While one building was designed to stand out from the others around it, the other offers nothing to remember it by.

Our questions have to do with the meaning behind the buildings: which looks more like a fire station? How are they different? Why the change? Why should two buildings erected by municipal governments to accommodate the same simple function differ so much not only in design but especially in character? The problem becomes more puzzling the more you look at fire stations around the United States. American fire stations include a remarkable variety of buildings of surprisingly high quality. Their designs range from outrageous adaptations of grand European palaces to rambling brick barns to cast-iron storefronts trimmed with gargoyles in the shape of firemen. Many others offer handsome examples of simple, everyday architecture handled especially well. And even though most fire stations built since World War II have followed the uninspired example of Engine 2 / Ladder 7 in Providence, a significant number still stand out as notable, innovative architecture. What is it then about the fire station that has generated such amusing, attractive, original, diverse, appealing, and quirky designs? When did it change? Why?

Traditional methods of architectural history offer only some of the answers. In the history of styles, the early fire station in Provi-

---

V. *Niagara Engine 2 (now Niagara Group offices), Providence, Rhode Island, 1866 (see also figs. 243, 244).* **VI.** *Engine 2 / Ladder 7, Providence, Rhode Island, 1952. Jackson, Robertson and Adams, architects. Two engine houses, built on the same street, show some of the changes the American fire station has undergone in the last hundred years.*

VII

VIII

dence is an example of Victorian taste for warm colors and rich, historically inspired ornament, while the later station's horizontal lines and band of ribbon windows follow the simple geometry advocated by twentieth-century architects working in the International Style. But these descriptions do not fully explain the change in attitude behind the two buildings. Fire stations are not the kinds of buildings that histories of architecture usually treat; their design and requirements have stayed so simple and so constant over the years that they have offered architects little room for creative manipulations of space and form. Because fire stations are usually modest buildings, commissioned by conservative bureaucrats and designed by lesser-known architects, they rarely display the radical innovation found in more symbolically important structures such as skyscrapers, houses, churches, or campus buildings. Fire stations usually reflect existing architectural trends instead of pioneering new ones. The reasons why these buildings look and have looked the way they do have as much to do with social history as they do with architecture. Many factors have contributed to their design.

One important influence is the history of the modern fire department and its administration. Firefighting originally was a community obligation—like nightwatch and jury duty —that was taken over by private groups at the end of the eighteenth century. By the 1850s, the volunteer fire company had developed into a fraternity or lodge, and the volunteers' fire stations were designed to be clubhouses. When municipal governments took control of the fire service after the Civil War, the fire station became a public building and its design and funding reflected political decisions. Some administrations chose to replace the extravagant houses of the volunteer fire companies with uniform, utilitarian structures. Others regarded fire stations as emblems of civic pride. Ever since that time the history of fire stations has been part of the history of public architecture in America.

The shift from private to public fire service also gave rise to the fire station's peculiar program. Once cities began to hire full-time firemen, they had to provide them with a place to sleep. The fire station's requirements became different from those of any other public building: it had to accommodate both men and machines, to include a heavy-duty garage for fire engines and pleasant living quarters for firemen under the same roof. Combining aspects of a garage, a barracks, and a home, it had to be public and private, institutional and domestic, ceremonial and functional all at once. As part of city government, the building somehow had to look more important than the garages where municipal garbage trucks are stored, yet appear less pompous than a city hall and less solemn than a courthouse. These requirements were made even more complicated by the fire station's location and relation to the buildings around it. Fire stations are the most ubiquitous of public buildings—until recently, no community, neighborhood, or section of town could do without one. They had to be designed to serve and fit in with areas

IX

ranging from suburbs to commercial districts, from swank residential neighborhoods to industrial parks. A fire station jammed between office buildings in downtown Philadelphia required a design quite different from one set on the town green in rural Connecticut.

Technology has changed the machinery inside the fire station and the shape of the building itself. Two important developments in firefighting equipment—from hand power to horse-drawn and steam-driven fire engines in the mid nineteenth century, and then to gasoline power before the first World War—have had repercussions on the design of fire stations. When compact automobile engines replaced horse-drawn pumpers and trucks, the fire station shrank, sometimes to the point where it could be disguised as a house in order to "blend in" with newly developed suburbs. In keeping with increasing worries about the hazards of the sliding pole, a change in size often brought a change in floor plan from two stories to one. The telegraph, electric light, and the radio all have affected the workings of fire stations; the periods of greatest change seem to have occurred in the 1880s and after

World War II. Technology also has determined the materials and construction techniques available to architects, an especially important factor in the last thirty years.

The other factor affecting the design of fire stations is the hardest one to define. It has to do with what people think a fire station ought to look like, and how we think about firemen. Beginning with George Washington, an active volunteer, firemen have held a special place in American mythology. The British journalist Charles Mackay put his finger on it when he visited the United States in 1857:

Whatever the Americans are proud of—whatever they consider to be peculiarly good, useful, brilliant or characteristic of themselves or their climate—they designate, half in jest, though scarcely half in earnest, as an "institution." Thus the memory of George Washington—or "Saint" Washington, as he might be called, considering the homage paid to him—is an institution . . . "sweet potatoes" are an institution and pumpkin (or punkin) pie is an institution; canvasback ducks are an institution; squash is an institu-

14

IX. *Detail over apparatus door, Engine 5, Cambridge, Massachusetts 1913. Newhall and Blevins, architects.* **X.** *"The Rescue," from* Harper's *magazine, October 1877. Fire stations are often characterized by a humorous touch, for many architects have enjoyed working "fire-manic" details into their ornament. The image of the fireman as a hero is a strong one that has changed little in the last hundred years.*

tion; and the fireman of New York, a *great* institution.

Since Mackay's time the fireman's image has gone through some changes. Firemen have been seen as rowdies, public servants, skilled professionals, neighborhood friends—but always as popular heroes. The fireman's popularity has made the fire station a place that people like to visit, whether to admire the fire engines or to sit around discussing politics over a cup of coffee. It also has shaped the way architects conceive the buildings themselves. More than merely providing a backdrop, the fire station has come to symbolize the "institution," and the best fire stations have some of that "institution" designed right into them. It sets them apart from every other type of building.

This book's bias is toward traditions, institutions, and fire stations that look like fire stations. The buildings illustrated in it have a kind of character that most recent public architecture lacks. Unlike the average modern municipal building, even the simplest old fire station could be recognized from across the street. In a time when architecture is becoming increasingly anonymous—when schools and banks and gas stations look more and more alike—the qualities that give a building such as the Niagara Fire Station in Providence its distinctive personality deserve more attention. Understanding where that personality comes from might help bring back some meaning into the everyday architecture around us.

X

2. *Relief Fire Station, Mount Holly, New Jersey, c1798.* **3.** *Grass Valley Fire Department, Grass Valley, California, 1974. Oldest surviving fire station in the United States, the Relief's building was used until the company replaced it with a more substantial clubhouse in the 1820s (their "new" quarters are illustrated in fig. 47). Thousands of volunteer fire departments in small towns still use a similar design—in prefabricated steel instead of clapboard (Photographs by Theresa Beyer).*

Before the Revolution there were no real fire departments or firemen in the colonies. Instead, fighting fires was a shared responsibility, just as night watch, militia duty, and maintaining the local roads were. Every citizen was legally obligated to contribute a certain amount of time to each of these tasks, or pay for a substitute. Fire had been a serious problem since the founding of the colonies; in crowded towns of closely built structures, flames might spread rapidly from wooden chimneys to thatched roofs. Therefore, some of the first laws to be passed in American towns regulated the use of fire. As early as 1638 Boston outlawed smoking "out of dores" since "fires have bene so often occasioned by taking tobacco." In 1647, New Amsterdam (the future New York) instituted a curfew that required all fires to be covered between nine at night and four-thirty in the morning. By 1715 it was illegal to carry an open flame in the streets of Boston, or store hay near the hearth in Charleston, South Carolina, or keep a private supply of gunpowder in Philadelphia, or display fireworks in Newport, Rhode Island.

Other laws, such as one passed by the General Court of Boston in 1679, prohibited the use of flammable materials in building. Wooden chimneys were an early target, and Peter Stuyvesant, director-general of the New Amsterdam colony, outlawed them in 1648. By the end of the seventeenth century most sizable communities had appointed "Viewers and Searchers of Chimneys," who were authorized to conduct regular inspections and to slap steep fines on householders whose sooty or poorly maintained chimneys presented a fire hazard. The city government of Philadelphia appointed a public chimney sweep in 1720.

Despite these precautionary laws all the colonial towns suffered major fires. Once a fire was underway there was little anyone could do to stop it; haphazard systems of fire alarms gave most blazes a good head start. To combat this, Peter Stuyvesant established a corps of men in New Amsterdam who patrolled the streets to watch for fires, and they gave the alarm by twirling wooden rattles. Most other cities relied on their regular watchmen to run or ride through the streets shouting the alarm. Bells then would be rung on churches and meetinghouses. In the early nineteenth century, residents of Cincinnati, Ohio, sounded the fire alarm by beating a huge leather drum mounted atop a local carpenter's shop. On hearing the alarm, most of the town's population would turn out at the fire with whatever buckets and ladders they could find. Fire marshals or wardens—"Brent Meisters" in New Amsterdam, "Alcaldes de Carrio" in New Orleans—were either elected or appointed to supervise activity at fires, and they had the power to fine any citizen who failed to cooperate.

Techniques for fighting fire in the seventeenth and eighteenth centuries were simple and none too effective, consisting mainly of dumping water onto the flames. To speed the process, fire marshals directed people at the fire to form two lines stretching from the burning building to the nearest source of water. One line passed leather buckets holding two or three gallons of water to men who heaved

2

3

19

4

their contents onto the flames; the other line, made up largely of women and children, passed the empty buckets back. Other people were given long-handled swabs to beat out fires on shingled roofs. When these methods failed (as they usually did), colonial firefighters used ladders, ropes, and curved iron hooks to tear down burning buildings in order to isolate and contain the fire. The decision to demolish or explode a building rested with the fire marshal or, in Philadelphia, with the justice of the peace.

Would-be firefighters could not always count on a steady supply of water. Before the Revolution only a few cities had waterworks or running water. Most relied on a network of public and private pumps and wells. As late as 1734 a law in Boston required every citizen to keep a barrel of water on his doorstep at night to be used in case of fire. In that year Benjamin Franklin wrote an article in the *Pennsylvania Gazette* complaining of Philadelphia's water supply, "*An ounce of prevention is worth a pound of cure.* . . . It seems to me some Publick Pumps are wanting."

In many colonial towns, individuals were expected to maintain a certain amount of firefighting equipment, not only for their own use but to lend others who fought the fires. In the aftermath of the great fire of 1653, the Boston town meeting ordered that each house be supplied with "a pole of about twelve feet long, with a good large swob at the end of it, to rech to the rofe," and a ladder long enough "to rech to the ridg of the house." In New York, thirty years later, each house with two chim-

neys had to be provided with one leather bucket, each bakery three, and each brewery six. At the sound of an alarm, citizens who could not come running would throw their buckets out into the street for others to pick up. The same sorts of laws came later in the Midwest as towns developed. In 1802 the council of the village of Cincinnati ordered each household paying a rent of $35 or more to keep a leather bucket for use in case of fire. A group of men with a cart and a large willow basket formed the Cincinnati Fire Bucket Company to collect and return the buckets after a conflagration.

Most towns also kept a certain amount of equipment on hand in a central location. The governor-general of New Amsterdam levied a special tax to import 150 leather buckets from Holland in 1658. These buckets were marked with the city's seal and hung outside city hall, the sheriff's house, and several taverns. A year later the city paid a carpenter to construct "a shed to keep the ladders under"—possibly the first fire station in America. The borough of Northampton (now Allentown), Pennsylvania, purchased its first supply of ladders in 1811 and soon had to decree that the ladders "must not be used for anything but fighting fires"— too many people were borrowing them to pick fruit.

With the introduction of fire engines, American firefighting gained in efficiency and sophistication. Once again Boston led the way. When fire destroyed fifty houses in that town in 1678, the aldermen met to investigate importing an engine from England. At that time fire engines were still in the early stages of development and relatively rare. Paris would not have one for another twenty years. The engine sent to Boston consisted of a rectangular wooden tub, about 18 by 18 by 36 inches, with a long-handled pump and a curved wooden nozzle at one end. The box rested on a pair of wooden poles by which two men easily could carry the rig into a burning building. Since there was no hose the engine still required a bucket line to supply it with water. The council hired a company of twelve men and a carpenter to keep the machine in working order and to exercise it between fires. "Ye engine lately come from England" was housed in a small wooden shed next to the municipal prison.

No other American city followed Boston's example until the eighteenth century. By the time Charleston, South Carolina, imported its English engine in 1713, the basic model had been considerably improved. The newer engines were set on wooden wheels and equipped with double-action hand- and foot-treadles that enabled several men to pump up and down together. The leading manufacturer, Richard Newsham of London, advertised "the most substantial and convenient engines for quenching fires which carry continual streams with great force." They came in several sizes, ranging from a "first-size" (for private use) on up. A "sixth-size" Newsham of the type ordered by New York in 1731 measured 6 feet long and could pump 170 gallons a minute in a 40-yard stream. A print from that period shows one of the engines in action: six or seven men are straining at the hand- and foot-pumps while another controls the nozzle that directs a stream of water into the building. A hastily assembled bucket line fills the engine from a nearby well, while other neighbors are puffing up to the line with more buckets.

Philadelphia imported its first engine in 1719. Before long, American craftsmen were constructing their own fire engines. In 1768 Richard Mason, a Philadelphia carpenter, designed an engine with pumping handles located at the ends of the tub rather than along the sides, thereby making it easier for the bucket lines to pour water into the engine. With seven men pumping at each handle the new "end-stroked," or "Philadelphia-style," engine could deliver a steadier stream of water than a Newsham did. As the Revolution approached and Americans became more reluctant to buy British goods, the demand for Mason's engines increased.

The purchase of a town's first fire engine marked a new level of municipal responsibility. Before the Revolutionary War the engines were major investments for towns already strapped by British taxes. A "sixth-size" Newsham cost £70, roughly the price of a first-class slave, or one-third the annual expenses of a family of six. Along with the engine came the costs of paying at least one man to maintain it (£3 per annum in Philadelphia) and of building a shed to house it. While in the past fines collected from violations of the fire-prevention laws had been adequate to pay for a community's supply of hooks and ladders, most cities now had to raise extra money for the new equipment. City officials resorted to levying additional taxes—on land, on buildings, or, in Savannah, Georgia, on hearths. Other towns simply assessed their population for the cost of the new engines. For many years the citizens of Somerville, Massachusetts, refused to pay any more taxes for fire equipment, and thus put off buying a new engine until 1849. In 1791 Savannah got around the problem by holding a public lottery to raise funds for a new engine and house.

For seven years, Philadelphia's fire engines stood out in the open, exposed to the elements, before the city corporation moved to erect a "proper shed" to house them. Other communities acted more quickly in building fire stations to protect their new equipment. Most engines were stored with the local supply of hooks and ladders in or near centrally located public buildings. Philadelphia's "proper shed" stood in the corner of a churchyard. In New York the two Newsham engines were housed in sheds behind city hall. Occasionally the quarters for the engine were combined with space for other civic functions in a more substantial public building, as in the combined fire station and meat market built in 1803 in Salem (now Winston-Salem), North Carolina. Philadelphia's New Market, a two-block-long brick building erected in 1804, included a storage space for an engine in its Head House. The simple wooden fire station (now demolished) in Westminster, Maryland, served a double function without any architectural embellishment. When a townsman became disorderly the engine would be rolled out and the offender locked in.

Owners of property had a vested interest in improving fire protection. Many communities acquired their first fire engines and fire stations from groups of wealthy, public-minded citizens who were dissatisfied with the haphazard fire service provided by the local government. In 1736 Colonel Godfrey Malbone, the wealthiest man in Newport, Rhode Island, presented that town with a Newsham engine. The town in turn appointed nine men to "at any Out Cry of Fire . . . bring out the Engine and attend the Working according to the order of their director." Later the town paid a carpenter £16 to build a shed for the engine. Newport received another engine in 1754 when a group of gentlemen raised a subscription on the provision that the town pay for a suitable engine house. In the nineteenth century, factory towns and newly founded communities from Collinsville, Connecticut, to Stockton, California, received their first fire equipment in the same way.

Interest in protecting property also led groups of prominent citizens to found America's first fire companies. Several cities claim the title of "Birthplace of American Firefighting"; Peter Stuyvesant's Rattle Watch and the crew of men assigned to look after Boston's first fire engine both assumed some of a fire department's responsibilities. The earliest fire companies were private, voluntary associations patterned after those set up in England after the Great Fire of London in 1666. The Boston Fire Association, organized in 1717 as a mutual assistance league, served primarily to protect its members' belongings from theft at fires.

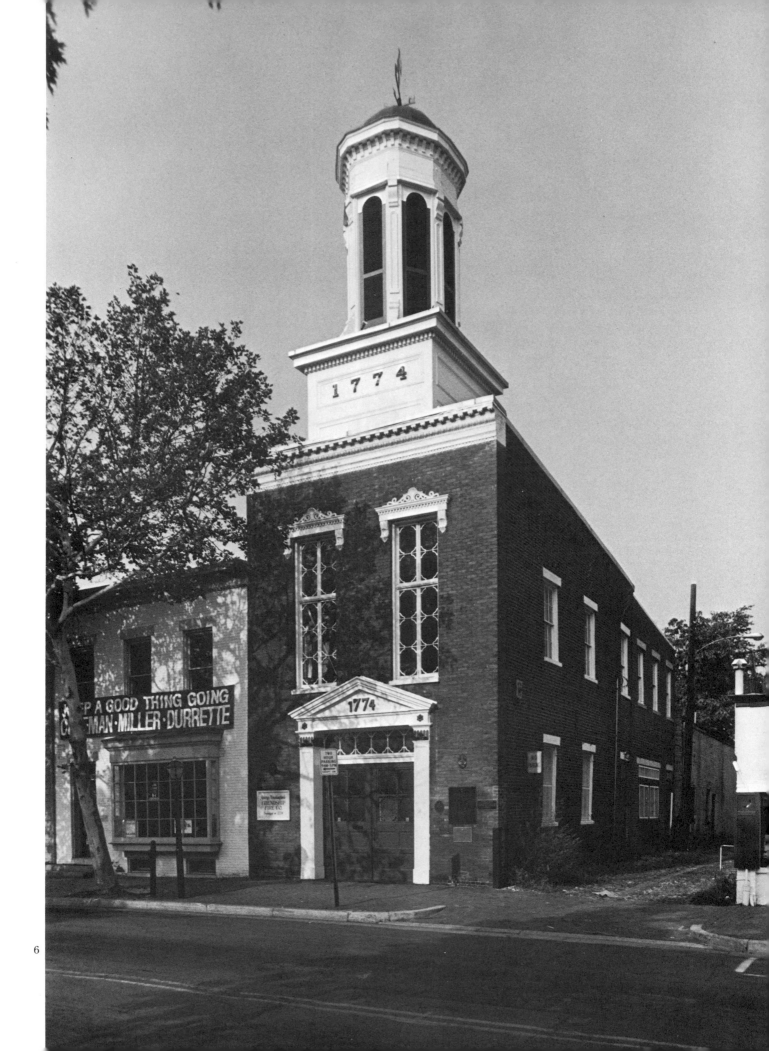

6

6. *Friendship Fire Company, Alexandria, Virginia, 1855. Volunteer fire companies, organized privately by groups of property-owners in the eighteenth century, claimed many prominent citizens as members. George Washington belonged to the Friendship, though he never saw this building—an example of the ornate nineteenth-century architecture discussed in Chapter Two. The original, much humbler structure probably looked more like fig. 2.*

Among its founders were the Puritan minister John Cotton and the merchant Peter Faneuil, who later endowed Faneuil Hall. Each member pledged to report to fires at the others' houses, bringing two buckets and two stout linen bags for salvaging goods.

When Benjamin Franklin inaugurated Philadelphia's Union Fire Company in 1736, he copied the organization of the Boston group but extended its coverage to include more active firefighting. According to Franklin's autobiography: "Our articles of agreement obliged every member to keep always in good order, and fit for use, a certain number of leathern buckets, with strong bags and baskets, which were to be brought to every fire; and we agreed about once a month to spend a social evening together, in discoursing and communicating such ideas as occurred to us upon the subject of fires, as might be useful in our conduct on such occasions." Members who came late or missed a meeting were subject to fines that were used to buy engines, hooks, and other equipment. Similar groups soon formed in other communities. At a meeting in the town hall of Mount Holly, New Jersey, in 1752, the Britannia (later Relief) Fire Company was organized "for the better protection of our own and our fellow townsmen's houses, goods and effects from fire." Its members were required to hang their leather buckets on an outside wall of their houses. The Fire Society of New Bedford, Massachusetts, founded in 1807, also extended its services "to assist not only each other when in danger, but the citizens at large as far as circumstances will admit."

By including the "citizens at large" these private organizations were already assuming public functions.

Since the membership in early voluntary fire associations consisted mainly of people with property to protect, "it was no uncommon thing" in Cincinnati and other towns, "to see the old solid citizens in their broadcloth and gold-rimmed spectacles tugging at the ropes" or pumping away at an engine. Most of the faculty of the College of New Jersey belonged to the fire company in Princeton. After Benjamin Franklin, America's most famous fireman was George Washington, who joined the Friendship Fire Company of Alexandria, Virginia, in 1774. Not only did rich and prominent men take an interest in forming fire companies, their dues and the fines levied on members were so high that less well-to-do citizens could not afford to join. Companies that met at local taverns (as Franklin's Union did) to "spend a social evening together" began to take on characteristics of private societies. New York's volunteers issued elaborately inscribed membership certificates, and in Wilmington, Delaware, the men designed their own red leather hats. As the Revolutionary War approached, fire companies acted as independent political cells. In Boston, the Anti-Stamp Fire Society agreed that if the local Stamp Office caught fire, "they would not assist in extinguishing it."

By 1790 the fire companies were changing the nature of American firefighting by taking it out of the hands of the average citizen. No longer a community chore, firefighting had

7, 8

These are to Certify that *Charles Stewart* is pursuant to Law nominated and appointed one of the Firemen of the City of *New York.*

July 2ᵈ 1787.

Robᵗ Benson, Clk

7

7, 8. *Membership certificates from New York fire companies, 1787 and 1799. By the late eighteenth century, volunteer fire companies were beginning to take on the characteristics of private clubs. Members designed their own uniforms, held regular social meetings, and received elaborate membership certificates. As ornate as a college diploma, the Neptune certificate is decorated with an allegorical picture of the water god surrounded by hoses (Museum of the City of New York, and Picture Collection, New York Public Library).*

9. *Interior, Eagle Engine Company 13, New York City, c 1790. Another wooden shed, but with a difference—the benches, windows, and fireplace are signs that the Eagle company held meetings inside their firehouse. This reconstruction is in the museum of the Home Insurance Company, New York. The engine and most of the equipment inside date from the 1830s.*

THESE are to certify that *Thos Franklin* is pursuant to LAW nominated and appointed one of the ENGINEE Firemen of the City of New York.

Decʳ 30ᵗʰ 1799

Robᵗ Benson, Clk

8

9

become the responsibility of a chosen or self-appointed group of specialists. Town treasuries provided funds for salaries and equipment, but inhabitants were no longer required to turn out for bucket brigades. Those who chose to serve as firemen were rewarded with exemption from militia, watch, and jury duty.

At first this shift in responsibility had no effect on the design of fire stations. Local governments and churches continued to provide sites for engine houses alongside important public buildings. Since the new, private associations held their meetings at nearby taverns and halls, the simple wooden sheds still sufficed for storing their equipment. Though wealthy and socially prominent members of the early fire companies spent considerable sums on engines, dues, and uniforms, they scrimped on their engine houses. Mount Holly's shed was built by a privately organized fire company, as was the slightly larger but equally humble building at York, Pennsylvania, depicted in a drawing from 1799.

1

Another engine house from the 1700s shows changes that were to come in the next century. Built by the Eagle Engine Company 13 of New York in 1790, the station has been carefully reconstructed in the museum of the Home Insurance Company. Like the other early stations discussed in this chapter, the Eagle's is a one-story building of unfinished wood with two large doors at the front. Unlike the other buildings, this one has windows. Further changes can be seen inside, where there is just enough room for a wooden fireplace (technically illegal under New York's building codes at the time) and benches along two of the walls. Members of the company must have sat there after fires, gathered there in their spare time, and perhaps held their meetings inside this wooden shed. The windows, benches, and fireplace signify an important change in attitude: once the firemen moved their activities inside the fire station the building became more than "a shed to keep the ladders under." The fire station was on its way to assuming a new architectural stature, and a new role in the community.

9

HIBERNIA FIRE ENGINE COMPANY. N°1.
OF PHILADELPHIA.

CHAPTER TWO

The Volunteer Fire Station in Its Heyday

1825–1865

When Benjamin Franklin founded the Union Fire Company in 1736, he had two purposes in mind: mutual assistance and social intercourse. By the early nineteenth century, social aspects of firefighting had become every bit as important as public safety— maybe even more so. From an association organized to realize a practical goal, the volunteer fire company developed into a kind of club that was part athletic team, part secret society, and part fraternity. Almost everywhere the annual firemen's ball was a major social event, and in Mobile, Alabama, the fireman's day parade rivaled New Orleans' Mardi Gras.

Firemen themselves enjoyed a new standing in their communities and a new role as national heroes. In songs, artwork, and plays, The Fireman took his place alongside Plymouth Rock and pumpkin pie as what the British journalist Charles Mackay termed an American "institution." References to fires and firemen turn up over and over again in

documents of the 1840s and '50s, and several foreign visitors published accounts of New York City fire companies in books about their travels in America. The volunteers' fire stations were becoming architectural statements of all that the "institution" had come to stand for. From lowly beginnings as a storage shed, the volunteers' fire station grew into something grand.

The last chapter mentioned that groups of property owners in the eighteenth century, dissatisfied with the protection offered by their local fire laws, had banded together to form their own mutual aid societies. The city of Philadelphia dismantled its municipal watch system and turned fire protection over to privately organized companies, and other communities followed this example. The ordinance passed by the St. Louis Board of Aldermen in 1825 is typical: "Resolved, that the citizens be and are hereby empowered and authorized to form themselves into fire companies, one company in each ward, as soon as fifty [members] shall subscribe their names, a meeting shall be called and officers appointed." Companies were approved one by one, as they formed: "Whereas, an association of the Middle Ward styled the Phoenix Fire Company have submitted a constitution and by-

10. *Hibernia Engine Company 1 assembled outside its firehouse in Philadelphia, c1857. Part lodge, part athletic team, and part militia, the volunteer fire company became an important social institution in the nineteenth century. Ornate fire stations with luxurious clubrooms inside were part of the companies' regalia; their design was a matter of pride (Historical Society of Pennsylvania).*

laws, therefore, be it resolved that this board do approve the constitution so subscribed and constitute the same as a Fire Company for said ward, and said company shall have charge of the engine now in the market house." Local governments organized the individual companies more or less loosely into volunteer fire departments, and reserved the right to incorporate the companies officially and to restrict their size. Some cities appointed a number of fire wardens to direct the volunteers at fires.

Provisions of any kind for public safety were irregular in the eighteenth and early nineteenth centuries—no American city organized a police force before the 1830s—and the administration and funding for fire protection varied widely from community to community. Along with exempting firemen from road taxes, militia service, and jury duty, most municipal authorities supplied volunteer fire companies with engines and a certain amount of equipment; some took charge of building firehouses or appropriated land and funds for them. Many cities followed the example of the eighteenth-century English police system that paid officers by reward instead of a fixed stipend. Boston offered a premium of fifteen dollars to the first company that put water on a fire, ten to the second, and eight dollars to all others that responded to the alarm (the city also allotted each fire company money for a yearly banquet). Mobile's fire companies received no set allowance from the city fathers, but asked for funds as they needed them.

New York City's firemen demanded and received a number of extra perquisites from the city, including a yearly clothing allowance for their children. Their colleagues in Boston had less luck trying to win larger appropriations from the local government. In 1825, when Mayor Josiah Quincy turned down their request for a $50 banquet budget, all the firemen went on strike—the first firemen's strike in history. The next day, Mayor Quincy, one of the first great municipal reformers, signed on twelve hundred new firemen and reorganized the department under one chief, who diplomatically declined the offer of a salary.

Cash bonuses from insurance companies provided another way for the volunteer companies to supplement the money they collected from dues, fines, and donations. The Philadelphia Contributionship for the Insurance of Houses from Loss by Fire, an association formed by Benjamin Franklin and a group of friends in 1752, was the first successful fire insurance company in America. Like the Union Fire company, it was patterned after the English agencies organized after the great fire of London, and like the English police system it offered protection on a fee-for-service basis. Once a subscriber's house passed inspection (Franklin's experiments with lightning prompted him to deny insurance to houses with trees nearby), it would be marked by a lead plaque with the company's emblem of four clasped hands. This "firemark" warned would-be arsonists that the house was insured, and told firemen that the Contributionship would pay a reward to the company putting out a fire there. Not only did a firemark encourage firemen to give their all in competing for the insurance company's payment, it also helped to guarantee that the house would be protected, since firemen were less inclined to save a burning house that had no firemark.

By the early nineteenth century the fireman's equipment had changed considerably. Buckets and wells hardly were used at all; most cities had underground water mains and regular fire hydrants. In the late eighteenth century, when they needed water in a hurry, firefighters had dug down to the nearest wooden water pipe, chopped a hole in it, and then stopped it up after the fire with a makeshift peg or "fireplug." When Philadelphia opened its extensive waterworks in 1801, the chief engineer commissioned a local foundry to cast a set of T-shaped fixtures that had a fitting for hose on one end and a drinking faucet on the other. These were the first true fire hydrants, and other cities quickly copied them.

Improved water supplies called for improved hose. The seams on the leather or linen hose used in the eighteenth century burst easily under stress, and in 1808 the Philadelphia firm of Sellers and Pennock introduced leather hose with copper rivets that could withstand the powerful pressure from hydrants. The fifty-foot lengths of hose could be coupled together and wound onto reels, which were wheeled to fires. New hose led in turn to the development of "hydraulions"—engines that used suction to pump water quickly. Now, instead of relying on a bucket brigade to dump water into a "tub" engine, firemen could set up a series of engines connected by hose lines to pump water from a distant cistern or hydrant.

The English traveler Captain Basil Hall described the new, more sophisticated equipment in use at a fire in New York City in 1827:

I succeeded by quick running in getting abreast of a fire-engine; but although it was a very ponderous affair, it was dragged along so smartly by its crew of some six-and-twenty men, aided by a whole legion of boys, all bawling as loud as they could, that I found it difficult to keep up with them. On reaching the focus of attraction, the crowd of curious persons like myself began to thicken, while the engines came dashing in amongst us from every avenue, in the most gallant and business-like style.

Four houses, built entirely of wood, were on fire from top to bottom, and sending up a flame that would have defied a thousand engines. But nothing could exceed the dauntless spirit with which the attempt was made. In the midst of tremendous noise and confusion, the engines were placed along the streets in a line, at a distance of about two hundred feet from one another, and reaching to the bank of the East River. . . . The suction hose of the last engine in the line, or that next the stream, being plunged into the river, the water was drawn up, and then forced along a leathern hose or pipe to the next engine, and so on, till at the tenth link in this curious chain, it came within range of the fire. As more engines arrived, they were marshalled by the superintendent into a new string; and in about five minutes after the first stream of water had been brought to bear on the flames, another was sucked along in like manner, and found its way, leap by leap, to the seat of the mischief.

A Currier & Ives lithograph from 1854 shows the kind of activity that Hall described at its height: the firemen already have pulled their huge, "Philadelphia-style" engines up to the burning building and connected lines of hose to hydrants. The foreman stands at the center, ordering the companies into position and shouting directions through a metal speaking trumpet. To help the engine companies keep up the rhythm of pumping (sixty strokes or more per minute), he calls out orders in cadence, like a sea chanty. Hosemen ply the water streaming from the nozzle onto the flames, and at the cry of "Men up to the roof!" ladder companies scale the walls. At the right, an anxious mother raises her arms in distress while a ladderman rescues her child from a third-story window.

Up through the 1820s, most fire companies continued to hold their meetings in taverns, rented halls, and private homes, and to store their equipment in simple sheds. In the late twenties and thirties, some cities began to build more substantial stations for the volunteer fire companies. Most of the new buildings had meeting rooms upstairs and a basement for storage. Fire companies in Savannah, Georgia, and Baltimore, Maryland, opted for two-story buildings of red brick, but Boston's Mayor Quincy, after reorganizing the fire department in 1825, commissioned a granite-fronted engine house "on the model of the Choragic

monument at Athens." Unfortunately, no picture of this building, which overlooked the harbor on Pemberton Hill, has survived. It was probably the first fire station designed to satisfy the taste of wealthy neighbors. Quincy explained:

> The Committee of the City Council selected sites for engine houses; not on the principle of economic and temporary expediency hitherto chiefly regarded, but such as were best adapted to facilitate easy communication with the most exposed or populous parts of the city. . . .
>
> The cost of this edifice [$2,300 for the building, $3,000 for the lot] was justified, in the opinion of the city government, by the circumstances under which the improvement had been effected; [and] by the satisfaction of a building so ornamental to the street gave to the proprietors of estates in the vicinity, who had objected to the erection of an engine house in their neighborhood.

Along with providing more space for the engine company it housed, this building marked a new stage in fire station design. Possibly for the first time, people were thinking of the fire department as a separate organization, worthy of its own quarters, and of the fire station as a monument in itself.

The choice of prototypes was an apt one. By the 1820s, architecture based on classical Greek models was the accepted style for any important American building. Architects and

11

laymen alike associated Greek architecture with the heritage of democracy and considered it a fitting style for a culturally independent nation; its popularity increased during the Greek struggles for independence from the Turks in the 1820s. The taste for monumental buildings with simple forms coincided with the development of the granite industry and helped to bring a new air of dignity to all kinds of public buildings. The Choragic monument also was the model for the cupolas on the Philadelphia Exchange building, the Tennessee statehouse

12

12. *Perseverance Hose Company, Philadelphia, Pennsylvania, c1830.* 13. *Spring Street Elementary School and Fire Station (now a fire museum), Portland, Maine, 1837.* 14. *Washington Fire Company 8 (now a roofing supply warehouse), Mobile, Alabama, 1851.* 15. *Narragansett Engine 3 (now a fire museum), Warren, Rhode Island, 1846–47.* 16. *Sacramento Engine 3 (now a restaurant), Sacramento, California, 1853 (photograph by Theresa Beyer). Early nineteenth-century fire stations gained a new stature as public buildings in their own right. Greek Revival architecture, with its associations with ancient democracy and modern government, gave these buildings a civic respectability. Builders adapted the basic shapes of a Greek temple's columns and triangular pediment in different materials as the style spread throughout the United States: granite in Maine; brick, wood, and wrought iron in the South; stucco in California; clapboard in New England. The Narragansett engine house originally was painted white, to suggest marble.*

13

15

16

14

17

18

at Nashville, and scores of churches.

The political symbolism of the Greek style made it especially suitable for the new Federal office buildings designed for Washington, D.C., and for local governmental edifices such as the female elementary school and engine house opened in 1837 on Spring Street in Portland, Maine. The building included an engine room and meeting room in front, a wardroom at the back, and a spacious classroom upstairs. This combination of functions might sound a little odd, but all three—public education, voluntary associations for public safety, and open political meetings—were considered uniquely American phenomena. The French observer De Tocqueville cited these three activities as examples of democratic developments that had no precedent in Europe.

When the building opened, the local papers boasted of Portland's free schools: "They are spacious, comely, ornamental, almost vying in magnitude with the temples consecrated to the worship of God. . . . The skill and care evident to the most careless observer convinced us that the supervisors of our public schools consider no money wasted that goes to promote common education among us." The building's stone front, one of several built in Portland after the opening of the Kennebunkport granite quarries in 1835, follows a simplified Greek order that architects often used for massive commercial buildings like the Quincy Market in Boston. The *Portland Daily Eastern* described the Spring Street building as "in a style of architecture substantial and pleasing"—fit terms for a small building that

housed three democratic institutions.

Fire stations in other parts of the country show how the Greek Revival eventually spread out from northeastern cities to become America's first truly national style. Where granite was not available, local builders adapted the forms to cheaper materials. Arriving in New York in 1831, De Tocqueville had remarked on seeing this: ". . . at some distance out from the city, a number of little white marble palaces, some of them in classical architectural style. The next day, when I looked more closely at one of those that had struck me most, I found that it was built of whitewashed brick and that the columns were of painted wood. All the buildings I had admired the day before were the same." And were it not for the remote location, one of those "little palaces" could easily have been a fire station. By 1851, when the quarters of the Washington Engine Company 8 opened in Mobile, a generation of Southern plantation owners had been building brick mansions in a similar style, with columns of painted wood. As architects and pattern books traveled west, buildings such as Sacramento's Fire Station 3, a stuccoed brick engine house that opened in 1853, were among the first permanent structures to be built in towns that had sprung up during the Gold Rush.

Elements of the Greek style also found their way into the more humble work of amateur architects. A white stucco front and a set of wooden columns were meant to bring some of the dignity of the Parthenon to downtown fire stations like the Perseverance Hose Company of about 1832 in Philadelphia. Carpen-

37

19

ters translated the style into simple clapboard houses and churches by turning the traditional frame sideways to the street, so that the gable end looked like a triangular pediment. The Narragansett engine house built in 1846–47 in Warren, Rhode Island, is an example of the kind of wooden fire station erected in small New England towns throughout the nineteenth century (like most of the others, it originally was painted white). Traces of the New England vernacular tradition live on in the Georgetown, Maine, substation designed by a local architecture student in 1977 and put up by people who live in the neighborhood.

By the time most communities built their first Greek Revival fire stations, volunteer fire companies were taking on many characteristics of exclusive clubs or fraternal organizations. Members had to apply to get into them, and all kinds of distinctions of class and status determined who could join. The fire companies in Mobile, Alabama, were patterned after the mystic societies that sponsored Mardi Gras festivities, and a prospective fireman had to be nominated by members of the company, be approved in secret balloting, and pay a hefty initiation fee and dues. Even today in towns like New Bern, North Carolina, where volunteer companies continue to use a nineteenth-century ballot box, an unpopular candidate still can be literally "blackballed."

Ambitious young fellows would choose a fire company carefully, since the most elite group could provide valuable social contacts. Merchant's Engine Company 4 was one of the wealthiest in Mobile, and Cincinnati's "Rovers"

were known also as the "Silk Stockings." Many a political career was begun in a volunteer fire company—the first foreman of the Metamora Hose Company was elected mayor of Chicago. Boss William Marcy Tweed of New York parlayed the alliances he made as a member of the Americus Engine Company 6 into a powerful political base in Tammany Hall; he chose for an emblem the tiger that originally graced his old outfit's fire engine.

Like lodges or clubs, fire companies often restricted their membership to one ethnic group. Milwaukee's Germania Company 2 was organized in 1840 to protect the neighborhoods where German immigrants lived. Philadelphia had both a Quaker company—the Harmony Hose, formed in 1784—and an Irish one. Members of the Hibernia Engine Company 1, established in 1752, wore green uniforms decorated with the company emblem of an eagle perched on a harp. Both New Orleans and Mobile had Creole engine companies by the 1820s. Mobile's company limited and defined its membership strictly: "That class of person commonly known as Creole, who by the Treaties between France and Spain and the United States were regarded therein as citizens of the United States . . . in contradistinction to any other persons of Color or mixed blood." In keeping with the tradition that later gave birth to New Orleans jazz, Mobile's Creole fire company arranged elaborate funerals for its members. The company's minute books record payments to bands hired to play in the funeral processions.

Fire companies in Southern cities were

racially segregated, though not always voluntarily. Slaves could be imprisoned or fined for failing to assist at fires. All-black companies such as Savannah's Tomo-chi-chi Engine 7 (whose membership included both slaves and free men) were required by law to have a white foreman. White fire companies in Charleston, South Carolina, received sixteen dollars an hour while working at fires in 1849, but black companies were expected to serve without pay. In 1825 the city council of Savannah, Georgia, passed a law requiring all black firemen to wear specially marked hats, and white companies petitioned later to prevent them from wearing uniforms.

While prominent citizens, professionals, and merchants continued to support volunteer fire companies after 1800, they usually held the title of honorary or "exempt" members. The roll of Philadelphia's Perseverance Hose Company in 1842 was typical: out of 110 members, 57 were honorary and 13 were contributing. An average of 15 "active" members turned out at fires. The actual firefighting was more often done by middle- or working-class members—tradesmen, shopkeepers, laborers, and artisans—some of whom formed their own companies, such as the "Mechanics" of Louisville. Mountain towns like Georgetown, Colorado, were an exception; since most of the men there worked in the mines during the day, the doctors and lawyers with offices in town fought the fires. In other cities, working-class men joined volunteer fire companies for their own reasons. They were willing to risk their lives fighting fires without pay not because

they had property at stake (most paid no taxes), or out of a sense of civic duty, or even just for the social advantages, but because they enjoyed it. As one engine company's motto claimed, "Our Duty is Our Delight."

Even the philosopher Henry David Thoreau could take time off from his studies to divert himself at a blaze. This passage from *Walden* describes a fire that probably took place near Concord, Massachusetts, around 1840:

Breed's hut was standing only a dozen years ago, though it had long been unoccupied. . . . It was set on fire by mischievous boys, one Election night, if I do not mistake. I lived on the edge of the village then, and had just lost myself over Davenant's *Gondibert*, that winter that I labored with a lethargy—which, by the way I never knew whether to regard as a family complaint . . . or as the consequence of my attempt to read Chalmers' collection of English poetry without skipping. It fairly overcame my Nervii. I had just sunk my head on this when the bells rung fire, and in hot haste the engines rolled that way, led by a straggling troup of men and boys, and I among them foremost, for I had leaped the brook. We thought it was far south over the woods,—we who had run to fires before,—barn, shop or dwelling-house, or all together. "It's Baker's barn," cried one. "It is the Codman Place," affirmed another. And then fresh sparks went up above the woods, as if the roof fell in, and we all shouted, "Concord to the rescue!" Wagons shot past with furious speed and crush-

39

ing loads, bearing, perchance, among the rest, the agent of the Insurance Company, who was bound to go however far; and ever and anon the engine bell tinkled behind, more slow and sure, and rearmost of all, as it was afterward whispered, came they who set the fire and gave the alarm. Thus we kept on like true idealists, rejecting the evidence of our senses, until at a turn in the road we heard the crackling and actually felt the heat of the fire from over the wall, and realized, alas! that we were there. The very nearness of the fire but cooled our ardor. At first we thought to throw a frog-pond on to it; but concluded to let it burn, it was so far gone and so worthless. So we stood round our engine, jostled one another, expressed our sentiments through speaking trumpets, or in lower tones referred to the great conflagrations which the world has witnessed, including Bascom's shop, and between ourselves, we thought that, were we there in season with our "tub," and a full frog-pond by, we could turn that threatened last and universal one into another flood.

In the days before baseball gained widespread popularity, firefighting served as one of the first American team sports. It offered risks, excitement, and the chance to show off physical strength before an admiring crowd. Members of a fire company had to work together as a team and, as with athletic teams, companies competed against each other. What began as an effort to win bonuses from insurance companies grew into a matter of honor.

No company wanted to arrive last at the fire, or to appear less brave than the others. Firemen raced each other to the scene, dragging their heavy engines and hose reels behind them, trampling any pedestrians or animals that got in the way. Hose companies would send runners ahead to hide the fire hydrant from others until they got there, or hire thugs—the original "plug uglies"—to "guard" the hydrant and ward off rivals. The greatest indignity an engine company could suffer was a "washing," which happened when another company pumped water into their engine tub faster than they could pump it back, resulting in an overflow. The only way to save face after such a disgrace was to "wash" the next engine in line. As taunts flew back and forth and rivalries developed into feuds, the competition grew more violent. Arguments sometimes turned into fights at the scene of a fire (see Chapter Three).

Volunteer fire companies took the matter of names and nicknames as seriously as clubs or athletic teams would. New York City companies devised some of the most colorful nicknames, including the Black Joke, the Red Rovers, the Honey Bees, and the Shad Bellies (named for the time the volunteers pushed their burning fire engine into the East River and jumped in after it). Other groups carried on the eighteenth-century tradition of patriotic names such as Union, Eagle, Columbia, Liberty, Franklin, and Washington. Names with allegorical reference to water—Neptune, Torrent, Niagara, Cascade, Oceana—were popular for engine companies. Some New

20

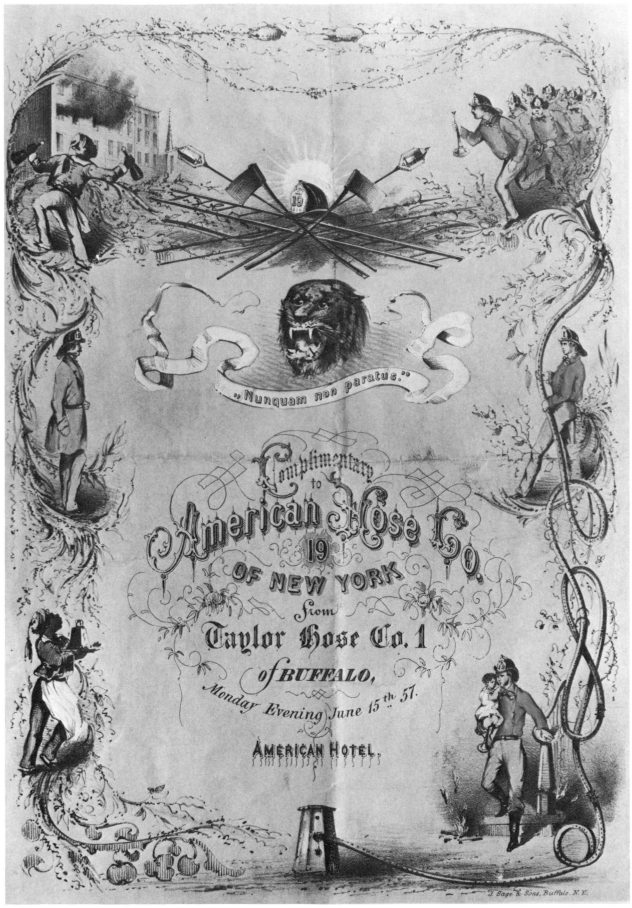

"Nunquam non paratus."

Complimentary
to
American Hose Co.
19
OF NEW YORK
from
Taylor Hose Co. 1
of BUFFALO,
Monday Evening June 15th '57.

AMERICAN HOTEL,

J. Sage & Sons, Buffalo, N.Y.

England companies chose local Indian names. High-flown names like Vigilant, Perseverance, Invincible, Defiance, Friendship, and Good Intent glorified the work of the firemen. And so did the company slogans: "The Public Good Our Only Aim," "When Help Calls It is Our Duty to Obey," "Fearless of Danger." Cincinnati's Rovers proclaimed, "Our War is with the Elements!"

Ritual and ceremony played an important part in the activities of fire companies of the 1830s, '40s, and '50s. The volunteers made firefighting into not just a job to be done but an activity worth celebrating in its own right. Not content with the equipment provided by the city government, firemen spent their own money to embellish the tools of their trade. The gray, standard-issue fire engines were painted over with stripes, scrollwork, and gilt-lettered inscriptions. The condenser cases on "Philadelphia-Style" engines formed a square box that made a perfect setting for oil paintings. John Vanderlyn, Thomas Sully, and John Quidor were among the major American artists who supplemented their incomes from more lofty work by painting panels for fire engines. Companies would pay up to $1000 apiece for depictions of classical scenes (usually featuring undraped goddesses), historical events (scenes from the Revolutionary War were especially popular), or portraits of military heroes. Spectacular blazes and pictures of firemen making dramatic rescues were also favorite subjects. Firemen first added bells and lanterns to their engines for safety reasons, but soon these too were dressed up with silver and brass. Hose wagons and ladder trucks offered fewer surfaces to decorate, but hose reels could be made to look like chariots. Some sported silver nameplates and ornamental sculpture cast in bronze.

Uniforms were another source of pride. After 1830 most firemen had two sets, one for work and one for show. Early nineteenth-century firemen protected themselves with leather top hats and short canvas capes, both of which could be brightly painted. The traditional working outfit of double-breasted red shirt, black tie, black trousers, and boots was introduced by New York's Protection Engine Company in 1840. The leather helmet with a decorative shield in front and an elongated brim behind goes back to an 1828 design by New York fireman Henry Gratacap, and it is still in use today. Firemen ornamented brass shields and belt buckles with their company's name and insignia, and their dress uniforms (worn at meetings, parades, and musters) could be as elaborate as imagination and money allowed. The men of New York's Jefferson Engine Company chose blue capes and trousers to match their fire engine.

Firemen turned out in full regalia for the ceremony known as "visiting," an early version of the business or political "convention," in which one fire department would play host to other fire companies for a few days of business and pleasure. A typical visit began with a triumphal departure from the engine house, with bands playing and banners (presented "on behalf of the female friends of the company") waving, and a march through the city to the

20

rail yards or docks. There the engine would be loaded onto a special car or stowed in a steamboat, and the company would embark. On arriving, the visitors would be met by a delegation of firemen from the host city and paraded to their quarters. Like most conventioneers, visiting firemen usually were put up at the local Grand Hotel. The next few days were spent in a round of receptions, processions, and endless collations ("wine and toasts passing freely around"). The highlight of any visit was the "muster" at which companies competed with each other to see whose engine could pump the tallest stream and which hose company could lay a line in the shortest time. The winners received elaborate trophies.

On a trip to New Orleans in 1842, members of Mobile's Phoenix Fire Company were treated to an evening at the St. Charles Theater, featuring "a 'Fireman's Address' and a 'Fireman's Song' written for the occasion." In three days they attended four banquets, including one with the "municipal Authorities," and "stopped to comply with invitations to drink from a number of the New Orleans Companies." The excursion would end with another parade, as the hosts escorted their guests to the dock or station, and there was more music and fanfare when the visitors arrived back home.

Visiting companies usually exchanged mementos, ranging from commemorative prints to silver punchbowls and trophies decorated with miniature replicas of ladders and helmets. One of the most popular testimonials was a full-size pewter or sterling silver speak-ing trumpet, engraved with suitable messages and adorned with a silken cord. Not only could these presentation pieces be displayed proudly at later visits, they also could be corked at one end and filled with champagne. The Washington Hose and Steam Fire Engine Company 1 of Conshohocken, Pennsylvania, still keeps an impressive collection of nineteenth-century trophies in display cases at their fire station.

Once the volunteer fire companies started functioning as clubs, members began to spend time at the station between fires. Some buildings included a bunk room where members could spend the night to be on hand if an alarm came in (there are a few reports of entire families moving into the engine house). More often, members just dropped in to socialize. The upstairs rooms that previously had been used only for scheduled meetings now became club lounges. The apparatus floor remained a plain, garage-like space, as the heart of the building moved to the sitting room. Off-limits to the general public, this room was the inner sanctum of the volunteer fire company—a place where all the fraternal activities were enshrined. Trophy cases, banners, and company portraits usually lined the walls, and easy chairs and card tables were arranged around the room. Firemen could gather here to receive visiting companies, or get away from the rest of the world.

No doubt many of these sitting rooms, like neighborhood saloons, matched the description a fireman gave of a small-town Rhode Island station in the 1920s: "It was a place where the men could spit on the floor and not

22

get yelled at, drop ashes on the floor, and go home only when the supply of coke brought for the evening had burned out." But in cities where the volunteer fire companies assumed a more formal role, firemen would spend as much of their own time and money as they could to make these rooms places of splendor —often far more palatial than the men's own homes. Early newspaper accounts that survive from the 1850s compare firemen's parlors to European clubs, and even Europeans were impressed. "The parlors are fitted up with a degree of luxury equal to that of the public room of the most celebrated hotels," observed the Englishman Charles Mackay on his visit to New York in 1857:

> At one of the central stations . . . the walls were hung with portraits of Washington, Franklin, Jefferson, Mason, and other founders of the republic; the floor was covered with velvet-pile carpeting, a noble chandelier hung from the centre, the crimson curtains were rich and heavy, while the sideboard was spread with silver claret-jugs and pieces of plate, presented by citizens whose houses and property had been preserved from fire by the exertions of the brigade; or by the fire-companies of other cities, in testimony of their admiration for some particular act of gallantry or heroism which the newspapers had recorded.

Visitors in other cities described reading rooms, billiard tables, and gilt-framed oil paintings. In St. Louis the engine house of Union Company 7, built in 1847 at a cost of $5,000, boasted frescoed ceilings and a floor-to-ceiling stained glass window.

As they did in most matters of ritual, the firemen of Mobile, Alabama, gave their buildings an extra touch of class: instead of having parlors they had ballrooms that opened out onto balconies. The ballroom of the Washington Engine Company 8, the only one from 22 its period to survive intact, is decorated with wooden door moldings that were meant to recall the entrances to Greek temples. This tradition of sparing no expense for interior decoration peristed in Mobile until well after the Civil War. The minute books of the Creole Engine Company record the lengths firemen went to in outfitting their engine house built in 1870. A separate committee on interior decoration was formed to investigate prices, and the Ladies' Committee held a fair to raise money for furniture. The entire company voted on a motion "that the Company have on the globe of the Chandelear [sic] the words 'Go Ahead' between the word 'Creole.'" And they did it all over again eight years later. At that time the room was redecorated and fitted with custom-monogrammed window shades and purple velvet carpets. In June of 1878 the hall committee reported, "it affords your committee pleasure now to present you with the most tastefully painted and finely furnished house in the department."

A number of stations that survive in New Jersey and Pennsylvania show how volunteer firemen decorated their parlors at the height of the Victorian era. Visitors to the Washington

23

24

25

26

23, 24. *Trophy case, and upstairs parlor, Washington Hose and Steam Fire Engine Company 1, Conshohocken, Pennsylvania, 1878.* **25, 26.** *Bunkroom, and trophy case, Laurel/Rex Fire Station, York, Pennsylvania, 1877–78. Beaton Smith, architect.* **27, 28.** *Chandelier, and podium, table, and chairs, Laurel/Rex Fire Station, York, Pennsylvania, 1877–78. The tradition of fitting out the volunteer fire station's upper stories as clubrooms continued after the Civil War. All the furniture, including the Washington Company's custom-made mirror frames decorated with hydrants, is original. The trophies were collected as prizes at firemen's musters or as gifts from visiting companies.*

brate with them. One hundred thousand people turned out to watch the Philadelphia Fire Department on the centennial of Washington's birth. Firemen in Mobile marched to welcome Henry Clay to their city in 1843, and they draped their engines in black crepe on the death of Andrew Jackson. When New York's fire companies decided to honor the Marquis de Lafayette with a parade on the occasion of his return to America in 1824, the general was obliged to stand in front of City Hall for hours, saluting and being saluted by every man who marched by. The firemen concluded a similar parade for the Prince of Wales in 1860 by inviting the honoree for a night of carousing. (He accepted.)

New York's firemen's parades may have held the record for length, but Mobile's set the standard for glamor. In that city, the anniversary of the founding of the fire department on April 9th was observed as a public holiday, and until the 1870s the annual Fireman's Day parade was a gala celebration. As with the later Mardi Gras revelry in New Orleans, numerous firemen's fancy dress balls were held weeks in advance of the great event. For the parade, fire companies bought new uniforms, hired marching bands, and decorated their engines with banners, flowers, and trophies. Some commissioned professional stage designers to concoct floats based on allegorical themes. To symbolize "Fidelity" in the 1875 parade, members of the Phoenix company covered their four-ton steam fire engine in white satin and dainty blue ribbons, built a canopy over the driver's seat, and placed a "most

exquisitely chiseled figure of a female figure caressing a little dog" above the smokestack. These doings always received copious coverage in the local press, and attracted spectators from all over the South.

The fireman's ball was another company function that involved the community at large. Begun as a way to raise money for new uniforms and buildings, it became an annual social event. For a ball held to benefit the Providence (Rhode Island) Fire Department's pension fund in 1877, the sponsors commissioned a complete program of dance music, including such numbers as "304 Alarms Last Year" (a quadrille) and the "Every Man With an Axe Waltz." Other departments started community traditions in the nineteenth century by sponsoring breakfasts, oyster suppers, levees, and "smokers." Conshohocken's Washington Company still drapes its station with bunting and holds a benefit picnic on the Fourth of July.

By the 1830s, fires themselves were becoming a form of popular entertainment. About the time that Thoreau was "running with the machine" in Concord, the New York diarist George Templeton Strong, then a student at Columbia College, described a fire in the city:

It's very amusing to note the view the loaferage (i.e., the majority of the lookers-on at fires) take of the subject. They consider it a sort of grand exhibition (admission gratis) which they have a perfect right to look at from any point they like and to choose the best seats to see the performance; the interests of the owners never seem to enter their heads, and any attempt to keep them back, or to keep a passage open, or any other effort to save property by which their freedom of locality or locomotion is impaired, they consider an unwarrantable interference, of course. . . .

Strong also was an avid "looker-on," as his diaries reveal:

February 3: . . . After tea went to the office and began to dip into Graham. Another alarm of fire, and as it seemed rather long and loud, I shut Graham and cleared out. Fire in Gold Street from Ann to Beekman, in a large six-story cabinet warehouse and manufactory extending from one street to the other. . . . This was not one of the gunpowdery, irregular, flashy fires that have been so common of late, governed by none of the acknowledged rules of the art, but a good, steady, old-fashioned conflagration, in which the dramatic interest was well-sustained throughout, and fire and water were "head on head" till the grand finale when the walls tumbled down in various directions with a great crash, and then fire triumphed, which as the hero of the piece it was very proper and perfectly regular that it should do. On the whole, this was a very fair fire. I'm getting quite a connoisseur.

April 16: . . . Quite a respectable fire in Water Street near Old Slip at five o'clock. Saw the new Philadelphia engines in action.

They are cumbrous, unwieldy things with their two ranks of pumpers (like a double-banked galley), but they throw glorious streams of water, and throw them with ease, over the roofs of the highest stores. I suppose they require each about thirty men, and probably two ordinary engines to keep them full. This was a dry-goods store, and all of it that wasn't burnt must have been soaked by the Philadelphia deluge. . . .

June 6: . . . I'm deuced lame and sore and stiff just from taking hold of an engine a little on Friday night. It's grand exercise.

Disasters held as much fascination in the nineteenth century as they ever did, and American families hung Currier & Ives prints of Great Conflagrations on their living-room walls. But for the people who turned out to watch fires in the 1840s and '50s, fire was not always "the hero of the piece." The actions of the firemen could be the most entertaining part of the show. The analogy with athletic events comes to mind again: firefighting was similar to a team sport not only for the "players" but for the spectators as well. Like sports fans, admirers would adopt fire companies and root for them as they competed at the fire, and sometimes firemen played to their audience. Basil Hall complained in 1827: "The chief thing to find fault with on this occasion, were the needless shouts and other uproarious noises, which obviously helped to exhaust the men at the engines, and the needless forwardness, or it may be called foolhardiness, with

32

33

32. *Torrent Engine Company, Boston, Massachusetts, 1859. John Roulestone Hall, architect.* **33.** *Phoenix Fire Company 6 (now fire museum), Mobile, Alabama, 1859.* **34.** *Steamer 5 (now fire museum), Richmond, Virginia, 1849. Rebuilt in 1863. The warm tones, heavy overhanging cornices, and rich carving of the Italianate Style offered architects a decorative alternative to the Greek Revival's severe lines. It proved especially popular for houses and commercial buildings. The Friendship Company of Alexandria, Virginia, and Philadelphia's Hibernia 1 (figs. 6, 10) were especially flamboyant examples.*

34

which they entered houses on fire, or climbed upon them by means of ladders, when it must have been apparent to the least skillful person, that their exertions were utterly hopeless." Young boys were the most devoted hangers-on, but not the only ones. The most famous fire enthusiast (or "buff") of the nineteenth century was the San Francisco socialite Lillie Hitchcock Coit, who began going to fires with the Knickerbocker Engine Company 5 when she was a girl. As an honorary member of the company, she wore a gold "5" pin until the day she died. In her will she left money to the city to build the Coit memorial, a 540-foot tall observation tower in the shape of a fire nozzle, on the top of Telegraph Hill.

In time, public enthusiasm went beyond an interest in fires and parades to an all-out glorification of The Fireman. Songs, stories, and plays celebrated his exploits with all the fulsome oratory of the day: "No body of men is entitled to deeper gratitude than that which bares its bosom to the fiery element, standing forth like the remnant at Thermopylae, the protectors of a community, if not of a nation. In time of war the cause of the masses is that of the individual, and the compact of defense is mutually binding, but not so with the fireman, who battles oftener for others than for himself. . . ."—and on and on. Popular illustrations such as Currier & Ives' series of scenes from the life of a New York City fireman helped bring the now-traditional images of the fireman ("Always Ready" and "Prompt to the Rescue") into thousands of homes, and into the national mythology. Of all the nineteenth-century trib-utes, Walt Whitman's lines in *Song of Myself* (written in 1855) have probably lasted the best:

I am the mash'd fireman with breast-bone
  broken,
Tumbling walls buried me in their debris,
Heat and smoke I inspired, I heard the
  yelling shouts of my comrades,
I heard the distant click of their picks
  and shovels,
They have clear'd the beams away, they
  tenderly lift me forth.

I lie in the night air in my red shirt, the
  pervading hush is for my sake,
Painless after all I lie exhausted but
  not so unhappy,
White and beautiful are the faces around
  me, the heads are bared of their
  fire-caps,
The kneeling crowd fades with the light
  of the torches.

But Whitman's description of a wounded fireman was unusual. Audiences at the time preferred a less vulnerable kind of hero, such as "Fire-fighting Mose," a character based on a notoriously rowdy New York fireman. Mose first appeared on stage in 1848, as an incidental figure in a play called *A Glance at New York*, and went on to achieve the same legendary status as Brother Jonathan, Paul Bunyan, and Davy Crockett. Like the heroes of tall tales, Mose was larger than life. Six feet tall, with a shock of red hair, he "loved that ingine better than his dinner," and battled fires with prodigious strength. Nearly every play ended with a conflagration scene, where actual engines would be wheeled on stage. As a typical "Bowery b'hoy," Mose was usually "bilein' over for a rousin' good fight with someone somewhere"; he wrestled bears and Indians, but mostly he brawled with rival firemen. His most famous line—"Get off dem hose or I'll hit yer wid a spanner"—was repeated by schoolboys everywhere. Of course, beneath the bluster, Mose had the obligatory heart of gold: "The fireboys may be a little rough outside, but they're all right here [touching breast]. It never shall be said dat one of de New York boys deserted a baby in distress."

Mose enjoyed phenomenal popularity; *A Glance at New York* was one of the most successful plays in the history of the New York stage, and over the next twenty years audiences from Montreal to San Francisco enjoyed his adventures. The character inspired twenty-three more plays, a ballet, and several circus acts. He traveled to China, visited France, panned for gold in California, and fathered a cigar-smoking son, Master Mose. In his own words, Mose was truly "far-famed and world renowned."

The "institution" that developed in the 1840s and '50s was an unusual one; the fireman was a heroic and brave figure in poems and legends, but he also lived in every community. Many poems compared firemen to soldiers, but firemen were more admirable than soldiers. They fought no human enemy; their goal was to save lives. Even more popular than the illustrations showing firemen in action was the picture of a fireman rescuing a fainting woman or returning a baby to its mother's arms. The fireman was seen as more self-sacrificing than a soldier, especially since he risked his life to save others without getting paid. Volunteers took pride in that image, and in years to come would refer often (in debates over establishing paid fire departments) to their "cheerful performance of our arduous duty without any compensation except that of the grateful feeling of our fellow citizens." (See Chapter Three.) "Public Servants, Not Hirelings" was the motto of one engine company in St. Louis.

But the fireman had his less heroic side, too. Mose spent as much time beating up other firemen as he did saving babies—and people loved him for it. Despite the flowery poems, firemen were not supposed to be sentimental sissies. Violence was part of the institution. In fact, because of the way firefighting functioned as a spectator sport with competing teams, people even expected to see a certain amount of brawling at fires in the 1840s. The closest parallel today would be with football or hockey players, whose fans allow for some fighting as part of the game.

Moreover, no one who watched a fireman's parade would believe that these heroes were entirely selfless; they clearly enjoyed everything they were doing. With their decorated equipment and their clublike organization, the volunteer fire companies of the nineteenth century turned an activity that had been a chore into a privilege, a game, and a sacred rite. Their ceremonies and pageantry set

firefighting apart from other civic duties that also had begun as shared obligations. Night watchmen were never known to ornament their alarm rattles, and road duty never inspired a play. Volunteer nurses earned everyone's respect, but they never had dances named for them. Even the police, who also have been thought of as heroes, never enjoyed the same widespread appeal. However, in the last fifty years policemen have inspired many more movies, stories, and television shows than firemen have— perhaps their work involves more moral conflicts. The fireman's job may be too predictable. But some of the difference in the way people perceive the two functions probably goes back to the heritage of the volunteer fire companies and their clublike activities. There never was an equivalent stage in the development of the police department, which grew out of the system of wardens and constables appointed to supervise watch duty, without going through a volunteer phase. Police work always seemed more serious, and nobody ever volunteered to be a policeman for the fun of it.

Keeping the unique character of the "institution" of nineteenth-century firefighting in mind, we can understand why the volunteers often built themselves unusual or eccentric fire stations. It was not just a matter of having the most comfortable and luxurious little building they could afford; firemen wanted their quarters to look more elaborate than the neighboring buildings but to stand out as well. Like the character of Mose, the volunteers' fire stations were larger than life. Because volunteer firemen saw themselves both as members of a private fraternity and as public figures, they treated their buildings as a kind of public statement, an architectural slogan or motto for the entire city to see. Just as volunteers paraded on the Fourth of July, they also proudly flew American flags from their fire stations. And for related reasons, fire stations that volunteers built for themselves usually displayed more signs and insignia than municipal buildings such as the Spring Street elementary school and engine house in Portland, Maine.

The Portland city fathers had elevated the fire department there by housing it behind the same kind of dignified facade used for important public buildings. Volunteer fire companies, on the other hand, tried to make their fire stations look different from any other type of building. Fire stations designed to recall the noble associations of the Greek Revival dressed up that style's severe lines with decorative molding and fancy iron grillwork. Engine companies in St. Louis topped their temple-fronted fire stations with ornate cupolas, one of which was crowned with "a figure half fish, half human, the idea being taken from the 'Tower of the Wind, Athens.'" A shift in taste that began in the 1840s brought new possibilities for flamboyant decoration as architects dissatisfied with the pristine white surfaces and rigid symmetry of the Greek revival turned to more "picturesque" Italianate styles. Using brick and brownstone they designed warm-toned buildings heavily ornamented with carvings, moldings, and cast iron. The former Torrent Company 6 built by the

42

32-34 city of Boston in 1848 shows a restrained use of the new ideas; Mobile's Phoenix Engine House and Steamer 5 in Richmond have the flat roofs supported by heavily carved brackets that are typical of the "Tuscan Villa" style.

10 A picture of the Hibernia Engine Company of Philadelphia assembled outside its quarters in 1857 shows the decorative effect at its most extreme. Compared to the houses next door, the narrow front of the engine house had enough brackets, scrolls, and fancy moldings to decorate an entire office block—or a theater marquee. Its sumptuousness is matched only by the decoration of the engine (note the painted panels on the sides) and the firemen's dress capes. As the company prepares to leave for a parade, silver trumpets and axes in hand, the neighbors lean out from their windows to gape. Also at the scene are the company mascot (posing solemnly near the engine) and three boys who try to look nonplussed but probably are awestruck at the combined magnificence of men and machines. The building that formed a backdrop for this splendid scene remained to remind people of it once the company departed. Anyone walking by would realize that the men who occupied the edifice thought pretty highly of themselves.

The new engine house built in 1855 by the Friendship Fire Company (George Washington's old outfit) of Alexandria, Virginia, still stands today and reveals that company's pride in its colonial heritage. All the overblown rhetoric of a toast at a fireman's banquet is reflected in the ornate facade, emblazoned with 36 "1774." The former Hope Hose Company in

Philadelphia is another fine example of a building that shows off. The lively, rich, and entertaining cast-iron front marks it as a building with some special kind of function (even without the twentieth-century paint job). And once the building has your attention, the giant fire hydrant built into the cornice tells you what its function is. The terra cotta lions' heads that adorn the Royal Fire Station in York, Pennsylvania, do somewhat the same thing. These buildings were meant to be just as idiosyncratic as the volunteers' uniforms, and like the uniforms they were meant to identify their owners.

Not only did volunteer firemen treat their fire stations as company emblems, they also carried company rivalry into their architecture. For example, the Gold Rush town of Nevada City, California, had two principal streets a block apart, whose merchants competed for prominence. Instead of cooperating on a network of fire protection, the Main Street faction installed a standpipe and organized its own fire patrol in 1852; the "Broad Streeters" responded by erecting a row of brick buildings they thought would never burn. When a bad fire in 1859 proved otherwise, the Broad Streeters' wives sponsored a ball and a theatrical performance to raise money for a fire station. Both factions then organized fire companies within a day of each other, but since the Main Street crew filed their papers first they won the distinction of calling themselves Nevada Hose Company 1. Their rivals already 37, 38 had cash in hand, however, and proceeded to build the town's first fire station—Eureka Hose Company 2—on Broad Street in 1861. Even

37

37. *Eureka Hose Company 2, Nevada City, California, 1861.* **38.** *Nevada Hose Company 1 (now historical society museum), Nevada City, California, 1861. Tower added 1880. Fire companies in Nevada City extended their rivalry to their buildings. The Number Two company had the more impressive engine house until 1880, when Number One added its gingerbread roof.*

though this one building probably could have protected all of Nevada City's tiny commercial district by itself, the Nevada Hose Company opened its own fire station a few blocks away on Main Street three months later. Eureka responded by erecting a 96-foot-high flagpole in front of their building and designing their own American flag (with the stripes the same but the stars forming a pyramid). One after the other in the 1870s, both companies embellished their stations with bell towers. The Nevada company eventually "won" with its marvelous gingerbread roof. This building was made over into a museum in the 1960s, leaving the number two station with the title of "Oldest Fire Station in Continuing Use," an honor the fire department still jealously defends.

The spirit of rivalry may also explain why the most ornate volunteer fire stations seem to have been built in clusters. Most city governments had no control over the location of fire stations (Boston was an early exception), and some sections ended up overprotected. As in Nevada City, there were parts of St. Louis, Philadelphia, and New York where the volunteer companies all chose to build miniature palaces within a few blocks of each other. The distinctive examples that survive today are mainly grouped within a few cities: Cortland, New York, has two fine old volunteers' halls; Mobile has three; York has two of the fanciest; Carlisle, Pennsylvania, has two; and Philadelphia at least four. It may be that once a city had one volunteer fire station worth boasting about,

39

40

41

VIEW OF THE UNITED STATES HOSE HOUSE & APPARATUS, PHILADELPHIA.

To the INDEPENDENT FIRE CO. of BALTIMORE & the FRANKLIN FIRE CO. of WASHINGTON, this print is respectfully dedicated, (as a slight token of appreciation of their generous hospitality)

by the UNITED STATES HOSE CO. of PHILADELPHIA.

42

43

every company that built subsequently tried to outdo it.

Towers gave the volunteer companies more ammunition for their architectural war. The principal reason for adding a tower to a fire station was not for a watchpost—which the city would maintain at central locations—but to provide a place to hang up hose to drain and dry. Leather hose rotted if not properly cared for, and firemen tried various ways to preserve it. For a time, Philadelphia's Humane Hose Company stored theirs in a pickle barrel. The most common system was to stretch the hose out on wooden racks, as Boston firemen did in the basement of the station on Pemberton Hill in the 1820s. Since so few records survive, it is hard to tell where or when the idea of hanging hose vertically originated, but some of the cupolas on fire stations built in the 1840s in St. Louis and Philadelphia may have been used for that purpose. By the fifties, towers equipped with pulleys, ropes, and hanging hooks were regular features at the back of buildings like the house of the United States Hose Company in Philadelphia. As this print from 1855 shows, the tower also could double as an auxiliary observation post or belfry.

Although these structures originally were built to serve a practical function, like towers on medieval palaces they offered another way to fly an architectural flag and call attention to the building from far away. Towers were often the most decorated part of the fire station. The one built by the Independent Fire Company of Baltimore in 1853 was especially spectacular; modeled after an Italian *campanile*, it transformed a simple brick engine house into a local landmark. The Alpine Hose Company of Georgetown, Colorado, achieved almost the same effect with simpler materials in 1880, when a local mining magnate offered to buy the company a bell if they would build a suitable tower to house it. In time, the tower became one of a fire station's typical identifying features (the oversized door was another). Playing up the tower architecturally was not only a way to call attention to the building but to make it look like a fire station. In the 1920s, however, when fire chiefs wanted fire stations to "blend into" residential suburbs, the first design change they made was to hide the tower.

When the volunteers decided to turn their fire stations into company symbols, local architects were ready to show them how to do it. Although there is no way of knowing who came up with the idea of building a sign into the top of the Creole Company's engine house, or who chose the ornament for the front of Hibernia Company 1, it seems safe to say that the firemen and the architects were probably of the same mind. Architects no doubt shared the enthusiasm for the "institution" of firefighting that poets, illustrators, and everyone else felt in the mid-nineteenth century, and they expressed some of that enthusiasm in their designs for fire stations. Like the institution itself, these buildings were pompous and ceremonial, but also flamboyant and fun. Fire stations like Philadelphia's former Hope Hose Company have an architectural exuberance not found in more solemn types of buildings.

ENGINE HOUSE

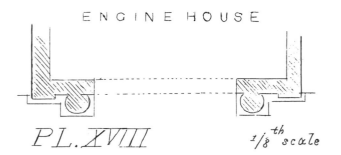

PL. XVIII $\frac{1}{8}^{th}$ *scale*

One architect spelled out his ideas about The Fireman explicitly. In 1853, when Mose was at the height of his popularity, Marriott Field of New York published a book entitled *City Architecture; or Designs for Dwelling Houses, Stores, Hotels* with the aim of "offering to the Architect, Builder and Capitalist, a variety of novel designs." His proposal for an engine house is one of the most elaborate in the book, far more fanciful than the dignified, classical façades he recommended for banks, houses, or even the "ice-cream saloon." Field's eloquent explanation of the design marks him as a man of his time:

 44

> We have here selected for our subject an engine-house, of which the general specimens are little superior to stable-buildings; and, by the addition of Sculpture . . . we have endeavored to compose something like an adequate architectural tribute to the meritorious Fire Department. . . . The appropriateness of the flame at the top of the pediment, the trophies of caps and trumpets, and the oak-leaf crown, the Roman award for saving the life of a citizen, will be readily appreciated. The lion's head, in the keystone, was emblematical of water among the ancients, and used for waterspouts on their temples; their most rainy period being when the sun was in the constellation of *Leo*. The *alto-relievo* represents a fireman just descended from the ladder, after having rescued an infant, and restored it to its mother's arms. Should such a design as this be erected, it would not be long before some

44

44. *Engine House from* City Architecture *by Marriott Field, 1853.* **45.** *Chief Director of the Mechanic Fire Company 1, Louisville, Kentucky, c1840 (J. B. Speed Art Museum).* **46.** *Fireman's Hall, New York City, 1856 (Museum of the City of New York). In his book of designs for urban buildings, Field recommended treating the fire station as "an architectural tribute to the meritorious fire service." Though no architect followed his advice to the letter, many did in spirit by adding "firemanic" ornament to their buildings. The eight-foot-tall wooden statue, painted like a cigar stone Indian, once graced the roof of a fire station in Louisville. Fireman's Hall, built as the central clubhouse of New York's volunteer fire department and later its headquarters, is still standing in lower Manhattan and slated for restoration as a fire museum.*

45

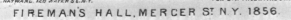

FIREMAN'S HALL, MERCER ST. N.Y. 1856.

46

RELIEF
1752   1892
1

47

48

47. *Relief Engine Company 1, Mount Holly, New Jersey, 1892.* **48.** *Decorative panel from the Emerald Hose Company, Cortland, New York, c1885. The taste for allegorical ornament continued in a more restrained way after the Civil War. Mount Holly's weathervane is shaped like a fireman's speaking trumpet; the plaque at Cortland is said to represent a fire god.*

similar instance of heroism might demand and obtain a similar monument; justly bestowed on those

Qui sui memores alios fecere merendo.

Who by desert have won a glorious name.

The design he illustrated is a perfect reflection of the institution it was meant to house. The ground floor is similar to one he recommended for a "Club-house or Private Mansion," while the upper-half with its sculptural group set into an arched niche looks something like his design for a theater. The two floors are joined and surrounded with an extra helping of "pleasing and characteristic embellishment."

No one fire station seems to have followed Field's recommendations to the letter, but many did in spirit. Whether or not they took the matter as seriously as Field did, other architects seem to have found a special pleasure in turning traditional ornament into the kind of symbol that later aficionados would call "firemanic." Just as Benjamin Latrobe had designed columns decorated with corncobs and tobacco leaves for the United States Capitol, now fire hydrants were sculpted in wood and buildings were trimmed with carvings of hooks and ladders. Some fire companies in St. Louis crowned their Greek Revival stations not with figures based on classical models but with life-size statues of firemen. The house of the Franklin Company 8 had a heroic sculpture of Franklin flying a kite on its roof.

An eight-foot tall painted wooden statue that once marked the house of the Mechanics Fire Company 1 in Louisville, Kentucky, luck-

ily has been preserved. This impressively bewhiskered "director" had a pivot in its knee-joint, so that firemen who climbed up onto the roof of the station could turn the figure around to point the way to a fire. The tradition of folk sculpture was carried on with the weathervanes shaped like trumpets and axes that volunteer fire companies placed atop the towers of their stations in the 1870s and '80s.

The architects of later fire stations went in for slightly more restrained decorations, like the plaques at the Emerald Hose Company in Cortland, New York, showing fire gods, dolphins, and a fireman rescuing a woman. Although this kind of motif originally was limited to volunteers' fire stations, by the late 1870s carvings of helmets and equipment were also built into fire stations designed for paid departments. Architects at the turn of the century sometimes preferred more allegorical references to fire and water (see Chapter Five), but as late as the 1930s some still could sneak fireman gargoyles into both "moderne" and "colonial" stations (see Chapter Seven).

Even without specific references such as keystones in the shape of lions' heads, the volunteers' fire stations of the 1840s and '50s effectively acted as symbols. Marriott Field's idea that a fire station could be designed as an "architectural tribute to the meritorious Fire Department" is an important one: it shows how closely architects, firemen, and the public associated the buildings with the "institution." As the social function of the volunteer fire company was to undergo major changes in the next fifteen years, the buildings would too.

CHAPTER THREE

Steam Engines, Paid Departments, and the "Storefront Style"

1853–1885

The bucket brigade, the hose line, and the hand-drawn, hand-pumped wooden engine were among the least efficient means conceivable for putting out fires. Yet throughout the 1840s and '50s, a time of remarkable mechanical and technical innovation in many fields, firemen adamantly stuck to these gimcrack arrangements. And while volunteer fire companies acquired increasingly elaborate engines, built more and more extravagant firehouses, and paraded about in ever-more outlandish uniforms, they failed with increasing frequency to stop the big fires that plagued America's growing cities.

By the 1850s popular enthusiasm for "the noble fireman" was waning; the public was disenchanted as much with the volunteers' bad manners as with their inefficiency. Though tradition-bound firemen violently resisted any suggestion of change, a fortuitous sequence of events finally enabled city officials to put the old volunteer establishment out of business.

---

49. *Truck 2, Chicago, Illinois, 1872. Storefront stations, erected by municipal building departments after city governments took over the fire service in the mid-nineteenth century, replaced the ornate structures of the volunteer fire companies. Designed to fit into crowded downtown commercial districts, their simple facades carried a symbolic, "no-nonsense" message.*

The invention of the horse-drawn steam fire engine and the ensuing system of municipally paid and administered fire service began a new era of professionalism in the history of firefighting and indirectly brought about new standards in the design of firehouses.

If not for the stubborn conservatism of the volunteers, change might have come sooner. New techniques had been available for some time: as early as 1829 a British engineer, George Braithwaite, had invented a steam fire engine capable of pumping water at twice the rate of a hand pumper. In 1841, a coalition of New York City fire insurance companies commissioned a steam engine ("the Exterminator") that shot a 166-foot stream of water over the top of the City Hall flagpole. Nevertheless, no volunteer company could be persuaded to use the invention. Firemen considered the very idea of employing mechanical assistance an insult to their manhood. In the 1820s Boston's firemen even resented using hose, preferring the danger of working in close to the flames. As one fireman explained, "the nearer the fire, the higher the post of honor."

For a similar reason firemen defended their "right" to haul the heavy apparatus to fires by hand. Before the 1850s the only time a company had used a horse-drawn engine was

50. *Fireman's Hall (now Stadium Restaurant), Cortland, New York, 1875. A. J. Lathrop, architect. Storefront fire stations were patterned after commercial architecture, with little of the flamboyance that had characterized the stations of the volunteers. Now that its apparatus doors have been covered over, this former fire station is almost indistinguishable from the buildings around it.*

51. *Ladder 122 and Engine 220, Brooklyn, New York, 1883 and 1907. The city of Brooklyn erected nearly a dozen identical fire stations in the 1880s. This simple structure was enlarged with the addition of a second building next door in the twentieth century.*

50

51

during an 1832 cholera epidemic in New York City, when the Mutual Hook and Ladder Company, its ranks severely weakened by disease, bought a black horse to pull its truck. Even under these extreme circumstances their fellow New York firemen sneered. One night a rival company stole into the Mutuals' stable, shaved the horse's tail and mane, and painted a skunklike stripe down its back. For the next twenty years, no fire company in New York or anywhere else dared hitch its engine to a horse.

What finally unseated the volunteer system and its methods was a combination of political and social pressure that grew as citizens became increasingly dissatisfied with the volunteers' behavior. As related in the last chapter, by the 1840s and '50s many volunteer fire companies had developed into social clubs. Fighting fires was merely one of the volunteers' concerns; at times, balls, parades, and "visiting" parties were equally important. As membership in fire companies changed from municipal leaders ("men in gold spectacles") to a younger, less savory crew, the new generation of firemen treated the job of putting out fires as a sport rather than an obligation. Like the character Mose, or the boys who had run along to watch the excitement Thoreau described, they regarded fires as opportunities to show off strength and derring-do: hence the volunteers' strong resistance to horses or any mechanical device that might upstage the firemen.

The fire station itself was changing from a private club to more of a neighborhood saloon, a place to stop by, to meet friends, and to socialize. In large cities firehouses began to attract gangs of young toughs (not always firemen) who gathered to carouse in the clubrooms or roam the streets looking for a fight. Chicago's volunteer quarters provided "a place of refuge for a floating, shiftless class, too often of a criminal tendency." In 1853, a Cincinnati newspaper deplored the situation: ". . . hordes of young brawlers and rioters . . . boys who had much better be at school, or learning some useful vocation, than clustering in crowds around the various engine houses, annoying the neighbors, and insulting every female who may chance to pass, with gross and indecent language."

This rowdy behavior soon spread beyond the firehouse and played on ethnic hostilities. In 1837 a scuffle between a Boston fireman and a recent Irish immigrant gave way to a riot in which volunteer fire companies ransacked the houses of neighboring Irish families. A few years later Philadelphia's Moyamensing Hose Company set fire to a tavern and hotel owned by blacks, then fought off with guns and axes the police and other fire companies who responded to the alarm.

The traditional rivalry among fire companies became more like gang war. In the preceding decades, people had grown accustomed to the sight of buildings being left to burn while opposing companies fought with each other to put "first water" on the fire. Now these set-tos erupted with disturbing frequency into full-scale riots that injured bystanders and killed more than a few firemen. Rival fire companies no longer limited their brawling to the scene of fires: on quiet nights one company might attack another's quarters, set off a false alarm, or even start a fire to stir up some excitement. Editorials in newspapers complained that firemen considered themselves beyond the control of the police.

The fires themselves were getting more serious. In 1835, a terrible fire in lower Manhattan destroyed an area of 17 blocks—the largest urban conflagration since the Great Fire of London. Over the next twenty years, crowded and newly built commercial and downtown districts across the country suffered disastrous blazes that volunteer firemen could or would do little to stop. The Great Pittsburgh Conflagration consumed 900 buildings in 1845; thirty-nine people died in a fire in Albany in 1848; In 1850, 600 buildings were destroyed in one night in Philadelphia. As property owners paid for inefficient fire service through rapidly rising insurance premiums they looked less kindly on the volunteer fire companies' escapades.

Meanwhile, fire companies demanded and received more pay for their services than ever before. Reports from New York and St. Louis indicate that firemen in those cities solicited "donations" from insurance companies and from "the grateful public"—we can only guess whether these contributions were entirely voluntary. Firemen also pressured municipal authorities for larger appropriations from the city treasury. In Providence, Rhode Island, all expenditures for fire equipment and buildings were controlled by an independent board of firewards, who were not subject to a city audit.

This unregulated system led to frequent abuses. In 1854 the city's finance committee complained that "Embarrassed by the sense of gratitude for the unrequited services of the firemen, the city council have made numerous grants of large sums for their gratification, amounting to nearly $50,000 in the last two years."

City officials found the prospect of restraining the firemen to be unwise, if not impossible. Fire companies controlled votes, and politicians who curried favor with firemen gained powerful political allies. If a promise to rally behind a certain candidate failed to get the firemen what they wanted, a threat to strike often did. Cincinnati's fire companies won several appropriations increases from the city council by staging elaborate hangings in effigy and mock funeral processions, complete with "political death warrants," for councilmen unsympathetic to their cause.

All over the country fire departments were getting out of hand. The audiences who chuckled over Mose's adventures began to complain about their own local fire companies—and found they could do little to control them. "No citizen should have any pride in the record of the Baltimore United Fire Department," fumed the Baltimore *Sun* in 1858, "and the less said about it the better."

The burning of a Cincinnati wood-planing mill in 1851 set in motion a series of events that ultimately ended the reign of the volunteer departments. This fire had been particularly severe and the firemen particularly ineffective. When companies came from neighboring cities

52

to help fight the flames, they found themselves caught up in an all-night melee. By dawn the mill was destroyed and six men were dead.

A few days later an exasperated group of city councilmen and newspaper editors began a concerted campaign to discredit the volunteer firemen. A committee was appointed by the city council to consider reorganizing the fire department, and it submitted a report early in 1852. Citing recent fire losses, complaints from insurance companies, and the fire companies' "corrupting influence on the young," the report recommended the formation of a city-administered, paid fire department, the first of its kind in the United States. (While the city of Boston had paid its chief engineer a salary since 1828, the Cincinnati proposal was the first to include a stipend for each fireman.) "In a dense population, our relations are more complicated, and however well it [the volunteer system] was adapted to our early history, it seems to be entirely unsuited to our present condition," the report argued.

To help sway public opinion in 1853 the Cincinnati *Daily Enquirer* and *Daily Commercial* ran a series of reports on "the increase of ruffianism and rowdyism, and blackguardism of every description." As the *Daily Enquirer* put it, "It is enough for the citizens to know that what they have heretofore regarded as an arm of protection from one danger has of late taken shape and become one of even more mischievous character. These rowdies, without responsibility, save what can be inflicted physically, are beyond the reach of moral sua-

sion, and seemingly as far beyond the reach of civil restraint."

In the meantime Cincinnati city councilmen had been investigating other measures. Convinced that more effective equipment could cut down on the number of men needed to put out a fire, they commissioned local inventors Abel Shawk and Alexander Bonner Latta to build a steam fire engine. At a public trial on New Year's Day, 1853, the 22,000-pound machine, with an operating crew of only three men, bested the assembled strength of the volunteer companies by producing six 225-foot streams of water simultaneously. Delighted with the new machine, the sponsors joked, "It never gets drunk. It never throws brickbats, and the only drawback connected with it is that it can't vote."

Seeing what was coming, the volunteers made several efforts to sabotage the new engine. But this time their protests were to no avail. With the new labor-saving engine at its command, the city could now afford to hire whom it pleased to fight its fires. A motion to establish a part-time salaried fire department was passed in March, 1853. Regular firemen received $60 a year to report to fires when needed. Several hosemen, drivers, assistant engineers, and a chief were appointed to full-time positions.

As news of both the administrative and technological innovations made in Cincinnati spread, other cities bought steamers and switched over to part-time paid fire departments. In Providence, a committee appointed by the city council recommended dismantling the volunteer system in November, 1853, following a riot in which an Irish-born fireman was killed. A paid department was proposed for Buffalo in 1856; volunteer companies slowly disbanded when a steamer was purchased in 1859. St. Louis made the change in 1857, Baltimore in 1858. Citing a recent bad fire, Chicago city councilmen argued for paying their firemen in 1857. A few months later they tried a steam engine, forcibly disbanded all the volunteer companies that marched to protest the steamer, then instituted a new paid department.

In the next few years Latta and Shawk refined their engine to make it smaller. Other manufacturers, including Amoskeag (established in 1859) in Manchester, New Hampshire, and LaFrance in Elmira, New York, improved on Latta's original design and were able to reduce the steam engine's weight below 8,000 pounds. But even these "lightweight" machines proved difficult to move. Before long cities made the logical step of bringing in horses to pull the engines. Some firemen protested; they still harbored the old resentment to "newfangled" labor-saving methods and liked even less the idea of sharing their firehouses with animals. A few companies held out and continued to pull the heavy steamers to fires by hand.

Those that consented to put up with the horses were not forced to get too intimately acquainted at first. In the early days horses were borrowed or "rented" from nearby owners as needed. It was only later that fire departments took responsibility for feeding and stabling the animals. There are some stories of city governments using the horses to get control over volunteer departments, by claiming that if the volunteers were not skilled enough to handle horses the city would have to replace them with firemen who could. Many of the first salaried firemen were essentially hired horse trainers.

The larger cities were slower to abandon the volunteer system. As mentioned above, the volunteers had considerable political clout, and they used this to maintain the status quo. However, speeches by firemen and politicians to defend the volunteer system would have us believe that their reluctance to change stemmed from higher motives. When the mayor of Boston sought to disband the volunteer fire companies after their riot in 1837, an eloquent captain had made this plea: "Do you think, Sir, that the citizens of Boston will ever submit to being prohibited from assisting a fellow townsman in distress? Such sort of laws may be obeyed in despotic countries, or in cities where the inhabitants do not feel for one another, but this is not the case, nor will it ever be in Boston."

In 1854 a Philadelphia writer again extolled the selfless volunteers (presumably not the same men who had earned a reputation for stabbing policemen a few years earlier): "Love, benevolence and glory would inspire and prompt them to fly to the rescue of property and life, when required, regardless of the imminent risks and hair-breadth escapes which they necessarily encounter . . . but the [paid

54

55

fireman] is moved solely by self-interest, and hence, the paid fireman would be incited to exertion just in proportion as he is paid. . . ."

His rhetoric was part of a sentiment that more and more people expressed as voluntary organizations were being replaced by professionals in many areas of American society. It helps to explain why policemen in New York and Boston refused to wear uniforms until the 1850s, and why volunteer nurses protested the formation of the Federal Sanitary Commission during the Civil War. A few years later, sports fans would use similar language to argue against paying salaries to baseball players; they complained that playing for money would kill the noble spirit of the game. The old traditions in the fire department died hard. Boston finally "submitted" to a fully paid fire department in 1860, while Philadelphia's volunteers held out until 1871.

During the Civil War the transition to paid departments came to a halt. Entire fire companies enlisted in the army. War slowed the production of steam fire engines, and demand for the machines decreased further when Southern fire departments went along with New Orleans' resolution in January, 1861, forswearing: ". . . our former course of folly in patronizing people directly or indirectly hostile to our institutions, manners and homes . . . [and to] hereby . . . have all various kinds of fire apparatus . . . made and manufactured south of Mason and Dixon's Line."

More cities established paid fire departments after the war—perhaps encouraged by the example set by the organization and admin-istration of the army. New York, the last major stronghold for the volunteers, instituted America's first full-time paid department in 1865. Other large cities followed suit.

A new professional attitude and paramilitary organization accompanied the newly created fire departments. Foremen and assistant engineers became captains, lieutenants, and sergeants, and blue uniforms replaced the traditional red shirts. "Water Witch," "Vigilant," "Good Intent," and other nicknames adopted by the volunteer companies were changed to "Engine 1" and "Hook and Ladder 3."

The revolutionary developments in equipment and organization at first had few direct repercussions on firehouse architecture. Most cities were able to buy or repossess the old volunteer stations and continued to use them with only slight modifications, usually involving an enlargement of the apparatus areas to accommodate steam engines. Cincinnati had to build an entirely new set of fire stations with huge doors and ground-floor rooms; and if the pictures of the period can be taken as true illustrations, the ceilings must have been at 53 least twenty-five feet high. St. Louis firemen met the problem of housing the new equipment in their old firehouses by hinging the tall smokestacks of their Latta engines so that they could .be folded down.

Other, more subtle developments reflected the change in personnel. When the volunteers left, they took their chandeliers, oil paintings, plaques, banners, trophy cases, and parlor furnishings with them. Since the new paid men worked only part-time or on a call basis and spent little time at the station off-hours, the old club–sitting rooms were converted into simple meeting halls. Plain tables and chairs replaced the overstuffed settees. An 1871 inventory (slightly abridged) of Cincinnati's Steam Company 19 shows the relative absence of creature comforts as well as the standard set of equipment typical in early paid fire stations:

One steam engine, one hammer, 1 vise, 10 oil cans, 3 chisels, 1 funnel, 1 jack screw and lever . . . 1 stove and heating apparatus, with platform coal box, poker and shovel, 2 coal buckets, 1 sheet iron smokestack, 26 feet ¾ inch rubber hose, 1 clock, 1 alarm . . . 4 dusters, 5 sponges, 1 mop . . . 4 leather pipes, 5 nozzles, 1 copper branch pipe, 4 spanners, 3 horses, 3 sets harnesses . . . 1 basket, 1 lantern, 1 Bible, 1 table, 6 common chairs, 6 cane bottom chairs, 6 beds and bedding . . . 1 Brussels carpet, 1 oil cloth, 1 bath tub with wash stand and oil cloth, 8 window and door curtains, 1 pick, 1 chamois skin, 1 Thomas cat.

In some stations part of the former lounge area was made over into an apartment for a full-time watchman or driver who sometimes moved his entire family into the station.

Changes were more marked when cities erected new stations to replace or augment volunteer houses. With municipal building departments responsible for their design, construction, and cost, the new fire stations were often less luxurious and less ornate than houses built by the volunteer companies. As if to present a no-nonsense exterior to the public, the stations designed for the new, professional fire departments followed the austere forms of factory and commercial architecture rather than resemble houses or clubs. Not surprisingly, the signs, statues, weathervanes, and identifying mascots that had graced older stations were early casualties. Even the tower, which in the past had served the function of making the fire station stand out from other buildings around it (see Chapter Two), was now treated as a simple shaft—or eliminated altogether in favor of drying racks.

49, 52

The new buildings were also more uniform than their predecessors had been. When each volunteer fire company had controlled the hiring of its own architect and the erection of its building, designs could be as extravagant as money allowed. Fire stations, conceived as symbols for the company, were designed to compete with the buildings of rival groups. Now that one public committee had responsibility for the design of all the fire stations in a city, the buildings began to look more alike. New Orleans and Brooklyn each erected groups of fire stations that seem to have been designed from one set of master plans.

51, 58

With city governments in charge, the names of the fire stations' architects became a matter of public record (a development that greatly simplified the work of future architectural historians). Annual accounts of the city of Cincinnati record payment to local architects Samuel Hannaford, Edward Anderson,

56

57

and Henry Bevis for plans and specifications from which six new engine houses were built between 1871 and 1876. Hannaford's obituary describes him as going on to become a leading Cincinnati architect, one of the founding members of the local chapter of the American Institute of Architects, the designer of Cincinnati's City Hall and "a great number of prominent residences."

Like Hannaford, most of the architects hired by city governments to design paid fire stations in the 1850s, '60s and '70s were respected locals who regarded the commission as no more nor less important than one for an office block or a private house. In the 1880s and '90s some cities adopted the practice of appointing one architect to design all of the city's fire stations instead of contracting separately for each building. The firms of Napoleon LeBrun & Sons in New York and Bruce & Morgan in Atlanta both made unofficial agreements with city officials that gave them monopolies on commissions for fire stations. Other

cities created the full-time salaried position of City Architect, which entailed responsibility for all public building projects.

One of the first and most distinguished of these officially appointed architects was Harvard-trained Major Benjamin Morgan Harrod of New Orleans, whose varied career ranged from captain of the Confederate engineering corps to consultant to Theodore Roosevelt for the Panama Canal. As City Surveyor of New Orleans between 1888 and 1892, he designed a number of fire stations that are still standing today. (Though New Orleans maintained a volunteer fire department until 1891, the city had taken responsibility for hiring drivers and erecting stations since the 1850s.)

With their stone fronts, heavy cornices, and rows of round-arched windows, Harrod's 58 fire station designs are based on a vaguely Italian-inspired style of architecture that was popular for American commercial buildings throughout the second half of the nineteenth century. Like many other fire stations erected

56. *Oceana Engine Company 11 (later Engine 13), New York City, 1881. Napoleon LeBrun, architect.* **57.** *Engine 54 (now a theater), New York City, 1888. Napoleon LeBrun, architect.* **58.** *Engine 6, New Orleans, Louisiana, 1886. Benjamin Morgan Harrod, architect. Like Bruce and Morgan in Atlanta, the firm of Napoleon LeBrun and Sons unofficially received most of the commissions for fire stations in New York between 1880 and* *1895. In addition to handsome, utilitarian storefront stations, they also designed the fire department headquarters (fig. 72) and several grander stations in the 1890s. LeBrun's most famous building was the Academy of Music in Philadelphia. Major Benjamin Morgan Harrod, former captain of the Confederate engineering corps, designed several stone-fronted fire stations during his tenure as City Surveyor of New Orleans.*

58

59

60

61

84

59. *Fire Station 8 (now Fire Station 4), San Francisco, California, 1916. John Reid, Jr., architect.* **60.** *Engine 5, New Orleans, Louisiana, 1907. Edgar Angelo Christy, architect.* **61.** *Chemical Company 1 (now Old Plaza Firehouse Museum), Los Angeles, California, 1884. W. H.* *Boring, architect.* **62.** *Engine 78, Chicago, Illinois, 1915. Charles W. Kallal, architect. The storefront type remained standard for downtown fire stations into the twentieth century. Depending on budget and location it could be simple or ornate.*

63. *Engine 17 (now a warehouse), Portland, Oregon, 1912. Lee Holden, architect. Holden was a Portland fireman whose first attempt at architecture was the design for a bungalow fire station illustrated in Chapter Six.*

by municipal administrations in downtown sections, these buildings drew on the simple design of stores and warehouses, dispensing with the elaborate towers, cupolas, and balconies (elements of more personal residential architecture) that had characterized the volunteers' houses.

This type of firehouse design can be termed "storefront style" and has its origins in such buildings as the Perseverance Hose Company of 1832 in Philadelphia (see Chapter Two). It became the standard for downtown fire stations for the next 100 years. Buildings in this style were usually narrow, two or three stories high, and squeezed between other buildings on a city block. Small personnel entrances or windows flanked the large front apparatus doors in an arrangement not unlike the symmetrical arrangement of a store's entrance and shop windows. Exterior ornament usually was confined to the ground floor, especially around the door, and a cornice that sometimes extended beyond the actual roofline to form a false front. The upper stories of the facade often consisted of rows of plain windows that let in as much light as possible for the meeting rooms and living quarters.

The interiors of the "storefront" stations followed the pattern established in earlier volunteer houses: apparatus on the ground floor, meeting rooms and living quarters (later offices and dormitories) above. Few had towers. New York City's fire stations of the 1870s and '80s were equipped with interior shafts or closets that extended the height of the building. The "towers" Bruce and Morgan devised for fire stations in Atlanta were actually narrow, two-story rooms with sloping floors lined with drying racks. Firemen in other cities resorted to stretching hose out on the floor of the station or on the sidewalk or, in Chicago, hanging it up in a nearby alley to dry.

The architectural trimming of storefront stations kept up with developments in surrounding buildings. The Perseverance's stucco front gave way to cast iron (Philadelphia and New York City), brick and brownstone (New York, Brooklyn, Chicago), and the stone facings found in New Orleans. For cheaper or less permanent buildings the style could be adapted in wood, as in the Alpine Hose Company of Georgetown, Colorado. A similar design of a plain brick front with corbel-patterned cornice made its way to cities as farflung as Los Angeles, Atlanta, and Providence. Though architects at the turn of the century sometimes came up with more flamboyant facades (see Chapter Five), the "storefront" fire station was almost always less monumental than stations constructed in other parts of the city.

With little modification, variants of the basic "storefront" type remained in use right up through the 1930s and '40s and finally went out of style when departments stopped building stations to house only one or two trucks. Today fire departments in Chicago and New York still use some of the "storefront" stations designed in the 1870s and '80s. With rising downtown land prices making the cost of bigger stations prohibitive, these plain and functional buildings, designed to house steam engines, serve their modern users well.

CHAPTER FOUR

The Red Brick Fire Station

Electricity, Horses, and the Romanesque

1865–1895

After the earliest paid fire departments took over stations already built by the volunteer companies, new buildings for paid departments were erected rapidly wherever space could be found, to improve protection for crowded downtown areas. By the 1870s and '80s municipalities were beginning to construct a different type of fire station. Taking up most of a city block, housing several fire companies together or a department headquarters, these were massive structures that stood out from other buildings in their neighborhoods as visual emblems of city government. Today they form the image most of us still associate with the "old-time" firehouse—big, square buildings with arched doors and prominent towers, almost always built of red brick. Of course, builders had constructed fire stations of brick before the Civil War, but after 1870 red brick architecture, incorporating new styles taken from industrial and commercial design, came to dominate municipal building. In these years

the red brick fire station became as ubiquitous as the red brick schoolhouse.

Changes inside the firehouse kept up with the latest designs. The era that saw the invention of the electric lightbulb, the telephone, and the automatic rabbit decoy also provided an arsenal of new equipment for the fire service. A profusion of novel devices were centered on the horse and the steam engine, which (despite the prejudices of the old volunteers) had developed into integral and well-loved features of firefighting. The fire service, in newly respectable quarters, made the change from makeshift to mechanized while restoring much of its earlier appeal to the public.

Some of the most impressive new stations were built in cities that developed after the Civil War, in the industrial and commercial centers that followed the spread of the railroad network into the Midwest. Small towns like Fort Wayne, Indiana, that formerly relied on a bucket brigade or a few volunteer companies were now faced with increasing population, expanding city limits, and new factories and rail yards to protect. The buildings these cities erected to replace their old frame fire stations (often their first substantial stations at all) were likely to be designed by architects brought in from a nearby big city and were opened with great public fanfare. The new firehouses were

---

64. *Fireman's Hall, Ann Arbor, Michigan, 1882–83. William Scott, architect. With its two-toned ornament and prominent tower, this station, built to house all of Ann Arbor's fire apparatus, combined Victorian taste with civic pride. The equipment inside was equally impressive. Electric lights, horse-drawn engines, and an arsenal of gadgets were developed in the 1870s and '80s.*

big buildings; unlike earlier stations built for individual volunteer companies, these housed several pieces of equipment and provided living quarters for more than one full-time crew.

With the siting of all of a city's fire stations now in the hands of one municipal department, fire chiefs could centralize stations. Replacing several volunteer houses with one large station permitted engine, hose, and ladder companies to answer an alarm together. However, downtown traffic, bad roads, and inefficient equipment still meant that stations had to be sited fairly close together for engines to reach a fire in time to do any good. Thus by the 1890s Columbus, Ohio, had a large fire station in thirteen of its fifteen wards. At that time most of the fire stations in Providence, Rhode Island, were located within a mile of each other, though some were small buildings left over from the volunteer companies.

There seems to be no record of how locations of new stations were determined. We can guess that fire chiefs were influenced then, as they are today, by petitions from people who either wanted or did not want a fire station in their neighborhood, by the availability of open land, and occasionally by politicians who had a special interest in the city's buying a particular lot. Furthermore, there seems to have been no accepted model for siting fire stations in the nineteenth century. Almost as many were built on side streets as on major arteries. Nevertheless, planners always followed two logical rules: the engines had to have enough room to maneuver in and out of the station (backing a twenty-foot ladder truck down a narrow alley

would not have made much sense), and the firemen had to be able to get to a fire as quickly as possible, usually by way of a wide, main street.

A typical red brick firehouse of this era is the central station in Ann Arbor, Michigan. The city's population had reached 10,000 when the aldermen decided to build a "firemen's hall" in 1882. They drew up a set of specifications calling for a sixty-foot-square ground floor to house a steam engine, a hook and ladder truck, and an old hand engine, as well as stables and coal bins. The second story was to include space for department offices, a hayloft, and a meeting room (later converted to living quarters for paid firemen). The city then sponsored a competition and awarded the project to architect William Scott of Detroit, whose compact, well-proportioned design stayed within the $10,000 budget and remains a downtown landmark.

By the early 1890s both Columbus, Ohio, and Fort Wayne, Indiana, had extended their city limits and outgrown their downtown fire stations. Both cities undertook building programs that included several large neighborhood stations in addition to huge new headquarters buildings. Fort Wayne saved on architects' fees by using one set of plans for three different stations (reversed in one case to fit the site); Columbus erected six different variations on the Romanesque theme of the headquarters, and each was more splendid than the one before. An 1894 publication of the Columbus Fireman's Pension Fund described the new gas-lit stations:

90

65

66

. . . of enduring brick and stone, chastely decorated and models of architectural compactness and beauty. They contain six ample apartments and stable, are finished in hard wood throughout, have water closets, bathrooms and dormitories. . . . the crew who man them are lusty fellows full of ginger and enthusiasm. . . .

It is doubtful if any city in the country can boast of a better outfitted Fire Department in any feature of equipment or housing. It is the boast of Columbus people that our engine houses would be a credit to any city in the world, and indeed there are few if any that can compare with them at all.

Combining a similar urge to boast with a need for practical, economical structures, less populous areas, such as the Western mining towns of Las Vegas, New Mexico, and Rock Springs, Wyoming, erected buildings that housed several civic functions, including the fire department, under the same roof. The Monumental Building in Sidney, Ohio, a village whose entire population was less than that of one ward in Columbus, is an early example. Built in 1875 as a memorial to the soldiers of Shelby County who died in the Civil War, it included space for a courtroom, a public library, a post office, a museum, and a high school in addition to a city hall and a fire station. The town raised the $65,000 cost of land and building by issuing bonds, levying additional taxes, and holding a public lottery that offered a new office block as first prize. Other cities were able to use their fire stations for

several purposes by adding an extra room. Unlike the private volunteer houses, city-built stations could double as public meeting places for the community. In Providence, Rhode Island, fire stations served as polling places and provided rooms for ward meetings. Ann Arbor's fire department helped cover the cost of its new station by renting out the upstairs room for temperance meetings. In less than a month one crusade convinced half the city's population to take the pledge.

Older, larger cities seldom had enough space for big new fire stations; those they did erect were usually on landfill or in newly annexed sections. The dearth of empty lots in downtown New York City forced the fire department there to rely on a network of new storefront and old volunteer stations that housed one or two companies and were located only a few blocks apart. By 1886, land in lower Manhattan was so expensive and hard to come by that fire commissioners considered a scheme to "rearrange all the [existing fire] houses so there is an extra engine in the basement, standing on a moveable platform, which could be raised to the first floor when the regular engine leaves." The department continued to build small stations downtown, but moved its headquarters and central alarm that year from the old Fireman's Hall on Mercer Street to a new building on East 67th, an area that was just beginning to be built up but "rapidly becoming central." The new building, a gorgeously ornate six-story affair complete with an Otis elevator and an observation tower with balcony and gargoyles, housed Engine Company

66, 68, 69

70, 71

93

68

69

94

68. *City Hall and Fire Station, Las Vegas, New Mexico, 1892–93. Kirchner and Kirchner, architects.* 69. *City Hall and Fire Station, Rock Springs, Wyoming, 1894. Martin Didicus Kern, architect (photograph by Mark Junge).* 70, 71. *Monumental Building, Sidney, Ohio, 1875. Samuel Lane, architect (opening day photograph courtesy of Dan Becker). Towns with no need or no budget for a large fire station combined several municipal functions in one substantial structure. The Las Vegas City Hall included a county courtroom; the Monumental Building, erected as a memorial to the Civil War soldiers of Shelby County, housed a library, a museum, and a schoolroom in addition to city offices and a fire station. The commemorative statue arrived too late for the building's opening in 1875.*

70

71

72

73

72, 73. *Fire Department Headquarters (now Engine 39/Ladder 16), New York City, 1886. Napoleon Le-Brun, architect. The headquarters built on recently developed land on 67th Street replaced the Fireman's Hall illustrated in fig. 46. Its sixth floor contained telegraphic alarm equipment for the entire city (see fig. 84). LeBrun paid particular attention to details such as the ornamental brickwork, decorative carving, and patterns worked into the cast-iron beams over the front doors (illustration, c1888, from the Picture Collection, New York Public Library).*

72, 73   39 and Hook and Ladder 16 on its first two floors, department headquarters and offices for the Building Inspection and Combustibles Bureaus above, a training school on the fifth floor, and the central alarm telegraph system under the mansard roof.

74   Boston's Engine 33/Ladder 15 and adjacent police station were built in 1888 on land that had not even existed ten years earlier. It was erected on one of the last sections to be reclaimed in Back Bay, in order to protect the new streets of that rapidly growing district. Starting with a clean slate, the fire department could choose how to orient the station. Unlike their counterparts in New York who put their headquarters on a side street, Boston's commissioners decided to front this building on a main thoroughfare (Boylston Street), with easy access to another main street (West Chester Avenue, now Massachusetts Avenue) around the corner.

A writer from the trade journal *Fire and Water* described the stations in Columbus, Ohio, as "imposing and complete"; while their exterior design awed the viewer, their interior fittings were equally impressive:

. . . they were all that was claimed for them. . . . In the headquarters building are the electric fire alarm apparatus and battery room. In this building is also the supply room and harness maker's room. All of the fittings in the interior are as perfect as those in an elegant private residence. The sleeping apartments are large and well-furnished and the plumbing work is of the most modern kind. The chief engineer and his assistants have their offices in the headquarters building, and the superintendent of fire alarm also has his headquarters here. In the cellar of the building is an Ahrens heater, which keeps the large building and engine supplied with adequate heat, and a water motor is here, which works the telephone connection. The equipment in this building consists of an Ahrens engine, a hose cart, and a Hayes

97

74

truck. The chief and assistant engineers have separate suites of rooms, handsomely fitted up, and the several men in charge of the apparatus, who sleep in this building, are better housed than probably any firemen in the country.

As this list of equipment and personnel indicates, the fire department of the 1880s and '90s no longer could be housed in makeshift quarters. Fire stations were becoming specialized buildings. The 1880s fire station followed the basic layout of a volunteer house but on a much larger scale. Cincinnati's giant engine room, described in the last chapter, showed some of the changes to come. Even the improved, smaller steam engines could be up to ten feet long; a hook and ladder truck needed at least thirty linear feet of floor space. Most stations kept a few pieces of outmoded equipment (such as Ann Arbor's hand engine) in reserve behind their newer apparatus, requiring an even longer apparatus floor. Further changes on the ground floor came with the introduction of horses into the fire station.

The last chapter mentioned the suspicion and even resentment with which volunteer firemen looked on the prospect of working with horses. In the 1870s and '80s horses gained acceptance among the men and moved into the fire stations. Firefighters had found that leading horses from an outside stable around to the engine wasted too much time, so it made more sense to build the stable right inside the fire station. Architects usually adapted the volunteer station's floor plan by

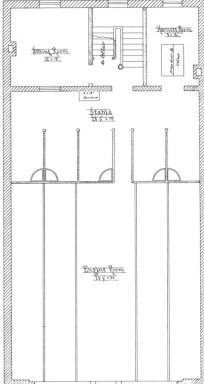

75

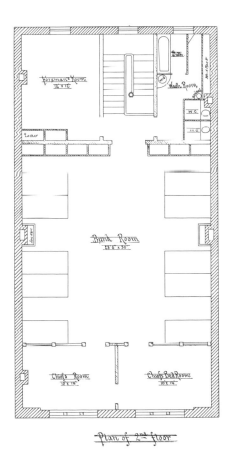

76

Plan of 2nd floor

74. *Engine 33/Ladder 15, Boston, Massachusetts, 1888. Arthur H. Vinal, architect. This fire station and the adjoining police station protected a newly created neighborhood in the Back Bay. Its round arches and rough textures show the influence of the Romanesque Revival popularized by H. H. Richardson. In 1974 the fire station was refurbished and the police station renovated as the Institute for Contemporary Art.*

75, 76. *Engine 6, Washington, D.C., 1857. An early example of the changes that took place when horses were moved into the fire station. Stalls were added at the rear of the apparatus floor, and most living areas moved upstairs (Department of General Services, District of Columbia).*

simply adding stalls to the back of the apparatus room—either in a separate wing behind the station or built right into the first floor. The 1857 plan of Engine 6 in Washington, 75, 76 D.C., shows an early example of a station designed to accommodate horses. It includes a row of five stalls—two for each piece of equipment and one for a reserve horse—behind the apparatus area. A passageway between the third and fourth stalls allows access to a stable area and harness room behind them.

Apparently this arrangement took a while to catch on: Providence (Rhode Island) city council reports from 1881 include a resolution to remodel the stables in Engine 17 to allow the horses to stand facing the apparatus (up to this time they had faced the rear wall and had to be turned around each time an alarm came in). An item in an 1879 *Fireman's Journal* notes that "the house of Hook and Ladder Company Number One in Baltimore is undergoing extensive repairs, the horses having been changed from the back part of the house . . ." (presumably moved up nearer the engines). Other stations placed several stalls along the side walls to keep the horses even closer to the front of the trucks. In New Orleans the horses never moved all the way into the station but stayed in stalls separated from the back of the building by a small courtyard. The stall doors lined up with two big rear doors to the station, so that when an alarm sounded the horses could run across the courtyard and take their places in front of the engines (see Chapter Five).

77. *Bunkroom of Engine 33, New York City, 1889 (Picture Collection, New York Public Library).* **78, 79.** *Locker room at Engine 20, Cincinnati, Ohio, 1888. Charles Fox, architect. The interiors of most red brick fire stations were simple, functional, and built to take heavy wear from a large crew. Men serving at Engine 20 today appreciate the spacious quarters and the extra details such as oversized wooden lockers and stained glass windows.*

78

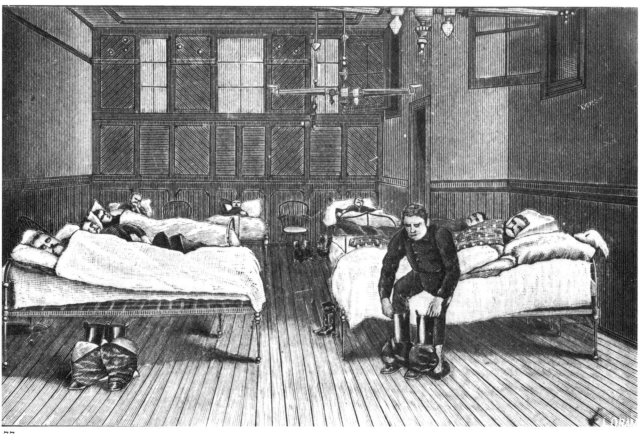

77

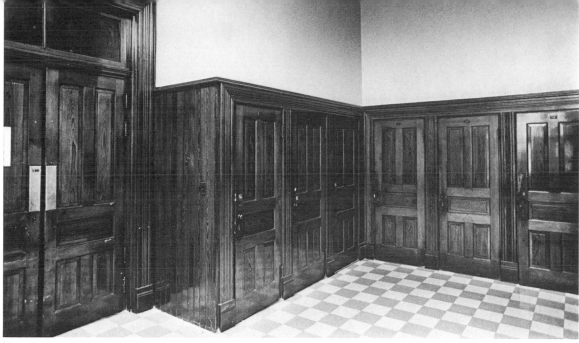

79

The introduction of horses brought several new rooms to the firehouse in addition to the first floor harness or tack room seen in Washington's Engine 6. Later stations included, at the back of the second floor, forage rooms and feed bins that connected with chutes and tubes to the stables below. Hay was stored in a separate upstairs loft, also at the rear of the building, which had its own outside loading doors. The old block-and-tackle arms still remain on many stations. Since horses have to be cleaned as well as fed, stalls and stables needed oversized floor drains. Manure pits and separate areas for bathing the horses could be located in the basement or in a yard behind the station. Benjamin Harrod's specifications for Engine 2 in New Orleans include detailed descriptions of a rolling pen—a 15 by 30 foot sandbox where horses could exercise—in back of the building. Pittsburgh's more elegant Engine 28, built in 1898, still has tile-lined pens in the basement.

As horses moved into the stations the men retreated by moving their quarters upstairs. Since most firemen now worked full-time, second and third stories were given over to living quarters, with the exception of the rear feed and storage rooms just described. Every company, whether of four men or twenty-four, needed a dormitory, a locker room, a good-sized bathroom, and some sort of lounge area. Officers usually had their own rooms, or sometimes separate suites. (The separation of men from animals did not always work: one lonely horse is said to have climbed a flight of stairs to visit the firemen in their card room, and he had to be lowered back to the ground through a broken window.)

Old pictures indicate that despite the "large and well-furnished apartments" described in the Columbus, Ohio, headquarters, the average living quarters usually were rather plain rooms with varnished wooden wainscotting and simple brass light fixtures. Harrod's specifications for Engine 2 called for pine wainscotting to be painted and grained to look like black walnut. As in the Cincinnati station described in Chapter Three, these rooms were furnished with plain oak tables and chairs, iron beds, and an ample supply of spittoons. *Harper's Monthly* described the bunkroom of a typical New York City firehouse of the 1870s as decorated with "severe attacks of scarlet-fever chromo-lithography, depicting conflagrations." An 1887 illustration of the bunkroom at Engine 33 in New York shows that station's windows covered with folding wooden shutters. In Washington's Engine 6 two rooms for chiefs took up the front of the second floor, with a 28 by 30 foot bunkroom for ten men directly behind. A row of lockers separated the bunkroom from the foreman's room and bathrooms in the rear. This early station included a 12 foot square sitting room on the first floor, directly under the foreman's room at the back of the building. 77–79

Moving the living quarters upstairs had its drawbacks, as can be seen in an early illustration (from the same article in *Harper's*) showing a typically disorganized alarm of the 1870s. As firemen, some still buttoning up their shirts, tumble down the stairs and over 80

80

their equipment, one man struggles to rush two frantic horses from their stalls while trying to hook on their collars at the same time. The sliding pole, invented by Chicago fireman David Kenyon in 1878, went a long way toward solving the problem of getting men down to the engines quickly and safely. Brass poles (earlier models were wooden) made their first appearance in Worcester, Massachusetts, stations two years later and soon became standard equipment.

Meanwhile firemen in St. Joseph, Missouri, came up with the "quick hitch" hanging harness, a device used to speed up harnessing horses to the engine. As refined by subsequent users, the system involved suspending harnesses from the ceiling and rigging them to drop down when horses were brought into position in front of the engine. Once the harness dropped, the sides connected automati-

82

cally beneath the horse—much the same way handcuffs close. A network of pulleys, springs, and counterweights would then pull the empty harness holders back up to the ceiling. Incredibly, this contraption shaved three minutes off the average response time and was used on into the twentieth century.

The introduction of electricity (first used for telegraphic fire alarms in 1839) gave rise to even more complicated devices for saving time. The year before Samuel Morse patented his telegraph, Dr. William Channing of Boston invented a system of numbered alarm boxes to be placed at public locations around the city. When triggered, each alarm box transmitted a signal back to a central alarm station, where dispatchers could relay that box's number to nearby fire stations. When the system finally was adopted on a large scale in the 1860s and '70s, the signal from the call box was trans-

80. *From* Harper's New Monthly Magazine, *October 1877.* 81. *From* Scientific American, *August 1884. Gadgets invented by firemen shaved minutes off the average response time and made alarms a bit more orderly. Both drawings depict firehouses in New York City; they show the changes that took place with the introduction of the sliding pole and the hanging harness in the 1870s and '80s. Notice the alarm desk and telegraphic alarm at the right.*

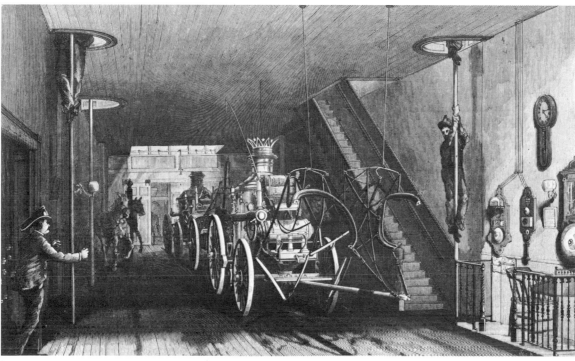

81

ferred by the central alarm office to bells in every firehouse, and they banged out the number in a series of strokes while registering the same information on a ticker tape. Thus an alarm from box 125 would sound out one ring, then two, then five, pause, and then repeat the pattern. Firemen receiving the message immediately consulted a call board for the box's address, to see whether their company was assigned to respond on the first alarm. More often the men recognized the numbers and knew the addresses by heart, as did people who lived nearby. Today most cities still use a similar alarm system, and firemen instinctively stop in the middle of a sentence to count out the numbers as an alarm comes in.

In individual firehouses, alarm bells and clocks were mounted on a wall in the apparatus room, with extra gongs on the upper floors to alert sleeping firemen. A watchman now sat at a desk near the ground-floor bell and registered each alarm in his log book. As time passed, the alarm apparatus increased and the watch desk grew from a railed-off area of the apparatus floor to a separate alcove, to sometimes an extra room.

Headquarters buildings had to make more significant structural changes, since central alarm rooms took up a good deal of space. By the 1880s a fire department headquarters also housed department offices and some central services (horse hospitals and blacksmith or harness repair shops that served the entire city's fire stations) as well as one or two engine companies to protect the immediate neighborhood. These buildings had to combine features of an office building with those of an enlarged fire station. By adding an elevator, the architects of New York's headquarters were able to stack four stories atop a regular two-story station.

82, 83. *Hale Hanging Harness and Horse Cover, 1893 (Snyder collection, University of Missouri–Kansas City Libraries).* **84.** *Alarm equipment in New York City from* Scientific American, *July 1887. Firefighting equipment that presaged Rube Goldberg: the hanging harness, invented by Chief George Hale of Kansas City, was rigged to drop down on a horse's back and hitch automatically when an alarm came in. It remained in use into the twentieth century. Hale's automatic horse cover had less success. The illustration at right shows some of the components of New York's telegraphic alarm system. Until very recently some cities still relied on a ticker tape to record the location of fires.*

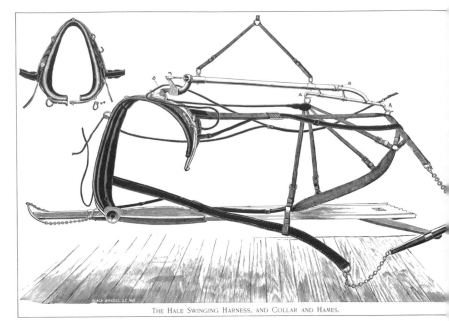

THE HALE SWINGING HARNESS, AND COLLAR AND HAMES.

82

The Hale Automatic Horse Cover.

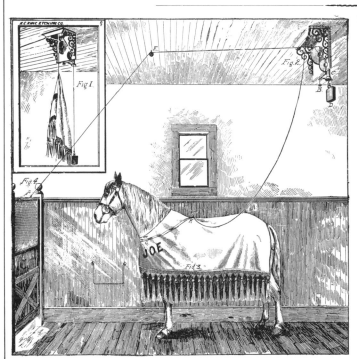

THE HALE AUTOMATIC HORSE COVER. "There are no flies on me!"

S OR the first time in the history of fire departments a device has been invented by means of which all fire horses may be kept covered and protected from the weather, dirt and the pestiferous fly.

On the opposite page is shown a cut of a horse standing in his stall and neatly and securely covered by the Hale Automatic Horse Cover. Figure 1 of the cut represents the cover and device the instant an alarm of fire is turned in.

In this arrangement a light weight linen horse cover is used, which is provided with a spring-wire collar or neck opening, which, with a cord attached to cover and being placed under the horse's tail, securely holds the cover in position on the horse while in the stall.

At a point on the forward point of the cover is attached a cord, which passes to a device secured to the ceiling, as represented in Figure 2 of the cut. This device is composed of small pulleys, locking device and weight. From it a cord passes to and is engaged with whatever apparatus is used for releasing halter straps, dropping stall chains, and opening doors. The turning in of an alarm of fire instantly sets the device secured to the ceiling in motion, and the cover is quickly carried from the horse to the ceiling.

The cord passing from the cover to the ceiling device is always slack and without the least strain on the cover, until the device is set in motion by the turning in of an alarm of fire or by manual interference, the latter method being adopted to relieve the horse of cover at any time it may be desired to do so.

With this arrangement, horses in fire departments may be securely and comfortably covered at all times, without the least reduction of speed in answering an alarm. The coat of the animal is kept clean, and the constant fighting and worry from flies is entirely prevented, thus saving much of the horse's strength and spirit.

Price: Cover and device, complete, per horse, $5.00.

83

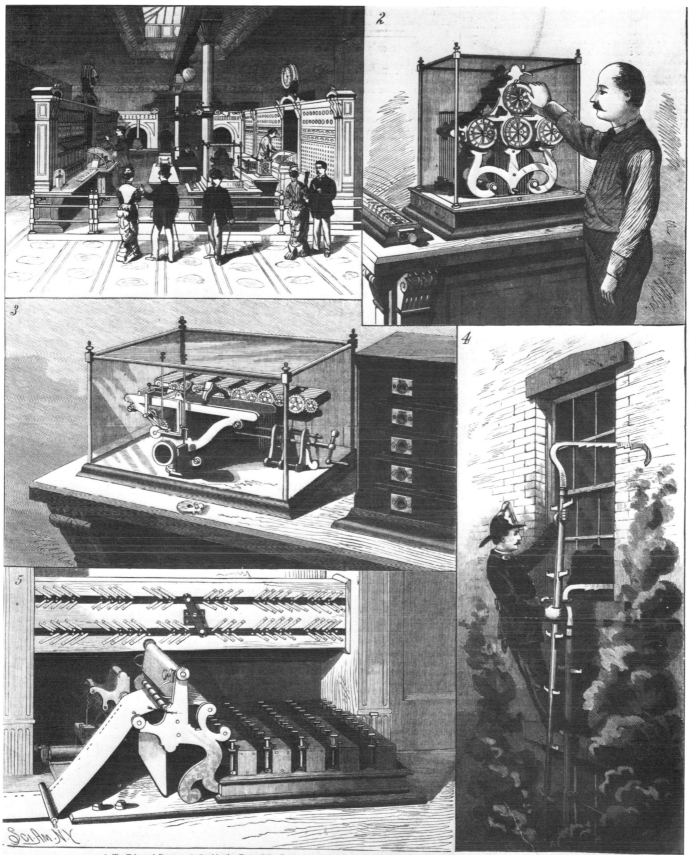

1. Fire Telegraph Room. 2. Combination Transmitting Repeater. 3. Button Transmitting Repeater. 4. Life Saving Corps. 5. Receiving Register.

NEW HEADQUARTERS OF THE FIRE DEPARTMENT OF THE CITY OF NEW YORK.—[See page 68.]

84

A GLIMPSE AS STEAMER FIVE'S HORSES.
86

85

Before long, someone got the idea of linking the drop harness to the alarm system so that the same electrical impulse sounding the bell would release the harnesses. Soon that current also switched the lights on and opened the swinging doors of the horses' stalls at the same time. In a fever of invention, firemen-tinkerers conjured electrical gadgets that no doubt awed the young Rube Goldberg. If electricity could open the stalls automatically, why not make it swing open the trapdoor that covered the hole for the sliding pole? (In the headquarters at Columbus, the pole covers were flat disks that shot up to the ceiling when the alarm rang.) Electrical whips urged the horses from their stalls automatically, and elec-

106

tricity could light a fire in the steamer as well as stop the station's clock to record the time of the alarm.

The ultimate time-saving device may have been the "Little Joker," invented by the men of Cincinnati's Engine 9 in 1881 to aid in rousing firemen in the dormitory. To operate the device, the beds were arranged "like the spokes of a wheel," with the covers attached to cords leading to an eighty-pound weight at the ceiling. When an alarm came in, a catch released the weight "and in the same instant the bedclothing is dangling in a united bunch half-way to the ceiling." A few years later Kansas City's Fire Chief George C. Hale adapted the same principle for his Automatic Horse Cover, "a device by means of which all fire horses may be kept covered and protected from the weather, dirt, and the pestiferous fly." As described in a glowing advertisement it consisted of a tasselled linen blanket with a spring-wire collar connected by cords to a collection of pulleys on the ceiling. "The turning in of an alarm of fire instantly sets the device secured to the ceiling in motion, and the cover is quickly carried from the horse to the ceiling." The cover sold for $5.00 per horse.

Several of the more commonly used improvements of the period can be seen in the "Interior view of a model engine house" that ran on the cover of *Scientific American* in 1884. In contrast to the earlier picture from *Harper's*, some kind of order prevails here: men slide down the poles and into position around the engine while the horses, released as the stall-doors swing open automatically, now run to their positions without any prodding. Their harnesses hang ready to drop down and hitch. The accompanying article describes a hidden network of mechanisms connecting the steam engine to a basement hot water heater that automatically shuts off as the engine pulls out.

The horses themselves became part of this smoothly run machine. The firemen trained them to move from their stalls to positions in front of the engines at the sound of an alarm, to wait there until the harnesses dropped down on their backs, and then to charge out at full speed to the fire. Stories are told of horses who learned to count out the alarms or were so eager to get going that they ran off to the fire and left the engines behind. The matched horses at Royal Engine 6 in York, Pennsylvania, reportedly relieved themselves into waiting shovels on schedule. A fire horse's reflexes were so well tuned, people say, that even when put out to pasture in old age a horse never forgot its former duties. Numerous anecdotes circulate about times when "retired" horses, hearing a distant alarm, ran off to a fire pulling a milk truck or delivery wagon behind.

Clearly horses had moved up in firemen's esteem since the days of the "skunk" incident in New York (see Chapter Three). Firemen gave their horses fond nicknames and taught them stunts. The Royal Engine Company's matched black horses lived in stalls with their names—Count, Duke, Czar, etc.—inscribed on marble plaques above the doors. The men in the New Bern, North Carolina, volunteer fire department will never forget Fred, a loyal horse who died in action after twenty-five

87

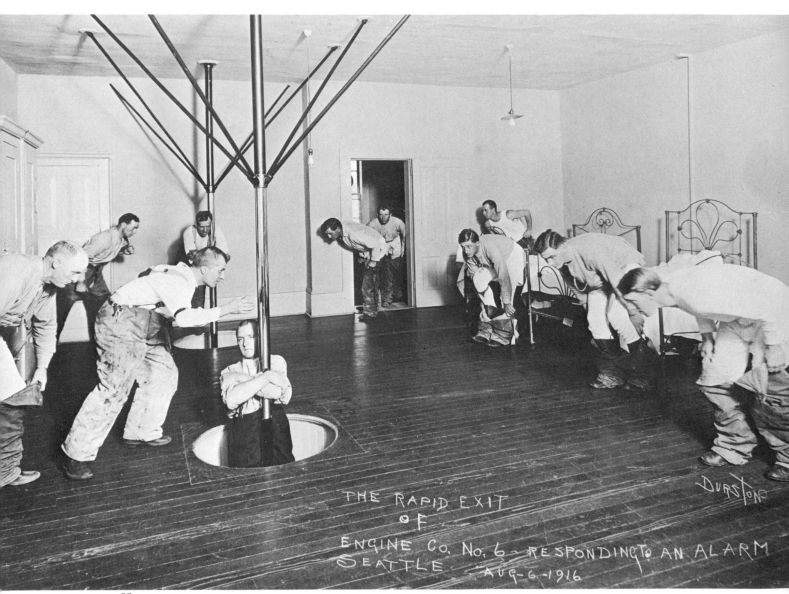

88

87, 88, 89. *Studio photographs taken at Engine 6, Seattle, Washington, 1916. "Live action" photographs arranged by a commercial photographer record life in a turn-of-the-century firehouse. Some traditions hardly have changed at all in the last hundred years. Firemen still sleep with their boots and pants beside their beds, and still play cards between alarms (Historical Society of Seattle and King County).*

89

90

years of service; he has been immortalized in taxidermy and put on display in the department museum.

In time the steam engine, that other enemy the volunteer firemen had protested against, also earned a place in the hearts of the firemen. Just as earlier companies had decorated their hand-powered engines with paintings and inscriptions, firemen and manufacturers now embellished the new machines with enough chrome, gold leaf, and fancy metalwork to rival a Mississippi steamboat. The *Fireman's Herald* published this paean to the steam fire engine in 1882.

> Behold! How she shines in her beauty,
> Resplendent in silver and gold;
> Ne'er shrinking from doing her duty,
> When worked by her members so bold;
> So peacefully-innocent standing,
> You'd dream not the work she can do;
> But when we her aid are demanding,
> She always proves faithful and true.
>
> Oh! dear shall she be to us ever;—
> For she's our companion and friend;
> She does her work neatly and clever,
> And labors, with zeal, to the end.
>
> The Steamer! We'll ever adore you;
> In praising you we never tire;
> Hand engines were nothing before you;
> Nor compared with you when at a fire.

As happened with the rest of the fireman's equipment, the engines had been refined and were capable of new feats. The steamer of the 1880s shot two 380-foot streams simultaneously and could pump for a day at a stretch. Manufacturers even developed a horseless engine, propelled by its own steam, that proved quite useful at the great Boston fire of 1871. Meanwhile the hook and ladder truck, originally a wagon heaped with equipment, had grown into a specialized machine in its own right. Equipped with telescoping 100-foot extension ladders mounted on rear turntables that swiveled into position, the improved ladder trucks were needed to combat fires in the new six- and seven-story office buildings and luxury hotels. Ladder companies were aided by the invention of the water tower, a 50-foot high periscope-like pipe that could direct a stream of water at the upper stories of a building. The ever-inventive Chief Hale of Kansas City patented a telescoping water tower that automatically raised itself to the desired height by means of water pressure. The late seventies also saw the development of the chemical engine, a pumper that worked on the principle of the fire extinguisher. The engine held two tanks of a solution of water and baking soda that would be mixed with a bottle of acid at the scene of the fire. The resulting chemical reaction propelled a stream of gaseous water strong enough to put out most small fires with less resulting water damage than a steamer would have caused.

It is hard to visualize the total effect of the alarms that set all of this activity—human, mechanical, and animal—in motion. Two staged "stop-action" scenes taken by a Seattle

90

87-89

studio photographer in 1916 illustrate some of the action: as the alarm sounds in "The Rapid Exit" the lights presumably have just flashed on. Men jump out of bed and into their pants and boots (left standing together beside the beds for just this purpose), pull up their suspenders, and dash for the poles. At the same time the doors on the horses' stalls downstairs swing open, the chains drop, and the animals gallop to the engines in time for the harnesses to drop. Sliding down to the apparatus floor and taking their positions around the truck, the men complete "The Hitch." If this truck had been a steam engine the engineer would be lighting some kindling in the boiler to start the pressure building. The men who had run ahead to open the station doors would jump onto the truck as it sped out. The whole process, from the time the alarm came in to the time the engine left the station, took less than a minute (*Scientific American* claimed times of "three, four or five seconds" for New York's engine companies). It must have been an amazing sight, only remembered now by members of our grandparents' generation—some of whom still can be persuaded to describe "seeing the engines, with the coal fires blazing under the steam boilers and the smoke billowing from the smokestacks, being pulled along the streets by charging horses."

Whether one of a group of identical neighborhood stations, or a stately department headquarters, or even a city's centerpiece, the fire station of the seventies and eighties was likely to be built of red brick and marked by a prominent tower. Historians have proposed several explanations for the advent of red brick in these years as the standard material, not only for fire stations but for houses and many public buildings. First came considerations of cost: the price of stone was rising in comparison to that of mass-produced brick, and the increase in wages for all laborers after the Civil War made hand-carved stone ornament even more expensive. But taste was an almost equally important factor. Even the wealthy volunteer Laurel Engine Company of York, Pennsylvania, chose brick for its elegant quarters in 1878—perhaps because by that time brick was no longer considered merely a cheap alternative to stone. With museums, theaters, city halls, and mansions all being built in brick, the fire station's design was in keeping with the latest architectural trend.

Red brick suited the era's taste for richly colored buildings, an outgrowth of the warm-toned "Tuscan" styles of the 1840s (as seen in the Hibernia Engine House and Boston's Torrent fire station described in Chapter Two). Unlike the Greek Revivalists in the first part of the century (such as the architect of Philadelphia's Perseverance Hose Company), who painted and stuccoed every surface in sight a pristine white, the Victorians preferred what they called "picturesque" variegation of pattern, texture, and color in furniture and clothing as well as in architecture. Following the dictates of the English critic John Ruskin, they decorated their buildings with insets of multicolored stone and tile (the architects of Firemen's Hall in Ann Arbor, Michigan, achieved the same effect at lower cost by painting parts

91

91. *Laurel/Rex Fire Station, York, Pennsylvania, 1877–78. Beaton Smith, architect. The mansard roof, spiky cast-iron railing, and tall proportions are all examples of Victorian Gothic taste. Placing style over practicality, the architect moved the tower from the back of the building, where hose is unloaded, up to the front, purely for visual effect (see figs. 25–28 for interior views).*

of their brick building to look like stone), and they added colored slate and cast-iron grillwork to lend interest to the roof. Red brick, especially when laid with black-tinted mortar, provided much more color than plain stone, and it could be arranged in fancy three-dimensional designs to break up the surface with even more texture and pattern. The old Tunxis Hose Company in Unionville, Connecticut, and Atlanta's Engine 6, both relatively plain buildings otherwise, feature some exceptionally fine decorative brickwork. Architects even were able to order ready-made surface texture in the form of pre-stamped pressed or cut brick, and molded terra-cotta ornament—as the designer of the Union Fire Company in Carlisle, Pennsylvania, used very effectively.

Love of the irregular was by no means confined to the buildings' surfaces. Victorian architects reshaped the buildings themselves to include jagged rooflines, and broke up the walls with projecting bays and balconies. Towers—big round ones, short spiky ones, glorified chimney pots, placed asymmetrically whenever possible—were a favorite device for all types of buildings: Mark Twain described a "bright new edifice" of the 1880s as "picturesquely and peculiarly towered and pinnacled—a sort of gigantic caster, with the cruets all complete." In a period when skylines sprouted spires and turrets as thickly as in a medieval town, fire stations were among the few types of building in which the tower served a real purpose. While the designers of earlier storefront stations had hidden their hose-drying equipment inside the buildings, archi-

tects now played up the tower for all it was worth. Responding to Victorian taste, they moved the tower from the back of the apparatus floor, where hose was unloaded, up to a front corner of the building. There was no way to justify this change in terms of function—if anything, the new arrangement was less convenient. It was all done for show. The architect who in 1893, designed Hose Company 6 in Pawtucket, Rhode Island, left a drying shaft at the back of the building but put his stairwell in a "tower" at the front to get the same visual effect.

Prominent towers also had the effect of making fire stations look like more important buildings than the "storefront" designs had been. The hose tower on the central fire station at Thomaston, Connecticut, designed to balance a similar cupola on the City Hall next door, links the station both visually and symbolically to the town's government.

Taste for the picturesque and a new sense of the fire station's architectural significance affected not only headquarters buildings but the less elaborate neighborhood stations as well. Unlike the storefront designs, which were patterned after commercial buildings, the "firebarns" of the 1870s, '80s and '90s are closer to industrial architecture. Towers—in this case to hold a siren—had been an integral part of factory buildings since the 1840s, and architects often used fancy tower decoration to offset the plain, functional design of the main buildings. Variants of Italianate decoration, sometimes with an admixture of pointy Venetian "gothic," prevailed as the most popular

92, 93. *Tunxis Hose Company 1, Unionville, Connecticut, 1893. Joseph Jetner, builder (photographs by Theresa Beyer).* **94.** *Union Fire Company, Carlisle, Pennsylvania, c1885. The red brick station at Unionville recalls factory architecture, but with unusually fine detail. Carlisle's Union Company boasts a decorative weathervane and a stained-glass window in the shape of a fire hydrant.*

93

92

95

96

97

116

98

95. *Engine 21/Truck 6 (now a private residence), San Francisco, California, 1893. Henricksen and Mahoney, architects.* 96. *Hose Company 6 (now a restaurant), Pawtucket, Rhode Island, 1896.* 97. *Engine 1, Albany, New York, 1892. Ernest Hoffman, architect. Henricksen and Mahoney took the basic lines of a building like fig. 94 and translated them into California redwood. Architects working in Romanesque Revival Style used large, simple forms and rounded shapes to give their designs an air of permanence.*

98. *Terra-cotta plaque, Harris Fire Station, Phenix (now Harris), Rhode Island, 1889.*

style for both factories and fire stations. The towers of the Palazzo Publico in Siena and the Ducal Palace in Florence were favorite models for adaptation, perhaps because the architects wanted their buildings to recall the palaces' historical function as civic landmarks. Those who preferred to copy elements of French architecture topped the same basic brick buildings with high mansard roofs. Even fairly simple fire stations such as the engine house in the factory town of Phenix, Rhode Island, or the false-fronted Alpine Hose Company in Georgetown, Colorado, could be dressed up with an elaborate cupola. Unfortunately these towers, often topped with delicate woodwork, proved vulnerable to attack from lightning, termites, rot, and even fire. Today very few survive intact.

By 1881, *American Architect and Building News* was advising its readers: "Black mortar is going rather out of date, joints colored with a Venetian red being much more agreeable in appearance, especially with the moulded and cut brickwork now in vogue, and more permanent." A new style, based on the Romanesque as adapted by the architect H. H. Richardson in the seventies, was gaining popularity. Favoring uniformly warm color, round arches, and large, simple shapes, Richardson had treated each building as one solid volume rather than an assortment of pieces or a group of accented walls. His Victorian love of rich surfaces translated into terra-cotta ornament and elaborately carved brick and brownstone trim. The new style never worked very well for factory buildings but came to dominate church,

school, and townhouse design. As they did in most matters of style, architects of fire stations stayed a good ten years behind this latest trend, but they eventually used the Richardsonian round arches and towers with great success. Boston's Engine 33/Ladder 15 and Hose Company 6 of Pawtucket, Rhode Island, are exceptionally attractive variations on Richardson's idea. Following another lead from Richardson, more pretentious fire stations featured the same basic shapes in rough-hewn stone with decoration in carved brownstone. In this way even relatively small buildings such as Steamer 1 in Albany, New York, and the Rock Springs (Wyoming) City Hall and Fire Station could convey the impression of massive, rocky fortresses.

With their increased bulk and their array of new equipment, these "imposing and complete" fire stations of the 1870s and '80s reflect the public's growing recognition of the importance of the fire department to community interests. Whether craggy piles of brownstone and brick, or factory-like "firebarns," they were far more substantial and often more expensive than the storefront-type stations had been. Even their towers indicated a certain amount of pride. The quantity of firemen's memorials and monuments erected in public squares during this period attests that people were beginning once again to think of firemen as heroes. Over the next thirty years architects would express the changing attitude toward the fire service by honoring the men, the horses, and the machines with increasingly elaborate buildings.

CHAPTER FIVE

Castles and Palaces

Eclectic Architecture, Politics, and Sentiment

1890–1918

One way to account for the look of the turn-of-the-century fire station is to say that the buildings' exteriors finally received as much attention as fire chiefs previously had given to the equipment inside. The electrical devices, alarm equipment, and apparatus perfected in the 1880s remained in use for the next thirty or forty years, so the fire station's basic program changed very little in that time. Nevertheless, the buildings did change—not so much in size or layout as in style. While a writer in 1893 had praised the red brick fire stations in Columbus, Ohio, as "chaste in appearance," the turn-of-the-century commentator would often compare new fire stations to mansions. The stocky, industrial designs of the red brick stations were left behind as firehouses began to resemble medieval castles, French chateaux, Italian palaces, and Swiss chalets.

These new buildings were every bit as "complete" as their predecessors had been, but rather than being "imposing" they could

best be described as "astounding." Their luxurious appointments would have made a volunteer company jealous; yet now city building departments were approving the designs and tax dollars were being paid for them. The reasons for this sudden boom of spectacular fire stations have as much to do with the politics and architectural taste of the era as with people's attitudes toward firemen. There has not been anything like it since.

By 1890 public sentiment was such that many people were willing to spend a little more for the comfort of their firemen. The image of the fireman as a rowdy menace had faded with the passing of the old volunteer departments; the picture of the fireman risking all to save a child from a burning building was utmost in everyone's mind. Public subscriptions paid for elaborately mawkish fireman's monuments in cities all around the country, but books of the time express this sentiment best:

He jumps at the flames, his blood is up in arms; his soul full of enthusiasm. Nor does he draw regular breath until his enemy is overthrown, till the flames are drowned and quenched in torrents of water. . . .

And the fireman! Who more gallant and brave? His calling is indeed a noble one. His

99. *Engine 31 (now a community center), New York City, 1895. Napoleon LeBrun and Sons, architects. Magnificent turn-of-the-century fire stations reflected the taste for eclecticism in municipal architecture. LeBrun's design copies the William K. Vanderbilt mansion, which in turn was based on a French chateau. Note the monogrammed gables and emblematic torches.*

119

100

100, 101. *Fire Department Headquarters, Brooklyn, New York, 1890–94. Frank Freeman, architect. "Complete in every detail," the Brooklyn fire department's new headquarters building was equipped with a complete gymnasium on the fourth floor and a sophisticated alarm system. But the most notable thing about the building was its magnificent facade. Using brick, granite, sandstone, terra cotta, and Spanish tiles, Freeman combined a tall silhouette, massive rounded forms, and intricate ornament in a highly original way. A contemporary writer called it, "the most striking architectural feature of all the city's public buildings" (postcard, c1895, Museum of the City of New York).*

first duty, to save life, his next, to protect property. Truly, an Evangelical mission. All the years of his life—the prime of his manhood and his more mature existence—are devoted to his calling. To be a fireman in the real sense he must possess qualities, physical and mental, which, when combined, form the real hero.

It must be remembered, too, that back of all the showy, valorous work at fires lies a long course of preparation and training, even of work that is dull, laborious and tiresome. . . .

He is naturally brave, loyal and progressive, thoroughly self-reliant, and too often, as tender-hearted as a child. He is a public servant of the highest order who cannot be too highly prized.

Authors would work their readers up to a fever of emotion and then hit them with this plea: "Give to them, then, if possible even more than what belongs to them. They are deserving of money, credit, and thanks. Encourage your firemen! 'Tis for your interest to do so."

Brooklyn's fire commissioner had found a sympathetic audience in 1894 when he proposed that stations include expanded lounge areas: "These new houses, when completed, will be a credit to the City and a boon to the firemen, who have long felt the want of comfortable quarters. There is no public servant so much confined to quarters as a fireman. . . . it is my desire to make their houses as comfortable as possible."

Finally, if an appeal for the firemen's comfort failed, a fire chief could resort to the argument of morality, as Chief Fillmore Tyson of Louisville did in 1904: "The best place for the formation of, and meditation upon, the purest ideals of life is where one is isolated from public view. This being true, every engine house of every fire system should conform to a happy home, so that the occupants thereof may be inspired by its very equipments to lead a consistent and useful life." The message was the same: whether from humanitarian concern or enlightened self-interest, the public owed the fireman the best it could afford.

Not since the 1850s had anyone proposed that citizens had any sort of obligation to firemen. In some ways the chief's rhetoric recalls speeches made by firemen before the Civil War, but with an important difference: the "real heroes" they referred to were municipal employees rather than volunteers. Firemen were now described as "loyal," "progressive," and "consistent"—their aim was to be "useful" to the public. If voters had not approved of the extra luxuries, few of the opulent fire stations of the turn of the century would ever have been built. Architects of the turn of the century once again designed fire stations as "architectural tributes to the meritorious fire service" (see Chapter Two) but now conceived of them as public buildings.

The story of Engine 31 in New York, the biggest and most expensive fire station in the city at the time it opened in 1896, is an example of turn-of-the-century building at its most extreme. Built on a 76 by 112 foot corner site

99

101

102

102

102. *Detail, Engine 31, New York City, 1895 (see fig. 99).* **103.** *Fire Department Headquarters (now Pine Street Inn), Boston, Massachusetts, 1892–94. Edmund Wheelwright, architect. Clever architects at the turn of the century adapted elements of historic European architecture to modern, "firemanic" uses. LeBrun worked torches and dolphins into the ornament of Engine 31 to symbolize fire and water; Wheelwright designed an elongated version of the ducal palace at Siena so that firemen could practice scaling the tower. The former headquarters in Boston now serves as a shelter for homeless men and women.*

three times the size of the average city lot, it was designed to house two engine companies, a water tower, a fuel depot, offices for the second battalion, and living quarters for its chief as well as seventeen horses—more equipment and facilities than any other station in the city. Though the building cost no more per square foot than smaller fire stations being erected in New York at the same time, its oversized lot and $80,000 budget inspired the fire department's architect Napoleon LeBrun to propose what local newspapers described as "a palace of stone with fittings such as only very rich men may enjoy at their own expense."

LeBrun's design clearly copied the William K. Vanderbilt mansion built on Fifth Avenue in 1879, which in turn was modeled after a French chateau. Like the Vanderbilt house the fire station had limestone-faced walls and a steep slate roof topped with copper cresting. Both buildings had dormers with triangular gables, but Engine 31's dormers were decorated with "F.D." monograms that comple-

102

mented the carved torches and dolphins (symbolizing fire and water) over the windows, and the decorative flames near the doors on the ground floor. The entire structure was supported by a steel frame, still an innovative technique at the time. Its overall magnificence is so unlike LeBrun's other, more sensible fire stations that one account credited the famous architect Stanford White with embellishing the design.

LeBrun spared no expense on the interior, either, specifying moldings of Italian marble, solid bronze railings, and a system of speaking tubes that connected the patrol desk to every part of the house. The sidewalk and apparatus floor were laid with a special beveled brick, imported from England. When set in a herringbone pattern it provided a secure surface for horses' hooves. Second floor bathrooms had mosaic marble floors and included two porcelain-lined tubs and a marble-enclosed needle bath. Up under the roof a "great sitting room" had twenty-five individual clothes closets—quite a change from the standard lockers. The *American Architect and Building News* congratulated "the authorities and the architects" for "acting wisely in erecting a building which will give so high a tone to the newer buildings that are to postdate it."

This building (notable in itself) was part of an even more remarkable trend in fire station design. Across the river in Brooklyn, builders had earlier completed a magnificent $140,000 fire department headquarters building, one of the finest examples anywhere of the Richardsonian legacy. In Boston, a four-story Italian palazzo fire station in yellow brick was being erected, and within two years Buffalo, New York, would have a set of chateau-like fire stations—slightly scaled down—in brick and pressed iron rather than stone and copper, but splendid nonetheless.

100, 101

103

104–106

Most of these stations opened as the country came out of the 1893 depression, which had slackened spending in all sectors and probably slowed work on Brooklyn's headquarters. By January 1895, the *Philadelphia Ledger* predicted "Hard Times Disappearing," and the *American Architect and Building News*

104, 105, 106. *Engine 26, Buffalo, New York, 1894. Frederick W. Humble, architect. For fire departments with some pretensions but a lower budget, the design of a French chateau could be translated into brick and stamped iron—though the effect was a little more convincing in the architect's drawings than it was in reality (original drawing from the City Architect's office, Buffalo).*

105

106

107

108

107. *Fire Department Headquarters (now Fire Station 2), Kansas City, Missouri, 1905. Albert Turney, architect.* **108.** *Engine 2 (now storage), San Francisco, California, 1908. Newton J. Tharp, architect. The City Beautiful movement advocated rebuilding the metropolis with wide streets, orderly parks, and dignified public buildings in classical styles. Not many plans included firehouses, but a few stations were influenced by City Beautiful ideals. Kansas City's headquarters was a smaller version of the train terminal that Turney designed the following year.*

reprinted the article, probably to cheer its readers (architects always have suffered during economic slowdowns). The period that followed, a golden age for fire station design, was one of extravagant building in both the public and private sectors. As personalities such as "Diamond Jim" Brady, Mrs. Potter Palmer of Chicago, and the Vanderbilts spent their fortunes on flamboyant public gestures, their taste influenced a wide range of American architecture.

The increase in cost and luxury for fire stations was also part of a larger trend in government policy. Budgets in all areas of city spending increased in the 1890s in line with an overall expansion of municipal services. Some of the impetus for civic improvements came from private booster groups, who hoped that increased amenities and beautified streets would attract business to the city. It was in the 1890s that most cities began to provide taxpayers with extensive sewer service, street lighting, playgrounds, and libraries; the modern high school is largely a product of that era. Budgets for public buildings grew enormously. Boston spent close to three million dollars on building projects between 1891 and 1894.

The World's Columbian Exposition held at Chicago in 1893 became the turn-of-the-century urban reformer's architectural ideal.

Its fairgrounds, laid out as a vast white city of orderly lakes and promenades, inspired private organizations like the Commercial Club of Chicago to commission plans to improve actual city centers along the same lines. Planners hoped to improve the quality of the citizenry's life by imposing ordered plans on the cities' streets and by opening up more space for public recreation. Their schemes usually advocated symmetrical arrangements of tree-lined boulevards, public parks, and grand lagoons. Like the pavilions at the fair, huge white buildings, emblazoned with inscriptions promoting the public good, were an important part of these plans. "Classical" and "Renaissance"-styled piles, approached by great staircases, and porticoed and bristling with white columns, were supposed to replace the "picturesque" structures of the Victorians. City halls and surrounding downtown areas in San Francisco and Denver, state capitols in Sacramento and Harrisburg, and the revival of L'Enfant's plan for Washington, D.C., all show traces of some of the grand plans partially carried out.

On a local scale the "City Beautiful" movement had a wide effect. Almost every city has at least one art museum, railroad terminal, public library, or courthouse that shows its influence—but probably not a fire station. Few fire stations fit the turn-of-the-century ideal for major city buildings. Most of the exceptions are department headquarters like the one in Kansas City, Missouri, built in 1905. An imperial edifice with four-story columns, its facade could pass for that of a high school or civic auditorium. The 1915 Central Fire Station in downtown Little Rock, Arkansas, takes its stylistic cues from the nearby city hall (1907) and courthouse (1912). The station's emblematic terra cotta shields and prominent inscription proclaim the building's civic importance. Fire stations usually followed another, less solemn, trend in turn-of-the-century architecture. The classical rigors of the City Beautiful ideal were offset by a rival movement of fanciful eclecticism, which borrowed stylistic elements from buildings of other times and cultures. While tycoons and members of chambers of commerce envisioned uniform "alabaster cities proud" in their plans for ideal public architecture, they preferred to live in houses like William K. Vanderbilt's New York mansion, a free copy of a French castle with Italian Renaissance dining room, Turkish boudoir, Japanese sitting room, and French parlor. Their private clubs looked like Florentine palaces, their stables like English cottages. The architects who served them had to be proficient in a number of styles, including the Baroque version of American "Colonial" much in demand after the Centennial.

This wave of eclecticism goes back to Victorian buildings such as Ann Arbor's Fireman's Hall, with its tower based on an Italian prototype (see Chapter Four), but differed in its use of historical models. While a Victorian architect could combine a French mansard roof with a vaguely Italianate cornice and translate both into American red brick, his turn-of-the-century counterpart had a more historically accurate approach. Though he might use details from several different palaces in one building he was careful to make faithful copies. The *American Architect and Building News* regularly published entire pages of sketches of assorted European towers, gables, or doors, and an architect could choose details to copy from the magazine as if it were a catalog. The very rich took this stylistic borrowing a step further by actually buying pieces of European buildings and shipping them home to incorporate into their new mansions.

In all branches of architecture lighter colors replaced the red brick and brownstone of the 1870s. Wealthy New Yorkers even put new limestone fronts on their old-fashioned townhouses. The use of steel frame construction meant that exterior walls no longer had to bear the weight of the entire building. New building materials—glazed brick, tile, colored terra-cotta—permitted architects to achieve a new range of effects at reasonable prices. In 1895, the *Brickbuilder* rejoiced that tile in "buffs and grays of several shades, white and cream-white, and the richer, warmer colors of fire-flashed old gold and mottled brown have come, and have evidently come to stay. Of the same colors are the bricks, in unique and graceful forms heretofore unknown among us, giving the architects much greater opportunity in the display of artistic taste than has ever before

109

110

111

112

112. *Chemical Company 5 (now private residence), Buffalo, New York, 1895. E. A. Kent, architect.* **113.** *Engine 21, Washington, D.C., 1908. Appleton Clark, Jr., architect. Without a fixed idea of the "proper" style for a fire station, architects took their inspiration from all sorts of sources: the mansion of the Albright estate adjoining Chemical 5 in Buffalo; a Spanish mission (for no reason at all) in Washington, D.C.*

been enjoyed by the profession." Even the brick schoolhouse of the 1890s was likely to be yellow, brown, or white, instead of red.

Boston's headquarters, Engine 25 in Pittsburgh, and the former Engine 45 in Cincinnati show some of the ways architects used the new brick and tiles. Brooklyn's headquarters is built of Roman brick, a longer, flatter, smooth brick that gave curved surfaces an uninterrupted, seamless quality.

The taste that influenced the Vanderbilts' mansions eventually trickled down to other types of buildings. Along with the increased range of building materials, eclecticism brought a new stylistic variety to American cities. Romanesque red brick often had not been all that different from Italianate red brick, but an accurately detailed Flemish bank build-

ing could not be confused with a hotel copied after a palace from the time of Louis XVI. Designs by City Architect Edmund Wheelwright for city buildings in Boston include a Japanese park pavilion, a bridge copied from one he saw in St. Petersburg, Russia, an Elizabethan-style lunatic asylum, and the Boston Fire Department Headquarters, which copies pieces from several Italian buildings. But the new vocabulary of styles did not permit architects the total freedom one would imagine. Underneath their eclecticism lay the doctrine of "appropriateness"—architects were to adapt elements from previous styles because they were thought to suit modern needs and the particular function of the building. For example, critics advocated copying Italian renaissance villas for modern country homes because

130

113

the villa originally was designed as a country retreat for rich and powerful merchants: "the sympathetic use of historic models [gives] propriety to our designs."

"Propriety" limited the choices of urban architects somewhat. There were few written rules, but for a variety of reasons certain types of buildings came to be associated with certain historical styles: armories copied medieval castles; school buildings followed Gothic or Colonial models; suburban houses adapted Tudor half-timbering. On the other hand, Boston architects considered "inappropriate" a public comfort station modeled after the music pavilion at Versailles. Sometimes architects adopted 249, 238 styles that reflected the heritage of different regions of the country. Many town halls in New England copy Colonial originals, Spanish styles were popular for all types of buildings in California and the Southwest, and Dutch Revival flourished in New York State. Still, very few types of public or commercial buildings were allowed the stylistic latitude permitted for private homes.

Fire stations were the exception. Their unique function and symbolism set them apart from other public buildings. Perhaps no other type of building illustrates the imaginative possibilities of eclecticism so well. Since there was no prevailing opinion on the "proper" style for a fire station, architects tried nearly all of them. The former Chemical 5 in Buffalo, 112 New York, copied its steep roof and tall chimneys from the Albright estate next door, and there are many other examples of stations with direct or indirect links to the fanciful styles

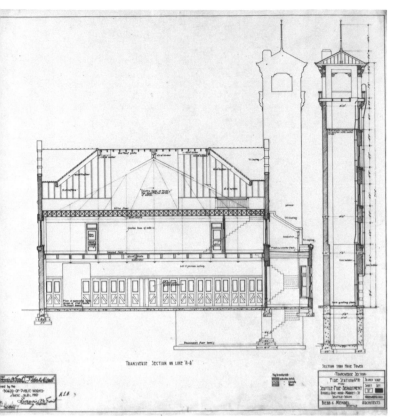

114

114. *Section through Fire Station 18, Seattle, Washington, 1910–11. Bebb and Mendel, architects.* **115.** *Engine 33, New York City, 1898. Ernest Flagg and W. B. Chambers, architects. Well-paying commissions for fire stations at the turn of the century attracted a high caliber of architect. Bebb, who had worked as chief engineer for Louis Sullivan, used his knowledge of structure to devise a truss system that allowed the ceiling of the engine room in Number 18 to be hung from the roof with no need for columns on the ground floor to support it. Flagg later used the idea of combining a giant arch and a narrow facade on his well-known building for Scribner's Bookstore on Fifth Avenue.*

of houses for the very rich. The architect Appleton P. Clark needed no historic justification for Engine 21, a Spanish mission he designed for a neighborhood in the middle of Washington, D.C.

113

Along with this increased variety of styles, fire stations of the 1890s show a new architectural distinction in their designs. Several explanations for the improvement come to mind. As budget appropriations for public buildings increased, the architects' fees involved became more substantial. Many profitable commissions for fire stations now went to leading architects who had trained at the Massachusetts Institute of Technology or the Ecole des Beaux Arts in Paris, the best architecture schools of the day. Charles Bebb had worked as supervising architect in the office of the great Louis Sullivan before designing Fire Station 18 in Seattle. Ernest Flagg, architect of New York's Engine 33, later designed the Singer Tower, for a short time the world's tallest building. Marcus Tullius Reynolds of Albany, New York, drew up that city's building code in addition to designing Ladder 4.

114

The fire station's relatively simple requirements permitted these architects a good deal of leeway. As *The Brickbuilder* pointed out in 1910:

> [The fire station] is exactly the type of building which is extremely interesting to an architect, being devoid of serious difficulties, and of a size and character which permit excellent results. . . . In many cases an opportunity occurs which is rarely offered in other buildings—that of a tower which is not only of use but is necessary, and is not an addition for the sake of fantasy only. . . . it would be wise for municipalities to realize that Fire Department buildings present possibilities which occur in but few civic buildings of small size, and that they can be made attractive and express an appreciation of civic care which should be apparent in all city work.

Unlike a school or a hospital, in which a complicated program dictates the shape of the building, arrangement of the windows, and placement of the wings, the fire station required only two or three stories, a big door, and some windows for the living quarters. Architects could experiment with bays, balconies, porches, and turrets as they liked. The

115

116

117

size and shape of the building may have helped them. Bigger than the average house but more compact than most public buildings, it was just about the right size for a plausible image of a private palace. The basic block shape provided a clearly defined surface for working out formal ideas. Pittsburgh's Engine 25, New York's Engine 33, and the former Engine 46 in Philadelphia are all experiments in fitting as much facade as possible into a limited space.

Sometimes the fire station's function as a city building called for special treatment. Fire stations may not have warranted the classical facade of a City Beautiful courthouse, but as an arm of city government the fire department still needed quarters that somehow looked official. Moreover, people had to be able to recognize a fire station when they needed one. Because fire stations were located in all parts of the city, they had to be distinguishable from commercial buildings, factories, and houses yet fit into their respective neighborhoods (a miniature version of a city hall would look out of place near the stockyards, and a shingled cottage did not belong next to a downtown office building). Though Washington's Engine 19 may not look like a

typical fire station, it is too singular to be confused with anything else.

Finally, some architects seemed to have approached the very concept of the fire station playfully, as an excuse for flights of architectural fantasy. Perhaps they thought that horses and engines would look "inappropriate" charging out of a building that looked like an art museum. Or perhaps some shared the public's sentimental feeling about firemen and their machines. As they had done before the Civil War, fire stations were again treated as a cause for celebration—or at least considered to be less serious than other public buildings. Architects tried out ideas on fire stations that would have been considered too outlandish for any other type of building; no one ever complained about a fire station being undignified. How else to explain the absolutely whimsical firemen gargoyles on former Engine 11 in Kansas City, Kansas? Or the crazy blend of Spanish tiles and mushroom-shaped gables of the fire station in Litchfield, Connecticut? Or the "Dutch Master" heads and pea-green beavers that decorate Albany's Ladder 4? They would never do for a courthouse, but somehow they fit the fire station.

135

118. *Litchfield Fire Station (now a boutique), Litchfield, Connecticut, 1891.* **119, 120, 121.** *Hook and Ladder 4, Albany, New York, 1910. Marcus Tullius Reynolds, architect. Not only were fire stations less solemn than other types of public buildings, they could be downright whimsical. The stepped gables and ornamental sculpture of Ladder 4, all cast in pea-green terra cotta, are meant to recall the Dutch heritage of upstate New York. Beavers symbolize the fur trade.*

121

119

122. *Fire Station 3 (now city offices), Seattle, Washington, 1903.* **123.** *Fire Station 33 (now private residence), Seattle, Washington, 1914. Daniel R. Huntington, architect. The growth of rail and streetcar service in the late nineteenth century helped spur the development of exclusively residential districts. For the first time, architects designed different types of fire stations for different parts of the city. Tudor was a popular style for suburban homes and fire stations (Historical Society of Seattle and King County).*

Architects now returned to the volunteers' tradition of incorporating firefighting symbols into the building's decoration. Like the earlier Emerald Hose Company in Cortland, New York, (see Chapter Two), Fire Station 3 in Sacramento, California, has terra cotta plaques with relief designs of hooks and ladders. The most extreme example of the fire station as architectural joke must have been San Francisco's renowned Engine 15 (now demolished), a gothic-styled structure adorned with sculptured heads of firemen and spires in the shape of hydrants.

Not every fire station was meant to stand out from surrounding buildings by virtue of its quirkiness. As American cities changed in the late nineteenth century, architects designed a new type of fire station especially for residential neighborhoods. The isolated residential district was rare before 1870, for boarding-houses and mansions often had stood only a few blocks away from sweatshops and stores. But with the increased number of city dwellers and the development of extensive streetcar lines, new neighborhoods, such as the Carrollton and Garden districts in New Orleans, grew up in suburbs and outlying areas. By the 1890s some of these new communities were big enough and far enough away from the city core to require their own fire stations. The new stations held one or two pieces of equipment, which often included a chemical engine, and followed the same basic floor plan as their downtown counterparts. Eclectic architects who chose to make these stations look like large houses discovered a new range of stylis-

tic possibilities. Just as cities were taking on more diversified streetscapes, for the first time the style of a fire station varied with its location.

One such new residential neighborhood was the area known as Russian Hill in San Francisco. When city officials decided to erect a fire station there in 1907 they asked City Architect Newton Tharp for a design that would "conform with the general architectural features of the private residences of the district." Tharp preferred Italian and Spanish references for his downtown fire stations, but for Engine 31 he used stucco and half-timbering to suggest a Tudor cottage or Swiss chalet.

In the mind of the turn-of-the-century architect these styles were suitable for houses but not for office buildings. Hence we find Tudor-style fire stations in the suburbs but not downtown. Other half-timbered stations, all in residential sections, include former Engine 33 and Fire Station 3 in Seattle, and Hook and Ladder 9 in New Orleans (like its counterparts in San Francisco, Engine 33 has been recycled as a private house). The town hall–fire station buildings in Lake Forest, Illinois, and South Orange, New Jersey, two small suburban towns, both use a kind of cuckoo-clock half-timbering.

Other architects adapted different residential styles in their designs for fire stations. Engine 1 in Newport, Rhode Island, copies the large shingled summer houses built there in the 1880s. In New Orleans, the huge roof of the Schackai house (former Chemical Engine 12) is based on Creole cottage design, a style

124

108

122, 123

125

126

247

122

123

124. *Engine 31 (now private residence), San Francisco, California, 1908. Newton J. Tharp, architect.*
125. *Town Hall and Fire Station, South Orange, New Jersey, 1894. Rossiter and Wright, architects. Tharp chose Tudor for an engine house sited between townhouses on Russian Hill—see fig. 108 for his design for a downtown fire station in San Francisco. The village fathers in South Orange, a community of lavish homes within commuting distance of New York City, requested "a quiet, unpretentious structure, many gabled and picturesque . . . as old villages were wont to have." Quarters for the local fire department were located around the corner at the back of the building.*

126. *Engine 1 (now offices of* The Newporter*), Newport, Rhode Island, 1887. S. S. Ward, architect.*
127. *Engine 3 (now private residence), Philadelphia, Pennsylvania, 1893. John Windrim, architect. The generous proportions of houses in the Queen Anne or Shingle Style adapted easily to rambling fire stations in red brick and shingle. Engine 3 is distinguished by especially fine brickwork.*

124

125

126

127

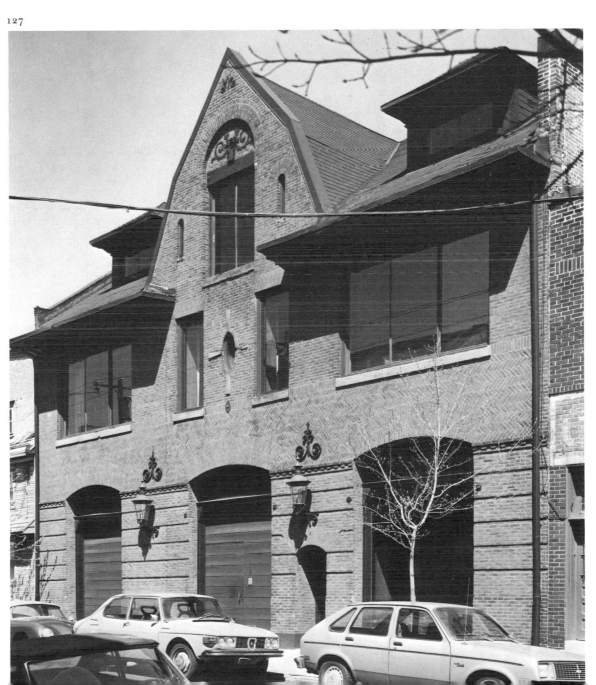

128

that was revived for more pretentious houses in the nineties. After the death of Napoleon LeBrun in 1896, New York's building department awarded commissions for fire stations to a number of different architects (including Ernest Flagg, Horgan and Slattery, and Percy Griffith) who also worked for wealthy private clients. By 1902, when the editor of the *Architectural Record* observed in horror that "there is practically only one class of private dwelling erected on the island of Manhattan—the dwelling intended for comparatively rich people," fire stations designed for residential sections of New York City copied the facades of luxurious townhouses.

The new stylishness was largely confined to the exterior of the station. Tongue-and-groove paneling and plain rooms remained the norm in turn-of-the-century fire stations. There were some exceptions: the apparatus room of Cleveland's Engine 1 featured iron pillars "prettily painted with fire-fighting emblems and inter-twining flowers." The men of Engine 10 in Washington, D.C., won a flag and the title of "Washington's Best Company" in 1906, partly in recognition of their efforts at interior decoration. Calling the station a "model of neatness and attractiveness," the *Fireman's Herald* reported: "The walls were all carefully painted, the halls neatly carpeted, well kept plants were in some of the rooms, and the color scheme was particularly noticeable; all of this work . . . having been done by members of the company." Officers of Engine 28 in Pittsburgh enjoyed a three-room suite that was approached by an elaborate front door and

128, 129

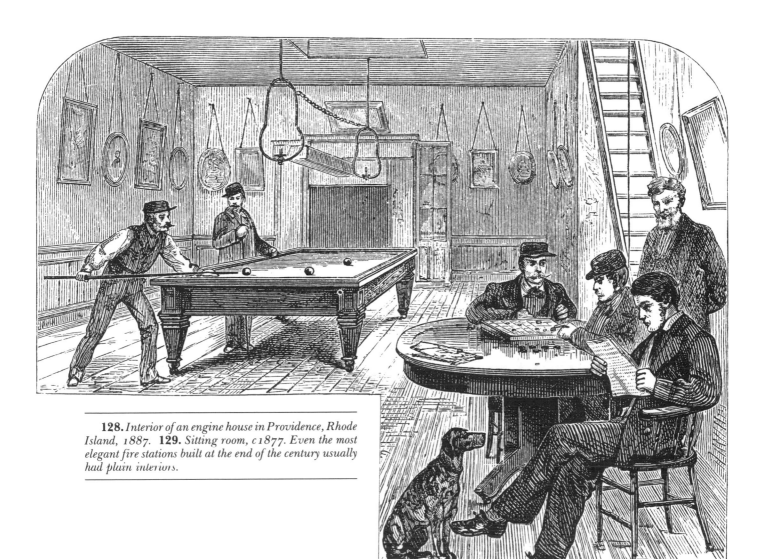

128. *Interior of an engine house in Providence, Rhode Island, 1887.* **129.** *Sitting room, c 1877. Even the most elegant fire stations built at the end of the century usually had plain interiors.*

129

miniature vestibule, and it had its own tiled fireplace and private pole.

Most of the changes in turn-of-the-century firehouse interiors involved improved amenities for the men (perhaps to keep pace with the increasingly comfortable accommodations for horses described in Chapter Four). In the 1870s New York stations had included a billiard room on the third floor, and eventually the third story became a standard part of the plan of fire stations all over the country. The *Brooklyn Daily Eagle* explained in 1894:

51

[Fire Commissioner Wurster], speaking to-day, said that there was not sufficient accommodation for the firemen in the engine houses heretofore built and he proposed to have new engine houses three stories high,

in order to give the men sitting rooms and reading rooms on the top floor. The present engine houses are only two stories high and the rules of the department prohibit the men from sitting in the sleeping apartments. This leaves them no place to sit during the day except in front of the buildings or near the stalls of the horses.

In addition to billiard and card tables, the third floor was sometimes fitted out as a library. Chief Manley of Dalton, Georgia, disagreed with that idea, arguing that "a good, fast fireman's basball team is worth a whole Carnegie library in creating and maintaining enthusiasm. (The library and reading room theory is popularly supported by those who haven't tried it to be the thing)."

130

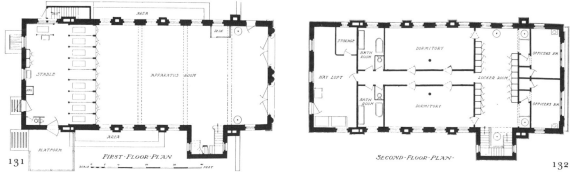

131   FIRST·FLOOR·PLAN   SECOND·FLOOR·PLAN   132

133

Even today, fire chiefs still debate the problem of lounge space for firemen. The quote from the *Eagle* suggests that Commissioner Wurster, like most of his twentieth-century counterparts, preferred not to see firemen sitting outside the station. On the other hand, turn-of-the-century fire stations in Atlanta were equipped with permanent outdoor canopies, somewhat like theater marquees, to shade the firemen when they sat by the front door. The high point in luxury must have been Boston's Engine 22, which featured a roof garden covered with canvas awnings and connected by sliding poles to the third-story gym.

By 1900 several fire stations had gyms on the third floor, but not so much to entertain the men as to keep them in shape. These rooms, as well as the idea that firemen should follow a regular program of exercise, owe their origins to the Civil Service reforms of the 1880s and '90s. In Boss Tweed's time, jobs in the fire department had been handed out as political favors. Under the new legislation prospective firemen were required to pass written and physical exams before they even could be considered for positions. Many cities also required their existing fire departments to take the tests, sometimes with surprising results. Denver's fire commissioner Ralph Talbot set up that city's first fire department gymnasium after overseeing Civil Service exams there in 1898

130–132

145

and finding "that there were on the pay roll of the fire department men who were drawing pensions from the government on account of physical disability resulting from service in the war of rebellion. I felt that this must stop. . . . My idea was to make the men active and strong, to strengthen the muscles and work off the fat." He persuaded the city to donate a room in a downtown building, then asked firemen to do the necessary carpentry on their own time. Once the gym was finished firemen reported there daily to go through this routine:

When the men meet at the gymnasium in the morning they doff their blue firemen's clothes and don a gymnasium suit . . . it consists of long, grey flannel trousers, short-sleeved black sweaters with a white edge, and gymnasium shoes, and in the uniform the men make a very neat appearance. [A captain stands in the center of the gym] and starts the men in a run around the room in a circle, beating time for them with a wand. . . . This running is what gives the men their wind and endurance. The director varies the monotony by occasionally giving orders that send the men running in the opposite direction, in convoluting circles, and in other forms. . . . Before the run is over they hop around the room a few times, first on one foot and then on the other. . . .

The men all take it seriously and earnestly and go in for all they can get out of it.

Talbot ordered "wall apparatus to be in each house for the use of the men while not at the gymnasium." Two years later the men of Hose Company 7 in Atlanta solicited donations to build a gym and bowling alley on a lot adjoining their station. The Prescott Neighborhood Center in Kansas City, Kansas, (see Appendix) now enjoys the use of that former fire station's gym, built in 1911. The exercise room is still intact in former Engine 11, one of the many stations built by Mayor Martin Behrman in New Orleans (see below). A photograph from 1911 shows men working out on rings and with barbells. As usual New York City set the standard for elegance: Flagg's Engine 33 contains not only a gym but fourth-floor handball courts as well. ¹³³

Opulent fire stations, like other showy civic buildings, constituted political as well as architectural statements. Responsibility for commissioning a particularly extravagant fire station sometimes can be traced directly to the wishes of a mayor. For example, Nathan Matthews, mayor of Boston from 1891 to 1894, took a special interest in public architecture, perhaps because he hoped to leave a monumental mark on the city. According to Francis Chandler of the School of Architecture at the Massachussetts Institute of Technology, Matthews "had a wide experience in building matters; and as an intelligent lover of the arts he fully appreciated the importance of constructing worthy municipal buildings." Following the advice of the Boston Citizen's Association (which suggested abolishing the city architect's department and contracting with private firms so that "the work of the city would then be done as private work is done, without the admixture of politics"), Mayor Matthews changed the job of city architect to permit the incumbent to continue a private practice on the side. In an inspired move he then convinced Edmund Wheelwright to accept the position. At that time Wheelwright was one of the most respected architects in Boston. His training included degrees from Harvard, the Massachusetts Institute of Technology, and the Ecole des Beaux Arts; and he had worked for the firms of Peabody and Stearns and McKim, Mead & White. During his twenty-year career in Boston he designed the city's Opera House, Horticultural Hall, and the Harvard Lampoon building, and served on the committee to study designs for the new Museum of Fine Arts building. Wheelwright must have taken a substantial cut in pay when he became city architect, but he, too, seems to have felt some special commitment to the work. Eventually he became an authority on school architecture and published several books on the subject. During Mayor Matthews' four-year administration the city erected twenty-three schools, four fire stations, fourteen buildings for the city hospital, and substantial additions to the city's institutions and jails, all from Wheelwright's designs. Matthews also initiated legislation to establish the first subway system in America; Wheelwright designed some of its stations.

103 Wheelwright's fire department headquarters ranks among his most striking designs. In four stories and two mezzanines this building housed central offices, alarm apparatus, and training school in addition to engine and water tower companies. The apparatus floor was covered with a tile dome, and the third floor gym had an elevated running track (29 laps to the mile). In true eclectic fashion Wheelwright adapted the building's tower from the Palazzo Publico in Siena, the windows and balconies from Venetian architecture, and colored marble shields from other Italian palaces. With typical turn-of-the-century practicality he then arranged these features so that trainees could practice scaling the 155-foot tower and rescuing each other from the marble balconies. Unlike its European prototypes, this building was designed with a steel frame and arch construction that made it fireproof throughout.

Matthews and Wheelwright won acclaim from local architectural critics, and four one-year terms in office. However, when Edwin Curtis succeeded Matthews in 1894 he abolished the office of city architect, and Wheelwright went back to private practice. A few years later Mayor Martin Behrman of New Orleans turned a similar architectural vision to political advantage. His story provides another example of a mayor's taking a special interest in expensive fire stations in that period. Behrman was a powerful political boss. Like Tweed of New York, he gained some of his earliest support from fellow volunteer firemen. His long administration (1904–1924) was marked by increased building and public services, which historians now interpret as an attempt to divert public attention from his corrupt system of political appointments. Behrman established the first city architect's office in New Orleans and was responsible for

134

135

148

136

134. *Rear yard and stalls behind Engine 37, 1910;* **135.** *Engine 31 (now Ladder 9), 1910;* **136.** *Engine 17 (now police station), 1912 (photograph by Theresa Beyer);* **137.** *Engine 34, 1917; all in New Orleans, Louisiana;* *Edgar Angelo Christy, architect. Some of the most spectacular fire stations can be traced to the wishes of a powerful politician. Boss Martin Behrman was responsible for erecting dozens of large public buildings during his five terms as mayor of New Orleans; he never failed to make a speech at opening day ceremonies. While City Architect Christy's designs for downtown fire stations were unexceptional (see Chapter Three), he turned out many gracious fire stations for residential neighborhoods. Instead of housing horses inside the buildings, he put the stalls in a yard behind the station. Notice the high ceilings and tall proportions that allowed air to circulate during hot Southern summers.*

137

138

139

134–137, 60 more than fifteen fire stations, including some of the most splendid residential-style stations ever built. Each bore a prominent plaque: "Erected Under the Administration of Martin Behrman, Mayor."

Unlike Wheelwright, New Orleans' City Architect Edgar Angelo Christy never attended an architectural school. He apprenticed with a local architect for two or three years and then joined the city's engineering department. Christy based his designs for fire stations on the fashionable mansions then going up in newly annexed residential districts. Photographs of these houses appeared regularly in *Architectural Art and its Allies*, a local trade publication that Christy no doubt read. In the early 1900s the magazine published many "examples of Old English timbered work, or its modifications; a style particularly satisfying and pleasing in its effects," and Christy used similar decoration in many of his fire stations. His handsome designs include some fine ornamental details, and critics praised the way in which "Every piece of timber and every course of brick seem as though they were moulded into one beautiful structure."

Like most big houses in New Orleans these fire stations have tall and ample proportions; architects "stretched" the humble English cottage prototypes to accommodate lofty 16- to 20-foot ceilings that helped keep the rooms

138, 139. *Fire Station 27, Hollywood, California, 1929. P. K. Schabarum, architect (interior photograph by Theresa Beyer).* **140.** *Engine 28, Los Angeles, California, 1912. J. P. Krempel and W. E. Erkes, architects. Grand fire stations in Los Angeles continued into the 1920s. The design for Number 27 was approved by the city's Municipal Art Commission while Mrs. Cecil B. DeMille was a member.*

140

141

cool during hot Southern summers. Some of the fire stations still use their original wooden ceiling fans to keep the air moving. The spacious interiors, finished in colored tile, were well-ventilated but fairly plain. What impressed contemporary visitors most were the "elegant tiled bathrooms with bath tubs of the most modern style and shower bath, etc., just as good as in any hotel." When shown the gym at Engine 11, one waggish reporter remarked on "a machine to reduce the corpulency of the firemen who may be getting too fat with all the other comforts of the house."

Christy's stations won acclaim from *Architectural Art and its Allies*: "both a comfortable home for the firemen and an ornament to each particular locality, the [stations] rid the community of some of its architectural nightmares." In their 1909 report the National Board of Fire Underwriters noted the "improvements" while deploring the "purely political administration of the department's affairs." Popular approval mattered more to Mayor Behrman, and he never missed a chance to make a speech at opening ceremonies for the new stations. Excerpts from an account of the 135 opening of Engine 31 show how he linked the new building's beauties with his administration's policies:

> [Behrman] said that the mayor and council are like the president and directors of a company and the people are the stockholders and can get just what they want if they go at it in a helpful way. . . . he added that the firemen are entitled to the best that the city

can give them and that the city administration is fortunate in having the co-operation of all subordinate branches, so that when such an improvement is needed everyone helps. . . .

Everybody said it was pretty enough to put alongside the library on St. Charles Avenue. The mayor said it was the handsomest engine house in the city, and everybody in the Third Ward is sure it is!

Relations among mayor, architect, and public were not always so cordial in the matter of expensive fire stations. The story of the corrupt officials responsible for Engine 23, 142 built in Los Angeles in 1910, shows yet another way that luxurious stations were erected at the turn of the century. This station cost $53,000 excluding the lot, was equipped with self-flushing stalls for the horses, a marble vestibule, and two elevators. The entire third floor was given over to a mahogany-paneled apart- 141 ment for the fire chief and his family. The press had a field day when the building opened:

> . . . the most elaborate and richest engine house west of New York and maybe the most ornate east of Santa Monica, in the whole United States or maybe in this or any other world. . . .
>
> SYBARITICAL EFFORT THIS
> . . . It is the interior which is a sort of Nirvana for a soulful legion of blue-shirted civil service graduates. . . . If you would reach the third floor properly, present yourself to the orderly at the wide entrance and he will

141, 142. *Engine 23 (now sculptor's studio), Los Angeles, California, 1910. Hudson and Munsell, architects. Fire Chief Walter Lips took the blame for this boondoggle, which caused quite a scandal in the local press. A $53,000 fire station with self-flushing horse stalls and two elevators, its crowning glory was a mahogany-paneled suite of officers quarters on the top floor.*

142

143

143. *Engine 61, Pittsburgh, Pennsylvania, 1915. John D. Brennan, architect.* 144. *Fire Station 3, Rock Island, Illinois, 1917. Cyrus D. McLane, architect (from Fireman's Herald, August 25, 1917).* 145. *Fire Station 14 (now abandoned), Kansas City, Missouri, 1905. Albert Turney, architect. Simple lines and overhanging roofs characterized buildings in the Prairie Style. These stripped-down buildings gradually replaced more elaborate types of fire stations in the years around World War I.*

New Station at Rock Island, Ills.

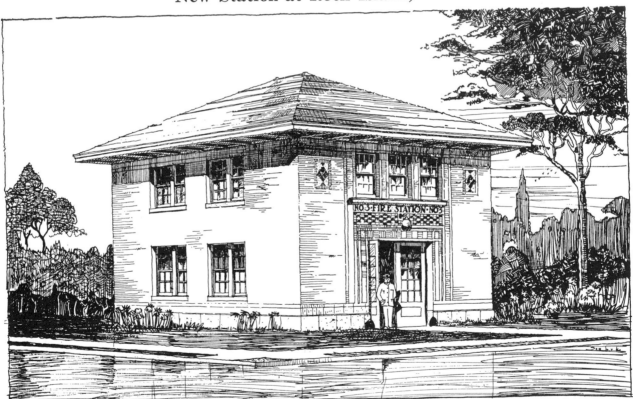

This new fire station is of brick with stone trimming. Wood cornice, composition shingle roof, apparatus room for motor truck only—no horses. It has a reinforced concrete floor, plaster walls and metal ceiling. The basement contains a heating plant and coal storage. The second story contains Captain's room, Firemens' room, toilet and bath rooms, and clothes lockers. A hose tower is provided in one corner of building.

Wood construction was used above the first floor line. The architect was Cyrus D. McLane, of Rock Island, Ills.

144

145

take you to the elevator. Elevator? Why of course—that is the passenger elevator for there is also a freight elevator. . . . Notice the Peruvian mahogany carefully and you will see that the heart of the log has been chosen and that its grain has been so placed that it gives the appearance of real flames. . . . a bath with a marble shower and a tub big enough for two large chiefs. . . .

It is likely that the house captain will wear evening dress after 6 o'clock at least, while the orderly at the entrance will perhaps wear knickerbockers. . . .

This house for magnificence is unrivalled except in New York, where they are jealous and are trying to outdo it with an engine-house with a banquet-hall. . . .

[Engine 23 is] the artistic spasm of a former board of fire commissioners. The mayor and the present board . . . think unkindly of the previous board when Engine House Number 23 is mentioned. . . .

It will be another one of those things for which Los Angeles is noted.

It is hard to reconstruct who was responsible for allocating funds for this "fire house deluxe" since no one wanted to take the credit. By the time the building opened in 1910, a new mayor and council who had run on a "Good Government" ("Goo-Goo" in the local press) reform platform were in power. They quickly disowned the station and canceled the dedication ceremonies. Blame eventually

fell on Fire Chief Walter Lips, who resigned under public pressure without ever getting the chance to enjoy his new quarters. A few months later the mayor asked the council to consider using one set of standard plans and specifications for all future fire stations. 138, 139

By the end of World War I the era of castles and palaces was passing. Shortages of labor and supplies curtailed all new building during the war, and very few fire stations were built in those years. When Edgar Angelo Christy designed his last mansion-like station in 1918, the type was already out of date; although some cities continued to erect elaborate, eclectic fire stations on through the 1920s, a new architectural style was coming to dominate fire station design. Based on the modernist aesthetic of Frank Lloyd Wright and other midwestern architects of the Prairie School, the style reached back to the industrial red brick architecture of the nineteenth century. Prairie Style stations like Engine 61 in Pittsburgh, built in 1915, are made up of clean, rectangular shapes with low spreading roofs and plain windows up close under them. Whether to save money (a similar station at Waukegan, Illinois, cost just $10,000 in 1911), to keep up with surrounding domestic architecture, or just to follow a new architectural trend, architects turned to the simple modernism of the Prairie Style more and more after 1910. By the time the war was over these plain buildings had just about replaced the eclectic fire palaces of the Gilded Age. 143

CHAPTER SIX

The Beginnings of the Modern Fire Station

Motorization and the Bungalow

1905–1940

The design of fire stations for residential areas changed dramatically between 1905 and 1940. Fire stations like Number 14, opened in Atlanta, Georgia, in 1913, presented an image quite different from the ample barns and baronial mansions discussed in the last chapter. With its flower beds and winding driveway, its overhanging roof extended to form a porch in front, this building imitated the informal design of a modest, middle-class cottage or "bungalow." Its floor plan was even more novel: all the rooms were on one level, with the apparatus floor to one side and a living area next to it. A locker room, toilets, and dormitory were arranged behind, with a new room—the kitchen—at the rear.

"Bungalow-type" fire stations owe their size and layout to the internal combustion engine, which replaced horse-drawn fire apparatus in the years before the first World War. But a wealth of other factors, including changes in the work day, changes in firefighting pro-

cedures, and changes in city planning also influenced their design. These buildings now show how firefighting and domestic architecture moved into the twentieth century.

The term "bungalow" comes from a Hindi word for a type of small house with a low-pitched, overhanging roof indigenous to India. American architects used it to describe the more substantial wooden or stuccoed houses designed by the followers of the craftsman/furniture designer Gustav Stickley after 1905. The style proliferated on the West Coast in the elegant low-roofed, handcrafted houses of the Pasadena architects Charles and Henry Greene, and it proved immediately popular in the South since it provided open shady porches and ample ventilation, which Southerners considered healthful. Eventually bungalow homes caught on in newly growing middle-class suburbs all over the country—their small size and simple plan ideally suited the needs of young families without servants. Early planned neighborhoods or "bungalow courts" left a permanent mark on American cities and set a new standard for one-family houses. The bungalow's low profile, casual look, and use of natural materials carried over into the ranch houses of the 1950s and '60s.

146

146. *Opening day at Fire Station 14, Atlanta, Georgia, 1913. Morgan & Dillon, architects. The automobile, a health craze, and the growth of the suburbs helped bring about fire stations designed to look like cottages. Firemen tended the gardens themselves (photograph courtesy of Chief Steve B. Campbell).*

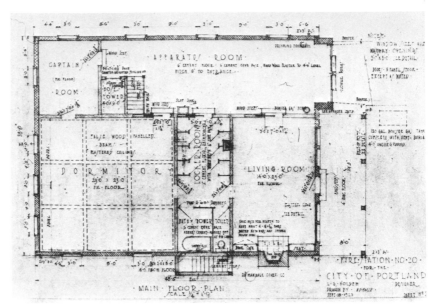

148

147

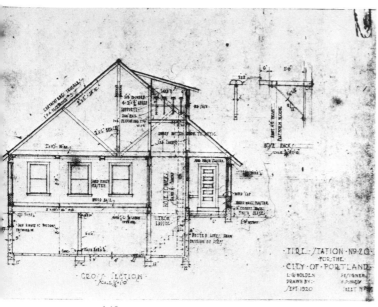

149

147, 148, 149. *Fire Station 20 (now Sellwood Boys' Club), Portland, Oregon, 1920. Lee Holden, architect. Replacing horse-drawn equipment with compact motorized engines made possible a radically new floor plan; instead of adding stories to separate living quarters from the stable, all the fire station's rooms now could be grouped on one level, with easy accessibility to the engine room. However, the introduction of the two-platoon work schedule brought about the need for a new room—the kitchen. This low-profile arrangement pleased neighbors, who claimed that three-story "firebarns" were an eyesore.*

Lee Holden, a Portland fireman, designed his first bungalow fire station in 1913, in response to complaints from wealthy homeowners about plans to build a station in their neighborhood. He hid the hose tower in a shaft descending from the roof to the basement. His idea proved so popular that other buildings like it were commissioned, including this example in modified Tudor style (original drawing from the Portland Bureau of Buildings).

Firemen's journals described "bungalows" as any one-story fire station designed to look like a house. The most striking characteristic of the early buildings of this type is how little they looked like fire stations. Their main exterior feature was not the apparatus door but the front door, entered by way of a porch and surrounded with flower boxes. Trucks left from a garage door tucked away in a corner or recessed off to the side as in a private residence. Like single-family homes, these stations were set back from the street with a landscaped lawn and garden. Architects actually disguised some of the fire station's more obvious attributes: they put hose-drying areas into sunken shafts inside the station to eliminate the tower, and even toned down the signs or lettering that identified the building. The name of Sacramento's Chemical Company 4 was spelled out in flowers; one station in Portland, Oregon, had only a hand-carved wooden plaque proclaiming "Ye Fire Station." The result of these changes was that, as one Seattle fireman recalls, the firemen themselves would often drive right past their own station without recognizing it.

155, 156 The small scale of the stations made interiors seem more like those of a private home rather than a cavernous hall. The mahogany and brass and dark wooden wainscoting used in nineteenth-century buildings gave way to white paint, porcelain, tile, and enamel. Lounges heated with radiators also had open fireplaces where firemen could pull up their

rocking chairs. From the inside, the new "sunken tower" resembled a large closet that 149 extended from under the peak of the roof down to the basement.

Fire stations of the bungalow type developed for several reasons. Most important was the change in layout brought about when motorized apparatus replaced the horse-drawn steamers. One of the first gasoline-powered chemical engines and hose wagons was tried out in New London, Connecticut, in 1903; three years later a fire company in Wayne, Pennsylvania, bought a motor-driven pumping engine. Because there were problems with the early equipment, the trend did not catch on in a big way until about 1912. By 1919 an article in *Fireman's Herald* on "the steady onward progress of motorization" noted that in the more than 700 American cities with populations over 5,000 surveyed by the editors, "practically no new horse-drawn equipment is being purchased," and "large purchases of [motor] apparatus are contemplated during the coming year." At that time Baltimore's headlines announced, "FINAL RITES FOR HORSES IN FIRE DEPARTMENT HELD. FINAL RITES HELD IN SALOONS AS KING BOOZE DIES." By the late 1920s only a few small towns and suburbs lacked at least one piece of motorized equipment, though many used makeshift "tractorized" machines mounted on an auto chassis or kept an old steamer in reserve to be towed behind a newer engine in an emergency.

With the shift "from oats to gasoline," the

150, 151. *Fire Station 48 (now Carthage Senior Center), Cincinnati, Ohio, 1913. Cincinnati's first bungalow station was built for a residential district that was annexed to the city in 1912. Its design combines grandiose ornament with a low profile.*

150

requirements of the fire station changed. As long as they had housed horses, fire stations essentially had been modified barns or at best, as one article described stations in New York City in 1912, "ornate and pretentious livery stables." Motorized engines eliminated the need for haylofts, feed rooms, stalls, hanging harnesses, and the high-ceilinged rooms that accommodated them. Since the engines themselves were usually smaller and lighter than the old steamers had been, the doors and the area that housed equipment in the new stations could be smaller. For instance, the apparatus floor in a bungalow station built in Portland, Oregon, in 1920 measured 12 by 32 feet, compared to the 34 by 60 foot floor and additional 34 by 25 foot area for stalls at Engine 22 in Boston. One "triple combination" engine consisting of a pumper, chemical engine, and hose wagon was often enough to meet the needs of a small community. Since a motorized fire engine called for a smaller crew than horses had required, even the size of the company could be reduced.

The new equipment removed the necessity for several rooms in the fire station related to horses and opened up more space in existing buildings. Removing the horses themselves made it possible to transfer the sleeping and living areas down to the first floor. Firemen had complained about the noise and smell of the horses ever since stalls had been moved into the stations in the 1870s and '80s. Second-floor dormitories had proved the best way to make the arrangement less like living in a stable. A speaker at the annual meeting of the New York State Association of Fire Chiefs predicted in 1908 that "The introduction of motor apparatus will cause a great improvement in the sanitary condition of fire houses by the absence of ammoniacal vapors, etc. It will add greatly to the comfort of the men not being disturbed by the kicking and stamping of the horses during the night." He suggested that the extra space made available should be used to provide a separate room for each fireman. While this idea never became very popular, many bungalow stations did include several small bedrooms for two to four men each instead of a single large dormitory.

The same concern for the health of the firemen that caused people to worry about "ammoniacal vapors" also led to other changes in fire station design. Preference was given to light colors and such washable materials as glazed brick or tile for walls and cement instead of wood for floors. Articles at the time showed a new interest in improving ventilation. Most important, the one-story design meant that "the dangerous sliding pole" could be done away with. Poles were losing their popularity, having been credited with causing everything from "hernias and ruptures" to "sprains and fractures." (The injuries usually resulted when firemen slid the poles while half asleep.) In 1928 poles were damned by a speaker at the annual meeting of the Association of Police and Fire Surgeons and Medical Service Commissions as "a menace to the health of the firemen and dangerous in the extreme to use." Poles remained a problem wherever the site, cost of land, or other factors prohibited the

148

151

construction of a one-story station. The Seattle Fire Department designed a two-story station with the floors connected by a spiral slide-chute, but this device had to be replaced with conventional poles the following year: firemen were wearing out too many pairs of pants. Today a few downtown fire stations are still designed with two stories (for instance, the Dixwell Fire Station in New Haven, Connecticut, discussed in Chapter Nine), but sliding poles have just about disappeared in the suburbs.

Around the same time that bungalow stations were becoming popular, a movement arose to change the firemen's work schedule by instituting a system of two alternating shifts or platoons. The design of fire stations was unexpectedly affected. A plan for rotating shifts that would shorten the firemen's working hours had first been proposed in 1888, but no action was taken on the idea until Omaha, Nebraska, instituted a two-platoon arrangement in 1907. Although some people opposed the system, arguing that hiring and training firemen to man the second shift would be unduly expensive, it attracted favorable attention. By 1918 the *Fireman's Herald* was running

weekly articles in support of two platoons with tallies of how many cities had adopted the plan in the previous week.

Until the early twentieth century, paid firemen were on duty twenty-four hours a day, seven days a week, with a few days or weeks off each year. Allowed three hours off every day for meals, the fireman would be penalized if late getting back to work, so he usually ate in a nearby restaurant (supposedly, certain restaurants near fire stations in Los Angeles were equipped with their own alarm systems—just in case), or he lived close enough to the station to walk or bicycle home for meals. In San Francisco, a retired fireman who still lives across the street from the engine house (now defunct) in which he had started work fifty years ago, reported that there are several other retired firemen still in the neighborhood and that the same pattern probably could be found in many older cities. Unless they visited him at the station, mealtime was the only opportunity a fireman had to spend with his family.

Under the two-platoon arrangement, each firehouse was assigned two companies of firemen who worked in alternating twelve-hour shifts. While on duty they were not permitted

152. *Fire Station 29 (now automobile salesroom), Kansas City, Missouri, 1917. Frederick Michaelis, architect.*
153. *Fire/Police Station 11 (now police station), Seattle, Washington, 1913. Daniel R. Huntington, architect. Architects also copied domestic types for larger fire stations designed to house horse-drawn equipment. In Kansas City, covenants established by the developers of the Brookside neighborhood required all buildings—stores as well as houses—to be in a uniform style. Seattle's city architect designed Fire Station 11 as an oversized version of the bungalow homes nearby (photograph courtesy of Seattle Office of Urban Conservation).*

152

153

to leave, which meant that at least one meal had to be taken at the station. At first the firemen brought a bag lunch or dinner and ate their other meals before and after work. But they soon improved this situation by installing kitchens in the station. Bungalow stations constructed at this time included a kitchen at the rear of the building. In older buildings the now unnecessary stalls could be removed, leaving room for a cooking and eating area. At a Boston station the men simply added a kitchenette in the rear of their smoking room, but in Champaign, Illinois, the arrangements were more elaborate. Partitions were removed from an area on the second floor, and a large gas range and oven, two sinks, kitchen tables, cabinets, dish racks, and cupboards were put in. "When completed," said an article from 1922, "the kitchen will be one that any housewife would be well pleased and proud to call her own."

A company would appoint one man as cook each day, leaving the other men to help out or wash dishes. Thus was born the traditional association of fire stations and good cooking in large quantities. The press was quick to applaud. *Fire Service* magazine sent two female reporters to dinner at the central station in Chicopee, Massachusetts. The ladies were as impressed with the "rare and spotless dining room" as they were with the meal, but had to turn down second helpings. The menu

for a special firemen's supper held in Boston in 1925 consisted of vegetable soup, sirloin roast, spaghetti, French fries, bananas, ice cream, cake, and cigars. In Worcester, Massachusetts, where an enterprising member of Hose Company 11 gained fame for inventing such dishes as chicken stuffed with hamburger and beef stew with oysters, the chief recommended in his annual report for 1923 that a kitchen be installed at headquarters. *Fire Service* reported: "The experiments which have taken the form of new fangled ideas in cookery have met with such apparent success that there has been little or no sickness among the firemen this year. The chief thinks that such progress should be encouraged."

Though the bungalow floor plan was well-suited to the new requirements of twelve-hour shifts and horseless fire engines, the decision to use a bungalow design for a station was often made by people who had no interest in the type's functional advantages. Rather, these people were concerned about how a new fire station would affect the look of their neighborhood. Some of the first bungalow stations were designed by city architects to appease irate residents of exclusive neighborhoods who did not want an ugly, institutional building on their block. In the newly planned communities of small-scale houses going up around 1910, a chunky red brick fire station, or even the large, rambling "residential" type used ear-

163

lier, would, in the words of a 1917 commentary, "stand out from the other buildings of the section like a sore thumb."

The typical residential section of the early twentieth century was usually more extensive than upper-class neighborhoods such as the Carrollton and Garden districts of New Orleans (see Chapter Five), but less expensive. "Covenants" drawn up by real estate developers and enforced by organizations in the community restricted the size of the houses, the distance they could be set back from the street, and sometimes even their design. In the communities developed by the J.C. Nichols Company in outlying areas of Kansas City, Missouri, between 1910 and 1920, all nonresidential buildings (schools, stores, banks, post offices, etc.) were grouped in small shopping centers decorated in the same style as the houses in the neighborhoods. Were it not for its large doors, the former fire/police station on Brookside Avenue in Kansas City—though built for horse-drawn equipment—would look exactly like the shops next door and the larger houses up the street from it.

As other architecturally uniform residential neighborhoods of this sort sprang up across the country, the small bungalow fire station proved increasingly useful. In 1912 the city of Denver erected an "artistic" bungalow fire station, complete with patio, in an area "filled with beautiful bungalow homes." According to newspaper reports at the time, the mayor and fire commissioner had decided that "since the residents of Park Hill had taken so much trouble in making their section uniformly beau-

tiful, it was up to the city to provide a fire station that would harmonize with the surroundings." Perhaps some of their good will resulted from predictions that the new type of fire station would cost less to construct than had the conventional, less artistic ones.

A few years later residents and landowners in the Inwood section of Portland, Oregon, actually complained to the city council about the fire department's plans to locate a station in their area, arguing that "the beauty of the neighborhood might be marred by the erection of a building out of harmony with the surrounding homes." Battalion Chief Lee Holden, an amateur architect whose sole training was an earlier stint as a coffin-builder, saved the day by offering to design a bungalow station (one of Holden's more conventional fire station designs is illustrated in Chapter Three). The new station had a sunken hose tower, apparatus doors disguised as bay windows trimmed with flower boxes, a circular driveway, and a lawn with an ornamental fountain in front. The widely circulated New York magazine *The American City* published an article about this station in 1917, reporting that "[the station] is not only free from objection artistically, but has the more positive effect of enhancing the attractiveness of this neighborhood. . . . the residents are greatly pleased with it."

A similar episode occurred in Shreveport, Louisiana, where a group of wealthy property owners presented a petition against the erection of a new fire station in their district. The "model fire station" eventually built there in

147-149

63

152

154

154

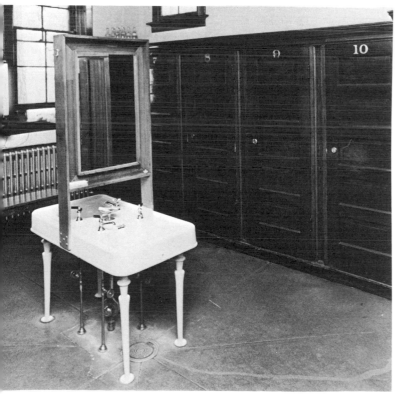

155

156

1922 was so congenial that 1200 neighbors turned out for the opening day ceremonies. Shreveport's fire chief reported: "The wealthy neighbors who are regular visitors now find praise enough that this station is so close to them and [admit] that they were so mistaken in their ideas of the character and life of the firemen." The station's "ornamental living room" with wicker settee, mahogany tables, and gas-operated fireplace became a gathering place for the entire community.

Throughout the 1910s and '20s, fire magazines described the aesthetic appeal of the new type of fire station with increasing enthusiasm:

The average American fire station is not a thing of beauty. . . . the reason probably is that in the larger cities such buildings are erected under the influence of individuals and boards who are familiar with the regulation type of public building which . . . was conceived by stodgy gentlemen after a very heavy meal. . . . with the construction of fire houses intended to be equipped with motor apparatus exclusively, a change for the better seems to be taking place. . . .

The evidence accumulates that the typical fire station of the future will not be the unlovely and usually unsanitary sort of building with which the present generation is most familiar. . . . It has dawned on the municipal mind that there is no imperative necessity for such structures to be so designed and built that it is not possible to occupy them without danger to health and that, moreover, there is nothing to compel a city or town to erect for the fire department buildings which cause the beholder pain. . . .

Providing a building design to harmonize with the surroundings of a residential neighborhood merits special commendation. In departing from the conventional brick building with flat roof, erected regardless of its environment, recognition is given to the growing demand for something that shall promote the development of beautiful suburbs instead of interposing structures that mar or clash with that purpose.

The advent of zoning laws, the policies enacted under Herbert Hoover's administration as secretary of commerce, and the increasing popularity of the automobile all encouraged the development of residential districts in the 1920s. In the words of a ruling by the California Supreme Court in 1925: "Residential zoning, especially single-family housing, ensures protection of the civic and social values of the American home. . . . any factor contributing to the fostering of home life doubtless tends to the enhancement not only of community life but of the life of the nation as a whole. . . . With ownership comes stability, the welding together of family ties. . . ."

Architects of firehouses in the 1920s and '30s adapted the forms of single-family housing to fit two-story as well as single-level stations. Since motorized equipment took up so much less space than had the old steamers,

166

Meets the needs of small communities~
The SEAGRAVE SUBURBANITE

The need for efficient fire-fighting service for communities, suburban villages, small towns and the residential districts of cities is adequately met by the Seagrave Suburbanite.

This speedy, light-weight apparatus is of the usual Seagrave high-quality workmanship and gives years of satisfactory service.

The Seagrave Catalog explaining the Suburbanite in detail will be sent to you upon request. Fire Departments in every part of the world are **equipped** with apparatus made by —

SEAGRAVE

The SEAGRAVE CORPORATION
Columbus, Ohio

BRANCH OFFICES AT:

Boston, Mass.	Birmingham, Ala.	Chicago, Ill.	Kansas City, Mo.	Seattle, Wash.
New Haven, Conn.	Philadelphia, Pa.	Dallas, Texas	Pittsburgh, Pa.	San Francisco, Calif.
		Los Angeles, Calif.		

158

158. *Fire Department Headquarters, Stratford, Connecticut, 1940. C. Wellington Walker, architect.* **159.** *Fire Station 24, Oakland, California, 1927. Dennison and Herris, architects.* **160.** *Fire Station 3, Santa Barbara, California, 1928. Edwards, Plunkett and Howell, architects (photograph by Theresa Beyer). As designs for suburban homes in the 1920s turned from the handcrafted look of the bungalow to more picturesque or exotic styles, fire stations followed suit. Fire Station 3 conformed to a mandate passed in 1925 that required all of Santa Barbara to be uniformly Hispanic. Oakland's engine house was intended as "an attractive fire station that would add to the value of surrounding property." Neighbors term the style "Hansel and Gretel" or "restrained Mother Goose"; the roof would have looked less like sugar icing when its original ridge of copper "flames" was intact. Stratford's headquarters is an example of the Colonial Revival that came to dominate public buildings, especially in small towns, in the 1930s and '40s.*

158

new two- or two-and-a-half-story fire stations could be as small as a modest home. One building of this type is shown in the illustration of an ideal "suburban village, small town or residential district" used in a 1926 advertisement for the lightweight "Seagrave Suburbanite" fire engine. Sited on a winding street and surrounded by planting, the fire station fits right in with the houses around it.

By that time, the low-slung lines and spreading roof of the bungalow cottage had given way to a more fanciful idea of domestic architecture. Firehouses from the later 1920s looked a good deal like the type of suburban development that Sinclair Lewis described in *Dodsworth*:

> Here, masked among trees and gardens, were springing up astonishing houses. . . . They were all imitative of course—Italian villas and Spanish patios and Tyrolean inns and Tudor manor-houses and Dutch Colonial farmhouses, so mingled and crowding one another that the observer was dizzy. . . . Here . . . was all the color and irregularity, all the twisty iron-work and scalloped tiles and striped awnings [one] could swallow, along with . . . all the mass-produced American electric refrigerators, oil furnaces, vacuum cleaners, garbage incinerators, over-stuffed chairs and built-in garages. . . .

True to form, Fire Station 3, built in Santa Barbara in 1928, is decked out in stucco, tile roof, and carved wood and wrought-iron trim to suggest "Spanish Colonial," and an example

of 1929 "pseudo-Tudor" in Shreveport has half-timbering and stained glass windows. The town of Stratford, Connecticut, built both its city hall and central fire station of red brick with white-painted wooden trim, shuttered windows, slate roofs, and numerous chimneys to affect an "Early American" look; a station designed for Providence, Rhode Island, in 1928 was decorated in brick laid in random patterns and a steeply pitched roof considered to be the essence of "Dutch Colonial." The local press hailed this last building at the time it opened as an "embodiment of beauty . . . a departure in municipal construction which presages a new era in building projects. . . ." Said a local zoning official: "Nowadays the public has recognized the advantage of guarding against monstrosities of architecture and of adopting aesthetic ideals."

While some architects continued to disguise fire stations as houses, others sought to make them into quaint ornaments to the community (see, for example, Fire Station 24 in Oakland, California). A few even emphasized the towers as decorative elements. When asked to design five fire stations for residential neighborhoods in Los Angeles in 1930, County Architect Karl Muck chose five different European models, from "French Provincial" to "Spanish Farmhouse," and explained: "[These stations were] so designed that they lent an added element of interest and a definite note of the picturesque to the general landscape. . . . Not always acceptable in exclusive residential circles, the fire house must get by on personality."

Under the New Deal, the Federal Housing Administration helped spur the growth of residential communities by making more money available for the building and financing of single-family homes. Many of the fire stations funded by Federal construction programs copied residential design, although their architects usually avoided the more elaborate ornament and exotic styles preferred in the 1920s. Since that time, the amount of detail lavished on the design of this kind of station has dwindled. In some cases the only difference between a fire station designed for a downtown area and one in a residential neighborhood is that the latter will have a pitched roof and some brick or shingle on the outside walls.

Just as the fire station was domesticated architecturally in the 1920s, the firemen themselves gradually became part of suburban life. Visitors to a bungalow fire station would find the firemen busy mowing the lawn, puttering in the garden, or trying out new recipes in the kitchen. After local matrons taught firemen how to knit socks for the "boys over there" during the first World War, firemen's journals reported a "knitting craze" in the firehouses. Men who did not already spend their spare time around the station building furniture or making toys took to knitting shawls for their sweethearts. Once again, the fireman's image was changing. A publication from the Denver Chamber of Commerce explained in 1929: "The fireman is a good neighbor. He is almost too good a neighbor, for demands upon his spare time are almost constant. Will he get the frightened cat down out of the tree? Can he open the bathroom door and extricate little Johnnie, who has accidentally turned the key? And can he anchor a loose wire (that turns out to be a clothes line)? Certainly he can, he will, he does. He is popular in his neighborhood." Instead of thinking of firemen as peaceful soldiers, mechanical wizards, or public servants, people began to see them as fixtures in the neighborhood.

The advent of motorized apparatus had one further effect on fire stations: namely, on the kinds of activities that went on inside them. The bungalow station did away with two of the best-loved traditions associated with firehouse life—the horses and the sliding pole—and even threatened the job of the traditional mascot. According to a gloomy article from *Fire Service* in 1921, most dogs were left behind at the station instead of being permitted to run alongside the engine to a fire. The poor animals simply could not keep up with the new apparatus (in time firemen remedied this by teaching their dogs to jump up onto the truck at the sound of the alarm and ride along). Ever sentimental, some firemen mourned the passing traditions. "Cut out the checker game now, and there won't be a darn thing left to bring memories back to the old-time fireman," a fireman from Lowell, Massachusetts, complained. One Baltimore fireman tendered his resignation when motorized equipment replaced the horses in that city. His reason: "There is nothing to it anymore. When they took the horses away, the pep and fun went out of the Department. It was the sorriest day in our history."

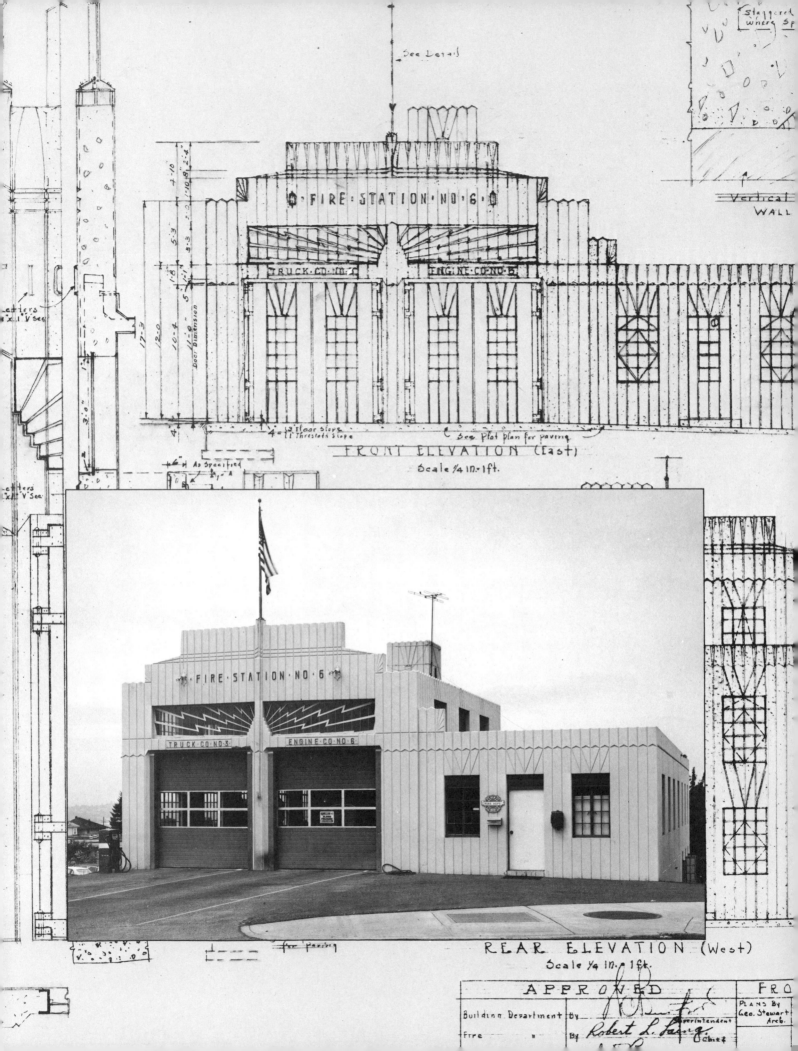

See Detail

Vertical WALL

FIRE · STATION · NO · 6

TRUCK CO NO 3   ENGINE CO NO 6

FRONT ELEVATION (East)
Scale ¼ in. = 1 ft.

See Plot plan for paving

FIRE · STATION · NO · 6

TRUCK · CO · NO · 3   ENGINE · CO · NO · 6

REAR ELEVATION (West)
Scale ¼ in. = 1 ft.

APPROVED

Building Department By _____ Superintendent

Fire   "   By Robert L. Laing   Chief

PLANS BY
Geo. Stewart
Arch.

CHAPTER SEVEN

Streamline and Specialization

Conflicting Ideas in the 1930s

1925–1945

Architects who designed bungalow fire stations in the suburbs during the first three decades of the twentieth century adopted nearly every style but one: modern. However, when it came time to build new stations designed for motorized apparatus in the cities, they often turned to an imagery different from the urban castles and palaces of an earlier generation. Buildings such as Seattle's Engine 6, designed the same year the Empire State Building was completed, projected a message that was anything but picturesque or quaint. With its lightning bolt design, solid concrete construction, and shiny metal trim, Engine 6 looks more like a radio than a cottage. It projected the message that firefighting was to be regarded as a technical business, involving new kinds of machines operated by highly trained men. The idea corresponds to a growing professionalism and specialization in the fire department and in city government as a whole.

But to some extent it was a purely sym-

bolic message. For all its electrical facade, Engine 6 was not even equipped with a radio to receive alarms. Fire departments remained remarkably conservative in the 1930s. The "technicians" who worked inside the "modernistic" buildings continued to do their jobs in much the same way their nineteenth-century predecessors had; and the interiors of some of the most modern-looking fire stations built in the 1930s and '40s are not much different from those designed for horse-drawn engines. Despite all the developments in other areas of technology at the time, the fireman's equipment hardly changed at all. Real "modernization" of the sort suggested by the design of Engine 6 came about only after World War II.

The fire stations built during the Depression show a number of conflicting ideas and images at work. Unlike the period that had given rise to the bungalow plan, there was little agreement among fire chiefs in the thirties as to a preferred layout or set of equipment. Neither did the public share one idea of how a fire station ought to look. More of the decisions seem to have been left to architects, who responded with a variety of designs. Some sought to emphasize the modernization of the fire department, with buildings that glorified the technical side of the fireman's work. Others stressed the familiar and traditional aspects of the fire service; because fire chiefs

162, 163. *Fire Station 6, Seattle, Washington, 1931. George Stewart, architect. Concrete construction, steel trim, and lightning-bolt ornament gave this "Flash Gordon style" station its "modernistic" look; but because conservatism lingered in the fire department itself, the equipment inside was quite old-fashioned. The floor plan is illustrated in fig. 174.*

were so conservative, many traditions remained. More and more architects, in confusion or in boredom, designed fire stations to be as unexceptional as possible.

The professional, the specialist, and the efficiency expert played increasingly important roles in American cities in the twenties and thirties. As part of the legacy of the Progressive era, volunteer charities were replaced by trained social workers. For the first time, universities offered professional degrees in city administration and planning. Efficiency engineers conducted time and motion studies that changed the arrangements of workers and machines in factories, and appliances in the home kitchen.

Trained professionals also moved into the field of city government, as voters sought to replace corrupt mayors and councils with disinterested experts. The success with which a state-appointed commission organized the efforts to rebuild Galveston, Texas, after its disastrous hurricane in 1900, inspired several hundred cities to experiment with various forms of government by boards of commissioners or by nonelected managers brought in from outside. While the former proved unwieldy, the council–manager system gained popularity after World War I, and eventually won the support of the National Municipal League. Throughout the twenties and thirties frequent articles in support of the "democratic, responsive efficient and economical" manager arrangement appeared in *The American City* (a new professional journal). Experts, the

articles argued, could take the appointment of employees out of the hands of "politicians who live upon office or political spoils" and rationalize the administration of city affairs along the lines of a modern corporation. Resulting changes would increase efficiency and save taxpayers money. For example, by consolidating all the jails in Denver county under one manager of "safety and excise," costs for the penal system dropped by more than half between 1911 and 1917.

Joining the commissioners and managers were a new crop of professional city planners. Unlike their predecessors who had laid out the grand schemes for Chicago and Washington, these specialists had training in economics and administration rather than in design. They claimed to be interested in the "city useful, efficient and liveable" rather than the city beautiful; instead of trying to replace existing city buildings, they concentrated on smaller-scale reforms that would "attempt to direct growth and development along sane and useful channels." *The American City* reflects the scope of the planners' concerns: articles range from studies of population statistics to hints on conducting traffic surveys to new designs for schools and public comfort stations. The power of city planners seems to have paralleled the growing popularity of the city manager form of government. By 1930, 691 American municipalities had established planning commissions. Planning projects received increased support under the New Deal.

The most far-reaching effect the new planners had in the twenties was to further widen the growing split between city and suburb. Until the Federal government made money available for public works projects in the thirties, modern planners had little opportunity to alter the layout of existing cities. But by working to direct future growth, they were able to confine industrial development to restricted zones and limit new housing to specially designated residential districts, most often beyond the limits of the city core. Their efforts gained momentum after the Commerce Department passed the State Zoning Enabling Act in 1923, providing a standard model for zoning laws in thirty states.

Starting from scratch, the planners of residential developments could pay more attention to the ideal location of services than their counterparts in the city did, and so the siting of fire stations came up in books on suburban planning long before the subject received any systematic attention in the city. Thomas Adams's *The Design of Residential Areas*, a standard text published in 1934, advised planners to provide each community with its own community center or hall, library, post office, schools, churches, stores, and theaters (the 1920s saw a boom in suburban movie theaters), as well as police and fire stations. It recommended that administrative buildings be grouped in one community center, preferably located near a park, and that stores and theaters be clustered in separate architecturally controlled areas. Fire, police, and utility buildings should be sited at a distance from the center of the town, and away from commercial zones where people congregated. Adams recommended placing them on the outskirts to allow more space and freer approaches.

Radburn, New Jersey, laid out in 1928, was one of the first suburban towns designed specifically with the automobile—as opposed to commuter rail or trolley line—in mind; its planners grouped houses on dead-end streets, and confined services to a few specially demarcated zones located near the main roads. As in the earlier planned suburbs in Kansas City (see Chapter Six), all the buildings followed a pre-set architectural style. Even though commercial buildings were physically separated from the houses, they shared the same design. The Radburn scheme proved very influential, especially with the growth of the highway system, and set the pattern for many of the new developments laid out in the 1930s. In Audubon, New York, a town built "on the Radburn plan" in 1929, the fire station was located in one of the commercial sections on the edge of town near schools and the country club. It sat at the intersection of two highways, separated from, but within easy access of, the houses on their winding culs-de-sac.

City planning and the reforms introduced under the council–manager system of government also had more direct effects on the fire department. Instead of receiving their jobs through political patronage, more chiefs were appointed by managers in charge of public safety functions and were required to pass Civil Service exams. More important, the trend to consolidate the functions, services, and administration of entire counties under one mayor and group of managers (following the

175

164

examples of Los Angeles and Denver in the early twenties) led to new cooperation among small-town fire departments.

The idea of mutual aid goes back to 1877, when the cities of Boston and Chelsea, Massachusetts, agreed to share one alarm system. But the genuine need for such arrangements became obvious only after the great Baltimore fire of 1904, when fire departments from as far away as New York and Pennsylvania sent equipment that was useless because their hose couplings could not be connected to Baltimore's hydrants. The resulting move to standardize hose couplings among neighboring localities went along with one to establish pacts by which a group of nearby communities would share the cost of certain equipment and respond to each others' alarms.

Under the agreement made by the towns of Everett, Revere, and Malden, Massachusetts, in 1927, apparatus from each community would automatically respond to all two- or three-alarm fires, or move into empty stations according to a pre-set pattern to "cover-up" for apparatus sent to the emergency. The New York State Emergency Plan law written in 1931 required that any town requesting aid take responsibility for compensating neighboring fire departments for costs, damages, and loss of lives. Such pacts were much more easily administered by one centralized department, and as more counties consolidated under manager systems in the late twenties similar schemes were adopted in Dallas (1921), southern Illinois (1925), northern Wisconsin (1931), and elsewhere.

But for the fire department, the influence of professional city managers and planners in the 1920s and '30s came as much from the changed *attitude* they brought as from any specific recommendations they made. Professional planners and city managers used a fresh approach to solving urban problems: their studies, surveys, statistics, and proposals were marked by a new kind of seriousness they considered scientific. While fire departments theoretically had been run by professionals since the end of the volunteer system, much of their traditional image carried over from the nineteenth century; most people still associated firemen with parades, monuments, and sentimental poetry. Now fire departments, historically one of the most conservative and tradition-bound branches of city government, tried to go along with the new spirit in municipal administration. New York's chief Thomas F. Dougherty wrote in 1931:

Say "railroad" to the Average American and he immediately conceives a mental picture of a tangible, concrete enterprise involving millions of dollars worth of capital and thousands of employees. But say "fire department" to the same man and his resulting vision is a soft-focus study of a group of blue-shirted men playing pinochle between occasional orgies of water squirting and axe-swinging. . . . it is a bit of a shock to discover that the operating costs of the New York Fire Department exceed the costs of any one of forty-two rather important railroads. . . . The fire department is a Big Busi-

165

ness. It is a highly specialized, scientific business combining the fascinating problems of engineering with the intricate tactics of warfare and the complicated organization problems of Twentieth Century industry.

To a certain extent the Baltimore fireman's doleful prediction cited at the end of Chapter Six was true: the "pep and fun" *was* going out of the department. Firemen's trade journals show the change. The *Fireman's Herald* was traditionally a source of poems, cartoons, and anecdotes about the fire service as well as conservative politics regarding labor issues. Along with stories about the eel caught in the hose, and what firemen ate for dinner, it ran articles protesting Civil Service and the platoon system well into the second decade of the twentieth century. But around 1930 it seems to have undergone a shift in editorial policy. Rechristened *Fire Protection*, it eliminated the folklore from its pages and confined its features to such skill-oriented topics as "Poisonous Gases which Firemen Encounter" and "High Voltage and Fire Streams." The year 1933 saw the launching of *Volunteer Fireman*, "the professional journal of the volunteer fireman's section of the National Fire Protection Association." Concerned with the purpose of "development of standard practices and methods," the only jokes to be found in its pages were the advertisements at the back.

In some matters the new attitude of professionalism in the fire department translated into changed policy. Most notable was the advent of training institutes or "fire colleges"

in the 1920s. In cooperation with local universities, cities established programs in which chiefs and firemen could take time off for an intensive course that ranged from two weeks to three months. Officers attending the college at Portland, Oregon, in 1931 studied "the construction of buildings, their desirable and undesirable points from the firefighter's standpoint, water supply and its distribution; fire hazards; . . . [and] the rudiments of chemistry." As part of the New Deal, many more cities instituted similar courses with the help of the Federal Vocational Training Act.

Among the subjects taught at fire colleges were some of the skills needed to battle the new fire hazards that accompanied twentieth-century technology. As the articles in *Fire Protection* indicated, gasoline, chemical fumes, and defective wiring had replaced carelessness with matches as the leading causes of fire by 1928. The growing popularity of movies presented new problems for firemen: not only was burning celluloid difficult to handle, but the electric speakers that made the "talkies" possible were housed dangerously close to the easily combustible screens.

Side by side with improved training for firemen came the idea of educating the public in fire prevention. Portland, Oregon, claims to have instituted the first city-wide fire prevention bureau in 1915; under its auspices firemen delivered lectures to school and civic groups on how to identify and eliminate fire hazards in the home. In 1920, President Wilson proclaimed National Fire Protection Day on the anniversary of the great Chicago fire. The idea caught on in the next decade as business groups—turning their attention from the City Beautiful projects of the turn of the century—supported fire prevention with Babbitt-like fervor. Articles in *The American City* in those years present numerous suggestions for ways in which the "Rotary, Kiwanis, Optimists Clubs, Press Clubs, Boy Scouts, etc." could get involved: ranging from sponsoring parades and clean-up weeks to getting local businesses to donate space for messages on menus and milk-bottle caps. Downtown stores in Columbus, Ohio, agreed to turn their shop-windows over to the state fire marshal's office for educational displays, including one that consisted of 175,000 half-burned matches that Boy Scouts collected from the city streets. According to the local press, they were effective: "All day long and at night, too, crowds stood in front of these displays. They set the Columbus people thinking. . . ."

Hoopla aside, by turning serious attention to seeking out and controlling fire hazards, fire prevention programs had a measurable impact. Statistically, they paid off in reduced fire loss and lower insurance rates. Writing in 1930, a representative of the National Fire Protection Association (a nonprofit research organization founded in 1896) could point with pride to the decrease in the average per capita fire loss in American cities with populations over 20,000 from $3.81 in 1920 to $2.70 in 1928. He attributed some of the improvement to the work of the N.F.P.A. itself, which in the spirit of specialization sent trained technicians out to towns across the country to conduct on-site surveys, train firemen, and make specific recommendations for improving fire protection.

Serious thinking about increasing the efficiency of the fire department's operations also led to changes in procedure. Since motorized apparatus could cover more ground in less time than horse-drawn equipment had, it was no longer necessary to group stations so densely in built-up areas. Departments could further centralize their stations and combine equipment from several smaller units into one building. During the thirties, for example, Allentown, Pennsylvania, cut its total number of stations back from eight to three. Following a trend begun in the 1880s (see Chapter Four), more stations were built to house ladder trucks, engines, hose wagons, and pumpers all under one roof. At the same time, realizing that extra men could be just as useful as extra equipment, a chief in Detroit devised the idea of the "flying squadron," a team of men who responded with the regular engine company and assisted as needed. Los Angeles adapted the idea for its Salvage Corps, a truckload of men who saved property from burning buildings, freeing other companies to concentrate on fighting the flames. In another variation of the idea, Chicago established the first rescue squad in 1913. Like the salvage corps and flying squadrons, these men were stationed in firehouses and answered alarms along with the regular companies, but once at the scene of the fire they concentrated on rescuing victims and treating firemen for smoke inhalation. Soon rescue squads became specialists; they carried their own forcible entry tools and oxygen equipment and began to receive special medical training. After World War II, more and more fire stations also included space for an ambulance.

A few new pieces of equipment were introduced in the 1930s. Portable floodlights and generators made nighttime firefighting a good deal easier; the fog nozzle, invented by a Los Angeles fireman in 1936, shot a mistlike spray instead of a stream. Motorized apparatus gained in length (in 1926 the average pumper measured 24 feet) and power (a twelve-cylinder engine could now pump 1,500 gallons per minute). Further experiments with combining several functions in one piece of equipment led to the development of the duplex pumper —two pumpers on a single chassis—in the 1930s.

The new mood of specialization and professionalism in government that affected the fire service extended to its architecture as well. The most striking example was George Ernest Robinson, a Boston architect who billed himself as a specialist in the design of fire stations. Trained at M.I.T., Robinson designed post offices, schools, and theaters but "made a particular hobby" of housing "the fire boys." He translated this interest into a careful study of the architectural requirements of the modern fire department and devised new standards for fire station design. "Strange as it may seem to the uninitiated," he told a meeting of the N.F.P.A. Firemen's Forum in 1944, "the fire station is extremely intricate in plan. . . . they must be carefully designed to house personnel

and equipment for the most efficient service to the community." A frequent speaker at the meetings of firemen's associations, he published his buildings and theoretical writings in both firemen's and architects' journals. As his reputation increased in the thirties and forties, fire departments throughout New England hired him to design their fire stations or consult with their architects.

One of Robinson's earliest and most publicized fire stations—the headquarters at Arlington, Massachusetts, completed in 1926—is 166–170 also one of his most interesting designs. It incorporates many features that Robinson either invented or was among the first to employ, which would characterize up-to-date fire stations for the next twenty years. And it shows the effects of some of the new methods conceived in the 1920s.

First of all, the Arlington station is a big building, orginally housing all of the city's men and equipment except for three engine companies assigned to outlying areas. Like many other cities that switched over to motorized apparatus in the 1920s, Arlington was able to consolidate several companies in one building. Robinson designed the new central station to house five pieces of equipment (including a police ambulance), with room for three more. The idea of planning a station with the future expansion of the city in mind was a new one, and shows the influence of the city planning movement at work. In his later articles, Robinson advised architects to allow room for auxiliary equipment, with a separate door to permit access without moving the other

166

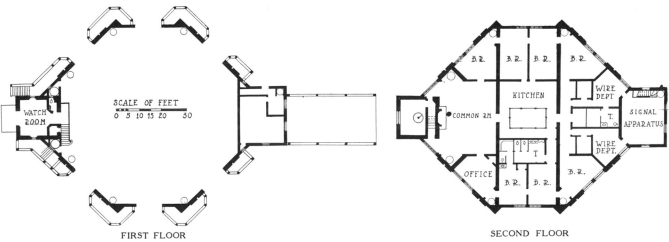

SCALE OF FEET
0 5 10 15 20   30

WATCH ROOM

FIRST FLOOR

167

B.R.   B.R.   B.R.   B.R.

KITCHEN

WIRE DEPT

COMMON RM

T.

SIGNAL APPARATUS

OFFICE   T

WIRE DEPT.

B.R.   B.R.   B.R.

SECOND FLOOR

168

PLANS, FIRE STATION, ARLINGTON, MASS.

apparatus. His suggestion caught on, as downtown stations were built with four, six, and even seven apparatus doors, and space was provided for more chief's cars, squad trucks, and rescue vehicles inside. By the mid-1930s only suburban fire departments were building stations for one piece of equipment; even in New York City, where the scarcity of land continued to dictate narrow fire stations of the storefront type, a two-bay plan became standard.

Robinson next came up with a startling new floor plan: the Arlington headquarters is probably the only octagonal fire station in the country. His solution was influenced in part by the awkward triangular site, and in part no doubt by a desire to see if he could pull it off. But the plan did introduce a new advantage: not only did it allow access to three main streets at once, it also made it possible for returning drivers to pull their engines right up into and through the station instead of having to back them in. This perfectly logical idea took a long time to catch on, in part because it required much larger sites with access on at least two sides, and it was not until the 1960s that the "drive-through" layout would be widely used. However, by the late twenties many fire stations built on corner lots included extra apparatus doors around the corner from the main entrance.

Not only did Robinson's plan permit trucks easier access to the building and the street, it also gave them more room to maneuver inside. He accomplished this by using a system of steel trusses in the ceiling, thereby eliminating the need for supporting columns. Charles Bebb had used the same technique back in 1910 for Engine 18 in Seattle, but Robinson was able to take advantage of more advanced steel frame and reinforced concrete construction to span a much larger area (75 feet across). Along the same lines, the enormous open engine room that Robinson designed for the central station at Gloucester, Massachusetts, was big enough for a 58-foot-long aerial ladder truck to drive in one of the front doors, turn around inside, and leave through another door without once backing up.

Other ground-floor rooms in Arlington reflected the changing needs of the department. The watch desk was expanded to a separate room, not so much to accommodate more equipment (the watch desk, alarm punch tape, and wall charts remained the same) but to provide a place where someone could be stationed full time to officially receive the public. It also included telegraphic alarm equipment tied into alarms in six nearby communities. The city's central alarm equipment was housed in a separate wing at the back of the building. In other stations with more conventional, rectangular plans, the watch or patrol area usually moved up to the front of the building, with offices or a lounge behind it.

Robinson fitted the basement at Arlington with a fully equipped machine shop, complete with hoists, where men could work on their apparatus. This idea had been suggested in city planning manuals as early as 1921: "Men are just as good firemen, and perhaps better, when, on an alarm, they drop useful tools to

181

169

170

fight a fire, as when they lay down a pack of cards." But unlike the would-be reformers, Robinson was not out to make things any more difficult for the firemen. If anything, he went along with the turn-of-the-century idea of providing them with as many comforts as possible: "Much of the discontent that one sometimes hears among the rank and file of the uniformed fire forces has been due to improper living conditions. Poor ventilation and lack of recreational facilities have made life irksome for the firemen who under proper arrangement of conveniences and harmonious, pleasing surroundings would live in a state of contentment and peace of mind." And so the station at Arlington had a skylit upstairs patio with record player, pool table, and open fireplace; other stations that Robinson designed included basement bowling alleys and, at Gloucester, a player piano. Robinson took especial pleasure in decorating common rooms and lounges with arrangements of antique equipment and memorabilia. To increase the firemen's comfort, he also advised including separate washrooms, laundry rooms, and cedar-lined closets for storing bedding.

But this aspect of Robinson's theory was anachronistic. More often, especially in the 1930s, new fire stations contained less elaborate lounge areas than provided earlier. Particularly in stations constructed by the W.P.A., built-in furniture and interior trim were kept to a minimum. In line with the new emphasis on training, classrooms replaced billiard rooms. More fire stations had libraries, though of a different sort from those of the 1890s: instead of being stocked with adventure stories and books on farming, they were now restricted to technical manuals. Since keeping in shape was still considered an important part of the fireman's regimen, stations built during the 1920s and '30s continued to include gyms or handball courts. But rather than provide a bowling alley they were more likely to have a training tower where men could practice firefighting skills (the one at Yonkers, New York, could be sealed off and filled with smoke to simulate "actual working conditions"). Unlike the tower at Boston's headquarters described in Chapter Five, these structures usually were separated from the main building by a drill yard and devoid of any architectural ornament.

Robinson stressed the importance of building fire stations with floors strong enough to support the heaviest equipment and of using materials that were themselves fire-resistant. Concrete and steel replaced plaster and lath throughout his buildings. But at Arlington and elsewhere he covered the steel beams with wooden paneling and faced concrete walls with brick, as if to hide the new material behind traditional Colonial trim. Similarly, he continued to follow the basic arrangement of rooms that had been used since the days of horse-drawn equipment. Even though he introduced new kinds of rooms, he kept the ground floors for apparatus and a few offices (with work rooms in the back where stalls formerly had gone) and confined all living quarters to the upper stories. He never designed a one-story fire station, never put any rooms on either side of the apparatus floor. Except for their extra

171

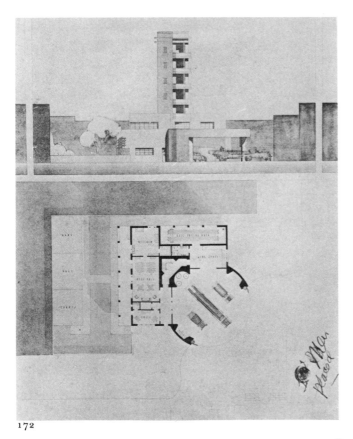

172

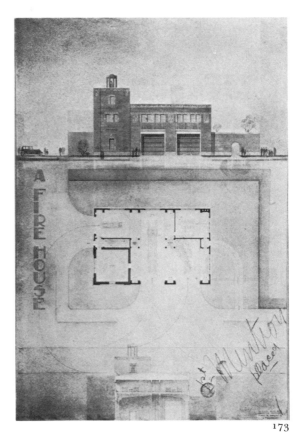

173

184

184

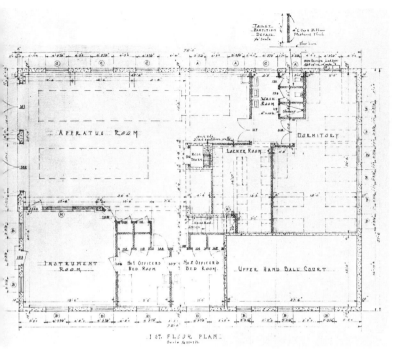

174

171, 172, 173. *Three entries from a competition spon-sored by the Beaux-Arts Institute of Design, 1929. These unbuilt designs were less traditional than typical student projects at the Beaux-Arts Institute, and far more adven-turous than most fire stations built in America. The asym-metrical, open plan of Fischer's design (fig. 172) is sur-prisingly close to advanced European architecture of the period.*

174. *Floor plan, Fire Station 6, Seattle, Washington, 1931. George Stewart, architect. Stewart's layout is an enlarged version of a bungalow plan. Notice the separate area for alarm equipment at the right.*

apparatus doors (and of course the octagonal plan at Arlington), Robinson's stations could pass for enlarged versions of nineteenth-century firehouses.

In the thirties, however, other architects devised new forms to reflect the changes tak-ing place both in the function of the fire department and in building technology. Rather than use new materials to imitate the building techniques and styles of the past, they turned to other models. Combining features brought about by changes in fire department policy with modern styles of architecture, they hoped to make fire stations that looked different from any that had come before.

Change was afoot as early as 1929. In that year the Beaux-Arts Institute of Design, prob-ably the most conservative architectural school in the United States, sponsored a competition in which students were asked to design a fire 171–173 station. The rules specified a two-story build-ing on a corner site to house an engine com-pany and a hook-and-ladder company: "Per-fect access to the street for apparatus is vital." This was a rather unusual assignment—most other competitions involved less utilitarian structures such as art museums, mansions, and war memorials—and it produced some unusual results. Rather than following the traditional, classical forms they preferred for almost every other project, the students experimented with a variety of new ideas. Some even broke a

cardinal rule of academic architecture and designed asymmetrical buildings. Perhaps tak-ing a hint from Robinson, one of the winners proposed a diamond-shaped structure for his corner site; another included a round appara-tus floor set at a diagonal to the rest of the building. The three prize-winning designs published in the Institute's *Bulletin* are much closer to the latest trends in European archi-tecture than any of the other student projects published that year.

Though none of the prize-winning designs was ever built, the fact that even the most conservatively trained architects thought that a fire station called for an atypically modern design is significant. It carried over into a few of the stations actually constructed in the 1930s and '40s. Seattle's Engine 6, for example, is 162–163, 174 built on one level as the bungalows had been, with kitchen and handball court in the base-ment. Larger than a bungalow, it was designed to house a pumper and a ladder truck, with a large instrument room up front next to the apparatus floor. The architect's specifications called for reinforced concrete construction with linoleum-covered floors, cement walls, and steel trim. And the building's exterior uses these materials for a new kind of decorative effect. Rather than manipulate the concrete and metal to imitate other materials, architect George Stewart made the most of their innate qualities. He specified that the concrete be cast in special molds to give it a grooved pattern. He then set off the flat walls with shiny polished metal and glass decoration on the doors and windows, and topped it all off with a lightning bolt-patterned transom and an antenna-like spire. The combination of metal decoration and stepped shape recalls either a radio case or a skyscraper, or perhaps the office of the *Daily Planet*. Critics called this kind of geometric ornament "modernistic." It does not hark back to any previous architectural style, either European or American.

164, 165

While George Robinson would have approved of the interior at Engine 6, he never would have used building materials in the way Stewart did. Neither would he have put the instrument room off to the side in a one-story wing. The position made sense, but Robinson's traditional architectural taste would not have allowed him to design a building with such an obviously asymmetrical front. Stewart was willing to make that break, though he was not quite sure how to do it; Engine 6 still looks like a symmetrical building with an extra piece stuck on the side.

Later architects played on the idea of asymmetrical floor plans for a deliberately new effect, in the same way that Stewart had devised an ornamental scheme emphasizing the novel qualities of his building materials. Fire stations designed in the variation of modern style known as "Streamlined" (popular in the late thirties and throughout the forties) combined asymmetrical plans with smooth lines and rounded corners to make them look sleek and new. Just as Victorian architects had moved

hose towers to the front of the fire station for visual effect, architects of this period found that the new flexibility in floor plans could be turned to design advantage.

The Central Fire Station built at Columbus, Indiana, in 1941 shows how an architect working in the Streamline Style could combine new firefighting features, new floor plan, and new building materials for a nontraditional and very dramatic look. In keeping with the latest theory it is all on one level, with a machine shop in the basement and an apparatus floor big enough to accommodate four trucks and a chief's car. It was equipped with automatic roll-up doors, just then coming into use. The dormitory and lockers are at the back of the building, the kitchen and dining room fill a small wing to one side of the apparatus floor, and a larger wing, set back from the front of the building on the other side, houses a lounge, offices, and signal room. The tower takes up the opposite rear corner. This asymmetrical floor plan allowed every room (except the bathroom and one of the offices) to open directly onto the apparatus floor, thus providing quick access to the equipment from any part of the building.

175-177

Not stopping there, the architect Leighton Bowers decked his building out in the latest materials. While Robinson had furnished the living areas of his stations with hardwood floors and imitation colonial furniture, Bowers chose linoleum, steel, and vinyl. The building's exterior is of glazed buff brick, laid flush to create a smooth surface of continuous curves, with corner windows made of curved plate glass and

176

177

175

glass brick. Instead of having a carved inscription, the station is identified by shiny stainless steel letters across the front.

The people of Columbus, then a town of 9,000 in the middle of the prairie, were quite proud of their "beautiful and commodious new fire station built in the modern manner." A Chamber of Commerce booklet, published soon after the building opened, explained that the glass corners and round hose tower, "unique features never before incorporated in a firehouse," were included for "practical purposes": the tower was said to hold more hose and the rounded corners enabled "the firemen to see Washington Street in front and for some distance north and south before starting to drive out." At the same time, the details "fit perfectly into the architectural effect." Today most people would assume that "architectural effect" was probably Bowers' first priority; there really was no functional reason for that round tower, but it is very impressive. However, in people's minds at the time, functional improvements and the "modern manner" seem to have been one and the same.

Buildings such as Engine 6 and the Columbus headquarters, and the designs of the 1929 Beaux Arts competition, are of special interest to a historian because they obviously were designed with history in mind. Instead of following historical precedent, they tried very hard to be modern in several ways at once. Not only did Stewart, Bowers, and their colleagues use new floor plans and new building materials, but the styles they preferred symbolized new movements in architecture. In a break 178 from earlier architecture (and especially from fire station design of the era of castles and palaces), these designs did not imitate any of the great buildings of the past. Instead, their simplified silhouettes and metal ornament were intended to evoke the image of machines, power, and energy. The lightning bolts above the door at Engine 6 are an obvious reference to new technology, while the curved glass walls at Columbus's central station resemble the windshield of an airplane. As historian David Gebhard has written of the general trend in design in the 1930s, "all of it conveyed the feeling that if it were not produced by a machine, it should have been."

Architects in the Streamline Style simplified the shapes of their buildings to resemble the outlines of high speed trains, dirigibles,

179

and, later, airplanes. Instead of the zigzag of lightning bolts they preferred long horizontal lines suggesting speed and motion. Like the automobiles of the time, their buildings were usually longer and lower than earlier models had been. Asymmetrical massing helped strengthen the effect. Engine 1 in Los Angeles, opened in 1941, is a good example of the streamlined look: its door is set off-center and

179

its ornament made up entirely of horizontals.

Modernistic and streamlined designs were not only of concern to architects. Almost every consumer product made in America in the 1930s and '40s shows their influence. Objects from toasters to cigarette packages to furniture to farm equipment—and of course automobiles—were redesigned with new shapes and more metallic trim. A glance through the pages of a 1930s Sears catalog conveys the message that metal, glass, and smooth lines meant modern, and modern meant new and improved.

In one of the oddest twists of all, industrial designers dressed up machines to make them look more machine-like. We can see the change in the design of fire engines. Up to 1935, most of them retained the boxy shape of the Seagrave Suburbanite (which in turn goes back to that of the Model-T Ford); like the steamers before them they were lavishly decorated with gold trim in filigree patterns. In the late 1930s the Seagrave Company introduced a new combination truck with a V-shaped grille. Though its basic mechanism, size, and pumping capacity were the same as in earlier models, it had a new exterior shell. The hoses and ladders were stored inside the truck, and many of the dials and knobs were now hidden behind doors—which theoretically kept them protected from dirt but also contributed to the sleek shape of the engine. Instead of gold paint, its ornament consisted of chrome bands. Windshield and bumpers both wrapped around the sides of the engine in continuous curves. Over the course of the 1930s, as other manufacturers "streamlined" their engines, fire trucks and fire stations began to look more and more alike. Ideas of design had changed considerably in the past hundred years: While the volunteers of the 1830s had hired artists to decorate their fire engines with oil paintings of scenes from classical mythology, architects of the 1930s designed buildings that looked like machines.

To a certain extent modern design was a matter of taste, and it played on the age-old desire to be in fashion. But in architecture the style meant something more than a choice of decorations. In 1890, eclectic architects had considered buildings that copied French chateaux to be more fashionable than buildings from the 1870s that had copied medieval churches. Modern design not only aimed to be different from what had come before it but also to be the single appropriate style for twentieth-century life. Little wonder that it became the prevalent style for movie theaters, gas stations, diners, industrial plants, and skyscrapers—buildings for which there were no precedents in the architecture of the past.

There was a good deal of fantasy mixed up in how the public perceived modernistic and especially streamlined styles, as witnessed by the fact that streamlined was the favorite form for luxury hotels, amusement parks, and movie theaters. Both the imaginary settings of Buck Rogers comics and the pavilions of the 1939–40 New York World's Fair ("The World of Tomorrow") employed elements of streamlined design. By the late 1930s this modern style would have seemed not only up-to-date but also a bit futuristic. It invoked dreams of a future world made better by technology.

The choice of streamlined design for fire stations in the 1930s and '40s takes on special significance when we realize that fire departments at that time were trying to convince the public that they were in step with the times—as efficient and effective as the new city managers and planners claimed to be. Why should a

190

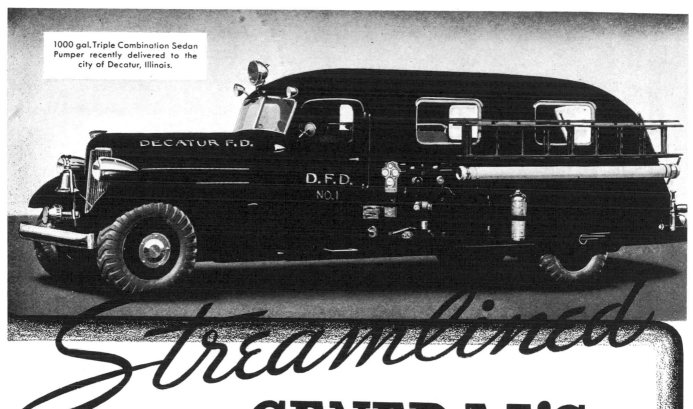

1000 gal. Triple Combination Sedan Pumper recently delivered to the city of Decatur, Illinois.

Streamlined
GENERAL'S
NEW SAFETY SEDAN!

The above photo illustration shows the FIRST *STREAMLINED* SEDAN pumper built in the United States.

Charlotte, North Carolina, pioneered the sedan fire truck, but GENERAL again establishes real leadership by building the FIRST *STREAMLINED* Safety Sedan Fire Truck built in America for the City of Decatur, Illinois.

The illustration clearly shows the beauty, completeness and modern design of this *STREAMLINED* 1000 gallon pumper.

Let us furnish you with full information on this latest GENERAL achievement.

SOME TERRITORIES NOW AVAILABLE. ADDRESS DEPT. B, IF INTERESTED IN SALES REPRESENTATION

180

modern organization be housed in a building that copied a European castle? What better image for the fire department than that of a machine, designed without frills to get the job done? Considering that most people associated modern design with "scientific" improvement, buildings like Engine 1 in Los Angeles show a new kind of optimism, and hope for the powers of the machine.

However, some of the visions of the future were premature. Architects could design buildings, consumers could enjoy "modern electric living," the National Municipal League could boast of the growing number of "forward-looking cities" that were instituting council-manager systems, but the nation did not "modernize" overnight. In the area of city government, for instance, boss politics and patronage prevailed in major cities throughout the twenties and into the thirties. Ironically, both Chicago's Big Bill Thompson and Mayor Jimmy Walker of New York continued the traditional connection between strong, corrupt mayors and increased city building budgets by erecting large numbers of fire stations. Building programs created jobs for voters and profits for construction interests with the right connections, and left a tangible mark on the city. While "Big Bill the Builder" followed in the tradition of Martin Behrman of New Orleans (see Chapter Five) by erecting expensive, luxurious stations like Truck 47, Tammany-linked "Beau James" aimed for quantity over quality. Twenty-three new fire stations opened during his administration, and plans for another seventeen were in the works when he

resigned in 1932. Among other charges leveled against him was the accusation that he accepted over a million dollars in "beneficences" from construction firms awarded contracts in New York City.

And despite the efforts at modernization and the decline in pinochle games, the fire departments resisted change most strongly of all. Since attendance at fire colleges was still optional, most firemen were not aware of new techniques. Nor were they aware of new technology. The most puzzling aspect of the history of firefighting from the 1920s up through the end of World War II is the reluctance on the part of fire departments to try any new kinds of equipment. This attitude was in marked contrast to the kind of experimentation that had gone on in the 1880s and '90s, when firemen themselves invented many new devices (see Chapter Four). Now, in a period when so many discoveries were being made in all areas of manufacture and communications, the fire departments lagged far behind. In 1927 alone, the first national radio networks began broadcasting, radio-telephone service was established between New York and London, the first underwater vehicular tunnel opened for use, the first "talkies" opened in theaters, television was demonstrated publicly for the first time—and Philadelphia's fire department was still using horse-drawn chemical engines. As late as 1936, an article in *Fire Service* complained, "even the lightest pleasure cars today have four-wheel brakes. Yet, but forty per cent of the fire trucks rolling on the streets are similarly equipped." Most fire sta-

181

193

tions probably had a radio set in the lounge but none in the control room. While the police were regularly using two-way radio to dispatch cars, the fire department hung onto the old ticker tape and gong system. Almost no fire department was willing to try using radio or even the telephone for announcing alarms until after World War II. Developments in the field of chemistry had even less of an impact: though synthetic fabrics and plastics were widely available by the mid-twenties, no one thought to improve firemen's bulky protective clothing or the rot-prone, cotton-jacketed rubber hose.

Not only did fire departments fail to take advantage of new inventions for their own use, they also failed to keep pace with the new fire hazards these inventions brought about. While skyscrapers soared to one hundred stories, the most powerful water towers could force water only to the sixth floor. Most surprising of all was the delay in developing new solutions for fighting chemical fires. Some of the worst conflagrations of the 1930s and '40s began with small chemical fires that got out of hand because firemen did not understand how to go about stopping them. The explosions and fires that devastated Texas City, Texas, in 1947 largely could have been contained if firefighters had known not to spray steam on burning ammonium nitrate. Lack of preparation, ignorance of new fire hazards, and the lack of appropriate equipment cost many lives.

In a way, the firemen's wariness of new techniques is not suprising. After all, nearly every innovation in firefighting equipment, from hoses to horses to the engines that re-

placed them, had met with suspicion and protests. At this point, however, conservatism was a matter of policy on the part of fire departments, and it contradicted their own professed attempts to bring firefighting into the modern age. It also conflicted with the image projected by buildings such as Engine 6.

Conservatism reigned in city building departments as well. Buildings like Engine 6 with its revised floor plan, concrete construction, and futuristic exterior were the exception rather than the rule. Inside and out, most of the fire stations of the twenties, thirties, and forties retained the characteristics of nineteenth-century buildings. Many of them *were* nineteenth-century buildings. In areas where there was no pressure from neighbors to rehouse the fire department in a smaller, less obtrusive station, the old "fire barns" continued to do their job. Once the stalls and haylofts were removed, large fire stations built for horse-drawn equipment had plenty of room for motor trucks. While chiefs might have preferred a slightly different layout with separate areas for an alarm room, office, library, kitchen, and locker room, most of these functions could be fit into existing spaces with the addition of a few extra walls. The fire department in Albany, New York, spent its W.P.A. money not on new stations but on new brick fronts for the buildings they had been using since the 1870s.

The storefront type described in Chapter Three—a long, narrow building with one open room on the ground floor and living quarters upstairs—remained the norm for fire stations

182

built on restricted city lots. Despite its machine-age trim, for example, Engine 1 in Los Angeles follows the basic layout of the fire station illustrated in the 1884 engraving from *Scientific American* discussed in Chapter Four. There is an open room in front, stairs to the right, and, instead of stalls, a kitchen in the back. In 1925, after much study, the New York City Fire Department adopted a standard floor plan that is essentially one of a nineteenth-century station. With no provision for horses, its simplified ground plan is closest to that of the volunteer firehouses built before the Civil War.

179, 81

Traditional floor plans continued to predominate in larger, more substantial fire stations as well. As noted above, when fire station specialist George Ernest Robinson rethought the arrangement of the modern fire station he chose to keep as much of the nineteenth-century layout as he could, and fit new rooms into it. Other architects used even more conservative plans than Robinson's. The headquarters 182 opened at Portland, Maine, in 1925 has a striking modernistic facade, but inside it is much the same as the Ann Arbor fireman's hall (see Chapter Four).

After the development of the bungalow station described in Chapter Six, the design of fire stations underwent little change at all in the suburbs. "Modern" design, with its symbolism of power, speed, and machinery, was always considered an urban style. People might drive Airflow cars and attend performances at Radio City Music Hall, but few wanted to live in a modern house. Even housewives who cooked in streamlined kitchens preferred early American living rooms. A 1923 article from *The Architectural Forum* on new housing developments in Holland criticized modern architects' attempts to use bricks to "symbolize the rapid movement of modern life": "As if it weren't bad enough to have to run after streetcars oneself without going home at night to a house which appears to be doing the same thing!" And as late as 1938, when *Life* magazine commissioned a group of architects to design model homes and then asked readers to pick their favorites, "traditional" designs won over "modern" ones by almost two to one. "Modern houses are like a flashy suit of clothes," one man wrote to the editor, "O.K. if you have several suits. But no good if you have to wear it every day." Looking back at movies of the period we see now that modern-style houses and interiors were usually the domain of loose women and sophisticated men who drove fast cars. Nice people lived in old-fashioned homes.

Part of the reason that people preferred not to live in modern-style surroundings is that they associated the new forms and materials with work (which explains why they chose streamlined designs for kitchens and offices, but not for the rooms where people relaxed). In the city, architects of modern-style fire stations used this association to glorify the difficulty, skill, and importance of the modern fireman's job. Buildings like the headquarters at Columbus, Indiana, called attention to the "modern and efficient" aspects of firefighting; other stations equipped with drill towers, libraries, and machine shops provided places where firemen could hone their special skills. But while the New York City fire chief urged citizens to think of their firemen as engineers, the old idea of the fireman as neighborhood friend lived on in the suburbs.

Since residential communities with their special zoning that separated the houses from the stores and factories were meant to be places where nobody worked, suburban fire stations emphasized the more neighborly aspects of the fireman's job. On the whole they were smaller buildings than their urban counterparts (in part because the areas they had to protect were less densely built-up). Few had practice towers or drill yards in the back; more had porches in front. They remained places where visitors were welcome. In keeping with prevailing taste for the traditional in domestic design, architects designed suburban fire stations to look deliberately old-fashioned. In a residential setting, a streamlined fire station would have seemed as unfamiliar, unwholesome, and unfriendly as a modern house.

Thus in 1937 fire departments in Hawaii encouraged their architects to "design a fire station to fit the surroundings, incorporating of course all the utilitarian essentials." *Fire Engineering* described the new station designed for downtown Honolulu as, "Modernistic in design, the towering doors of shiny metal and the exterior stone trimmings add height to the appearance of the two-story structure, in keeping with the larger buildings of the downtown area." But the station opened at the same time in residential Waikiki Beach followed a differ-

ent model altogether: "Did one not know it to be a fire station the natural reaction to its beauty of design and floral background would be to believe it a private home." Here the firemen still spent their spare time not in the machine shop but tending the garden.

Even in downtown districts, modernistic exteriors were not always preferred. The fanciful eclecticism of turn-of-the-century fire stations continued to be popular throughout the free-spending 1920s, especially for buildings in prominent locations. Baton Rouge's Central Station, with its gothic-style terra-cotta trim, 254 and the "English of the Stuart period" stations built under Big Bill Thompson are as ornate as any of the "palaces" of the 1890s. In Los Angeles the spirit of the City Beautiful movement continued through the 1920s in the Municipal Art Commission, which had the power to control designs of all civic buildings (Mrs. Cecil B. DeMille was a member). The fire stations they approved tended toward elegant combinations of Spanish and Italian 138–139 Renaissance architecture. And as late as 1931, the architects Madorie and Bihr chose an Italian Renaissance design for Engine 31 in Kansas City, Missouri. As a newspaper article at 183 the time explained, the buildings department was able to take advantage of a depressed market to incorporate such expensive details as a stone facade and apparatus doors "rustic in effect . . . made up of oak timbers." The final cost of $39,000 was well under the original estimates.

Though the demand for architecture in historic styles continued through the 1930s,

184

185

184. *Fire Station 2, Albuquerque, New Mexico, c 1935.*
185. *Fire Station 9, La Jolla, California, 1937.* **186.**
Fire Station 23 (now abandoned), Albuquerque, New Mexico, 1936. E. H. Blumenthal, architect. Although the Works Progress Administration had no official policy on architectural styles, the designers who worked for the government often tried to emulate the architecture native to different regions of the country. Fire Station 9 in a suburb of San Diego recalls California mission architecture; Number 2 evokes the "territorial style" of buildings designed by early white settlers in New Mexico; Fire Station 23 is an imitation pueblo, complete with false wooden beams or vigas *attached to the outside wall. Blumenthal also designed an airport even more outlandish in Pueblo Style.*

186

buildings like Engine 31 were among the last of a breed. Few buildings designed after the crash imitated European architecture of the past. Instead, architects of the 1930s turned to revivals of American traditions. They may have been inspired by the new-found nationalism that was changing American music, art, and writing. Or perhaps the old eclecticism reminded people too much of the extravagant tastes of turn-of-the-century robber barons. The new emphasis on native styles dictated mission style for California and the Southwest, with pueblo and Territorial Revival continuing on in New Mexico. For the rest of the country "Colonial," "Georgian," and "Federal" became the rule, even in regions where there had been no architecture at all in the eighteenth century.

In an effort to make their designs blend in with existing buildings, architects of fire stations from Stratford, Connecticut, to Hinsdale, Illinois, complied obediently with the change in taste. Instead of looking to the future, their steel-framed concrete fire stations with brick walls, limestone trim, and slate roofs recall the exteriors of eighteenth-century buildings such as the Head House in Philadelphia (see Chapter One). These traditional designs have a "back to basics" mood that is quite different from the exuberance of the Streamline Style.

Finally, a growing number of architects preferred to avoid the issue of style altogether by designing fire stations in no style at all. Returning to the tradition of unornamented industrial architecture, they combined elements of factory design with the simple aesthetic of the Prairie School (as seen at Engine 61 in Pittsburgh, discussed in Chapter Five) and the plain surfaces of the modern movement. They aimed to design "utilitarian" buildings that were neither monuments to the fireman nor architectural statements in themselves. The interiors were correspondingly bare. The W.P.A., with its concerns for simple design and solid construction, funded many of this type.

The "no-style" fire station reflects a new image for the fireman: that of the faceless laborer. Instead of glorifying the fireman as a hero or as a skilled technician, or encouraging visitors to regard the fireman as part of the neighborhood, these buildings practically ask to be ignored. While earlier chiefs had defended the need for elaborate buildings by claiming that we owe firemen the most comfortable quarters we can give them (see Chapter Five), these designs seem to say that we owe the fireman only what he needs to get his job done.

Between 1933 and 1943 the Federal government undertook a number of building programs as part of the New Deal. Among the projects funded by the Public Works Act and the Works Progress Administration were 525 new fire stations. The government had almost no control over the design of these buildings—its programs were set up to provide financial support for projects conceived by state and local authorities, designed by local architects, and constructed by local labor. In recommending applications for funding, Federal officials looked for projects that were well-

188

conceived and would benefit the community. There was no mandate from Washington about how a building ought to look except one:

The WPA followed the newer tendencies toward simplification in architectural style. Simplicity of design was best suited to the limited skills usually available for WPA work. The WPA urged upon sponsors the elimination of ornate architectural features, intricate structural designs, and elaborate trim. Types of design were suggested which would not require highly skilled and specialized workers, where these were not available from the relief rolls. In order to employ the maximum amount of WPA labor, sponsors were encouraged to use methods which would require the least equipment consistent with efficiency. . . .

Reinforced concrete was used very extensively in new construction work, in designs which fitted the local architectural traditions (as for example, in our originally Spanish southwestern communities). When other structural materials were used, they were generally native to the region, easily accessible, and not expensive.

The fire stations built under the W.P.A. include examples of all the different trends in design at work in the 1930s. They range from streamlined to colonial to renovations of nineteenth-century structures, with an assortment of domestic styles in the suburbs. Their floor

plans and equipment vary widely. The only thing they all have in common is that they lack some of the decoration and built-in furniture found in other fire stations, and they are all extremely well built. The Federal government did not scrimp on their budgets—the construction projects were meant to put as many people as possible back to work. The W.P.A. spent 188, 189 its money on sound construction and high quality materials. Today most firemen agree that W.P.A.-built fire stations such as Engine 41 in Seattle, nicknamed "The Rock," have lasted better than the flimsier buildings erected in the 1950s.

Compared with other types of public buildings funded by the Federal government, the fire stations show a greater variety of design, which goes along with the general confusion about an appropriate image for the fire department that prevailed before the Depression. Some of the W.P.A. fire stations follow the traditional styles used for schools and community centers. Others look more like hydroelectric plants. Still others, like the headquarters at Greenwich, Connecticut, follow a severe ver- 190 sion of modernistic design known as "stripped classicism" that architects used for museums, courthouses, and other major public buildings in the 1930s. This style was considered a new alternative to the classical designs preferred by the City Beautiful movement, an American response to the modernism practiced in Europe in the 1920s. In actuality it presented the same symmetrical plan, the same large scale,

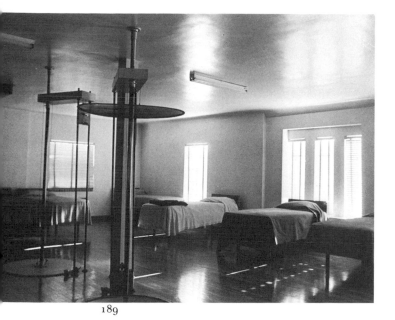

189

188, 189. *Fire Station 14, Denver, Colorado, 1937. C. Francis Pillsbury, architect. The WPA encouraged labor-intensive construction and put its money into high-quality building materials. Firemen have carefully kept this building in perfect order since the day it opened, and not even the swing-out apparatus doors have worn out in the last forty years.*

and the same marble columns of earlier monumental architecture, but stripped of all extra detail—and of all human content. Instead of decoration, the new style offered solemnity and bulk. When blown up to the enormous scale favored for Federal buildings, it sometimes recalled the overwhelming severity of Fascist architecture. Executed on the smaller scale of the fire station, American stripped classicism fared even worse. Following the line of reasoning that saw modern firefighting as a utilitarian function, architects often turned out fire stations that looked like limestone-covered warehouses.

The government realized early on that not all of its public buildings were of the highest architectural quality, and even came close to apologizing for them: "The PWA [Public Works Act] does not undertake at any time to assume any responsibility for, or to make any changes in design or specifications unless it may be obvious that the plans are technically or economically unsound. . . . Although some of the buildings erected by WPA labor are admittedly not of good architectural design, in the main the WPA has had an influence, recognized as good, upon public architectural standards." Architectural critics were more harsh. Writing in the *American Magazine of Art* in 1933, F. A. Gutheim complained:

It seems safe to report that public building will continue upon the same low level of mediocrity which has characterized it in the past. . . . The reason for the unimaginative dullness of most public buildings has been due to irrelevant political influences, to a complete lack of taste upon the part of members of representative bodies, to the conservative leanings of most public administrators . . . and to the bitter fact that public architecture cannot rise higher than the unfortunate state of the art itself. . . .

The great majority of public buildings have been characterized by a dusty formalism and routine flatulence; our worst architectural failing of all is a sentimental pretentiousness, and in public buildings this is carried to its extreme point . . . .

Gutheim did single out a few buildings as worthy of praise ("Here and there, almost accidentally, good modern public buildings are being built"). Among them was the Central Station at East Orange, New Jersey. But as for the question of a suitable style for monumental buildings, "The general observation one might make concerning this state of affairs is that the public works program finds architecture in a bad state of indecision and change. . . . Unless this situation is remedied by the designers themselves, nothing of consequence can result in the architectural design of public works in America."

Keeping Gutheim's remarks on public buildings in mind, it is interesting to compare the fire stations of the 1920s and '30s with gas stations—a building type with a very similar

191

190

program, but designed for private businesses. Both types of building provided garage space with an attached office area, and both were built in residential as well as urban areas. Like fire stations, gas stations were protested by residents of exclusive districts in the 1920s, and had to be quaintly disguised as houses. Architects of both types of building used machine-age imagery in their designs for downtown locations. But while the modernistic fire station of the 1930s usually remained a massive symmetrical building supported by load-bearing walls, gas stations were among the first American buildings to use the kinds of radical designs and construction techniques that European architects explored in the early twentieth century. Like some of the unbuilt competition entries from the Beaux-Arts Institute of Design, gas stations followed asymmetrical plans that were determined by the functions they accommodated. Many looked like greenhouses with light, panel walls and large expanses of glass, hung from a metal frame.

Part of the structural difference between fire stations and gas stations stems from the way the buildings were erected. As Gutheim hinted, conservative municipal building departments preferred not to take risks with unknown contractors and technology. Then there were differences in how the buildings were used: a fire station was built to be more substantial than a gas station because it had to last longer under heavier wear. But part of the reason that architects did not experiment with more advanced designs for fire stations in the 1930s may have to do with the fire station's

role as a public building. As oil companies competed for motorists' attention in the thirties, gas stations were designed to advertise—their glass doors acted as flashy shop windows, their panels as billboards. Fire stations, on the other hand, were still seen as part of civic government. Whether they evoked speeding trains or colonial mansions, they were public buildings and they still had to maintain a tradition of authority and permanence. The problem architects faced was how to convey a sense of the fire department's stability in a "bad state of indecision and change."

Distinctive fire stations from the 1930s and '40s are hard to find. But a few show that some communities and their architects still thought fire stations were worthy of imaginative designs. Buildings like those at Seattle and East Orange combine practicality with optimism in a way that sums up part of their era.

That optimism presents a paradox. The fantasy of 1930s modernism, as translated into fire station designs, was entirely different from the creative eclecticism of the turn of the century. The new buildings exalted not the fireman's heroism but his skill (the stripped-classical stations built by the W.P.A. conveyed the same message with more solemn forms). But whether designed to look like an airplane or a factory, the 1930s fire station retained the basic interior of a nineteenth-century building. Real change did not come for another generation. The period after World War II brought technological developments in firefighting that would rival a Buck Rogers vision—and buildings that no longer embodied any vision at all.

192

193

CHAPTER EIGHT

The Modern Fire Station

1945–

Since World War II, the promise implied in the machine imagery of the 1930s has been fulfilled: technological developments in the last thirty years have brought significant improvements to the fire service. In addition, new groups of experts have devoted serious thought to the methods and operations of the fire department and come up with far-reaching recommendations, which include the first serious re-thinking of the layout of fire stations and the first comprehensive system for siting them. The advent of computers promises to alter fire department traditions even more in years to come.

But while engineers and inventors have turned their attention to rationalizing the design of the fire station and improving the equipment inside it, the buildings themselves have lost whatever architectural distinction they once had. By the time the United States entered the space race, the American fire station,

192. *Engine 112, Chicago, Illinois, 1977–79. Jerome R. Butler, Jr., architect.* **193.** *Engine 18, Shreveport, Louisiana, 1973. Walker & Walker, architects (photograph by Theresa Beyer). A shift in priorities has robbed the postwar fire station of its former architectural distinction. The box and the ranch house are now the typical designs for city and suburbs.*

though filled with an impressive array of equipment, was likely to be one of the least impressive buildings in the community. And somehow the public—architects, city building departments, neighbors, and the firemen themselves—had come to expect no better. By a series of strange twists, people came to regard bad architecture as a sign of good municipal behavior, and to associate the "institution" of the fire service with an ugly brick box. Fire stations were not the only buildings to undergo this kind of change. Their history is part of a larger trend of the last thirty years and reflects a general decay in the quality of public architecture in America.

The W.P.A.'s construction program ended in 1941, when all building projects slowed down as energy and resources were devoted to the war effort. But early in 1945 fire officials began to make plans for postwar improvements. In contrast to the conservatism expressed during the Depression, that year a speaker at the annual conference of fire department instructors held in Memphis, Tennessee, looked forward to the new technology made available through wartime research. Soon, he predicted, fire departments would make use of new plastics and synthetic rubber, methyl bromide (used by the British air force for extinguishing air-

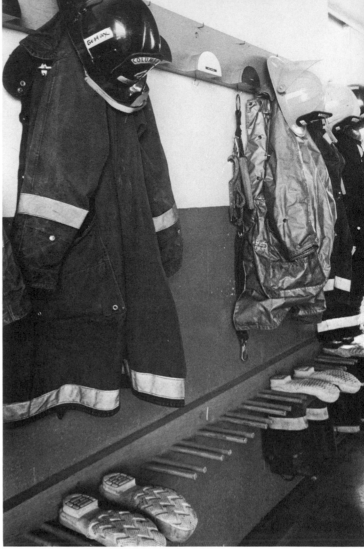

194

plane fires), and chemical additives that in effect made water "wetter" by reducing its surface tension. He also foresaw increased use of two-way radios and walkie-talkies. Advertisements appeared in trade magazines for Mearl-foam 5, "the war-born blended multi-protein foaming agent [developed by the U.S. Navy] for high-speed extinction of gasoline and other serious fires."

With the end of the war, all these predictions and more came true. Fire departments experimented with a wealth of new technology and ideas. Navy personnel offered to instruct local fire departments in the use of foam and fog nozzles and other equipment developed for wartime firefighting. Fire colleges adopted the Navy training technique of constructing temporary rooms and buildings that could be "burned down" again and again. The self-contained oxygen masks originally invented for high altitude flying were soon adapted for use in fighting fires. In 1945, after years of delay, the Federal Communications Commission finally passed an act designating thirty-five radio channels for the sole use of municipal fire departments. Before long radio equipment was devised not only for announcing alarms in fire stations but for enabling both headquarters and fire stations to communicate with chiefs' cars and individual pieces of apparatus. The old resistance to technological change was rapidly passing away.

This changed attitude toward invention was part of a widespread movement in American culture. The 1950s, like the 1880s, were a time of fascination with technology. As the cold war prompted an increase in government funding for research in defense and space travel, private industry kept pace (the research and development department flourished in this period). Spin-offs from research reached consumers in the form of new synthetic materials such as latex, plastics, and nylon, in new uses for aluminum alloys, and in new developments in home appliances. Among the uses firefighters found for these products were improved protective gear—lightweight, fire-resistant turn-out coats and helmets, with phosphorescent markings for higher visibility, in materials that could withstand chemical spills—and improved hose. Various blends of Dacron, nylon, and cotton jacketing reduced the bulk and weight of fire hose while increasing its strength, durability, and resistance to mildew. Lightweight aluminum couplings made hose easier to handle and store. Manu-

195

facturers began to produce new sizes and types of hose: five- and six-inch diameter hoses to handle high pressure streams, smaller one-and-a-half inch hose for use with chemical agents. On apparatus, tools, and in the firehouse itself, aluminum and plastic replaced heavier brass, chrome, and steel.

Changes in apparatus went beyond the skin-deep streamline styling of earlier years. While prewar fire engines had used the basic chassis of a touring car, the growth of the commercial trucking industry brought significant improvements in heavy-duty automotive construction. In 1939 the Cummins Engine Company of Columbus, Indiana, introduced the diesel fire engine, and within the next few years the city of Columbus purchased diesel aerial-ladder trucks and pumpers. Diesel fire engines took some time to catch on—in those days fuel economy was not reason enough to switch engines—but by the late 1950s several fire departments were using them. In those years, firemen began once again to tinker with their equipment. The "snorkel," an aerial ladder with an elevating platform conceived by Chicago's Fire Commissioner Robert Quinn, went into production in 1958. Suggestions from other chiefs led to the development of the quad truck (pumper, hose wagon, water tank, and aerial in one) and the Super Pumper, an 8,000 gallon-per-minute behemoth used in Chicago and New York in the early 1960s.

Postwar technology reached the firehouse as well, in the form of new building materials. Vinyl tiles, asbestos siding, acoustic plaster, and Plexiglas skylights are just a few of the inventions of the 1950s. More building parts were available as prefabricated units, from pre-hung aluminum windows to "pre-engineered" walls to entire buildings that could be ordered from a catalog and assembled in a day. While advanced techniques of steel-framed, curtain-wall construction had been used mainly for exceptional buildings like gas stations in the 1930s, now lightweight beams and panels and large expanses of glass became available to the mass market. As will be shown below, these developments in building technology helped give rise to the boxy, lightweight, standardized fire station of the present.

A 1945 article in *Fire Engineering* was right on the button when it predicted that "automatic features and gadgets galore" would be "outstanding features in tomorrow's fire stations." Fire chiefs hurried to install automatic heat detectors and sprinkler systems to avoid the embarrassing spectacle of a burning fire station (it did happen). Some of the gadgets came from industry: air conditioners, concealed fluorescent lighting, dishwashers, and garbage disposals all came to fire stations at about the time they reached the private home. Others developed in response to the specific needs of the fire department. As radio replaced telegraphic equipment, new electric devices were connected with the alarm system to record incoming alarms on tape. Thermostats automatically regulated the heating system when firemen were called out of the building. After 1959 it was increasingly common for alarm desks to be equipped with devices to control surrounding traffic lights. And by 1960 the television set was an unofficial fixture in almost every fire station.

In the fifties, two electrical devices introduced just before the war nearly did away with the fire station's most recognizable architectural features—the arched doorways and the hose tower. The new automatic roll-up door, manufactured of aluminum and glass, saved space, time, and energy. It was especially welcome in northern climates, where ice and snow piling up in the winter might block the old swing-out doors. When equipped with a timer and photoelectric switch, the doors could close automatically after the engines pulled out, thereby preventing more heat from escaping. Metal doors could be made to span much larger openings than wooden ones had, to the point where one wide door could be used for the entire front of a two-bay engine house. The new doors were manufactured only in rectangular shapes, though a few diehard traditionalist architects occasionally would have them custom-made for arched doorways. As fire apparatus has continued to expand in girth, more and more fire chiefs have been ordering that the arched openings of older stations be altered to accommodate larger rectangular doors, much to the regret of older firemen and preservationists alike.

As with the automatic doors, the Circul-air electric hose dryer dates from the 1940s but did not achieve great popularity until after the war. The six-foot-tall metal cabinet with racks, heaters, and blowers inside could dry a truckload of hose in seven hours, 2,000 feet in a day. According to the manufacturers, this machine saved space and construction costs by eliminating the need for a hose tower—the cost of electricity used was not yet a consideration—and it prolonged the life of the hose:

> With the thousands of dollars of construction costs saved by CIRCUL-AIR you can provide much needed additional equipment, such as two-way radio . . . additional alarm boxes, high pressure fog apparatus, salvage and first aid supplies, or possibly another small pumper.

> Your architect—and your building committee—will readily appreciate the limitless possibilities in planning a building without a hose tower or drying rack, one that will combine the most in beauty and functional design.

Circul-air promoted the machinery in an aggressive advertising campaign in the trade journals and in the pages of the new publication *Fire Station Design*, "a symposium of ideas, plans, and sketches for better housing of firefighting personnel." The magazine was supposed to provide fire chiefs and architects with "suggestions and ideas which we feel might be helpful in developing a really modern, functional engine house." Actually, it seems to have served mainly as a promotion piece: every building illustrated was equipped with a Circul-

255, 256

air. The general articles consistently advised prospective builders: "No more unsightly hose towers or racks—drying cabinets are preferred."

The publication did not say *who* preferred them—writings in other magazines and studies of fire station design show that then, as now, fire chiefs had mixed feelings about the machines. A poll taken in 1958 indicated that fifty-eight percent of the chiefs responding still preferred to dry hose on racks or in towers. Even today many would argue that it takes longer to wash, drain, and roll hose for loading into a cabinet than to hang it up in a tower to dry. While the initial expense is greater, a tower is permanent. Drying machines require maintenance and eventually need to be replaced.

Despite misgivings on the part of some chiefs, the magazine *Fire Station Design* was very influential. The 1959 edition reported 11,000 copies sold. To further spread the message, the Circul-air company regularly sent press releases illustrating buildings featured in their publication to firemen's journals, where they would appear as news items. As a result, very few fire stations with towers were published anywhere. Since 1950, fire stations across the country have reflected this manufacturer's advice.

Just as the modernization of equipment predicted by styling changes in the 1930s was not actually realized for another generation, so too the kind of rationalized re-thinking of fire department operations promised by city managers and planners before the war did not have its real impact on firefighting until the 1950s. Up to that point, firefighting had been conducted reactively—a fire would occur, and then officials would decide what to do about it. Changes would be made after an existing method or piece of equipment proved inadequate, and new fire stations usually were built only after a series of disasters showed that a certain area needed more protection. However, around 1953, fire departments finally began to analyze their needs systematically and make comprehensive plans to meet them in advance.

The first step toward reorganizing the fire department was often the preparation of a master plan for the location of fire stations. Fire chiefs found that existing stations and equipment could not keep up with the leap-frogging growth that American cities underwent in the 1950s and '60s, as automobiles and highways changed the ways Americans traveled. A planner in Phoenix, Arizona, described the trend in typical jargon: the postwar city was experiencing "a major decentralization of retail activity" due to the new "automobile dominated transportation emphasis." Unlike earlier expansion, which had followed an orderly progression outward from the urban core along streetcar and rail lines, new communities like Phoenix grew in disconnected patches, with clusters of industrial development or residential districts separated from downtown and from each other by highways. Older cities also decentralized, as stores and entertainment followed the population out to suburban shopping centers. Manufac-

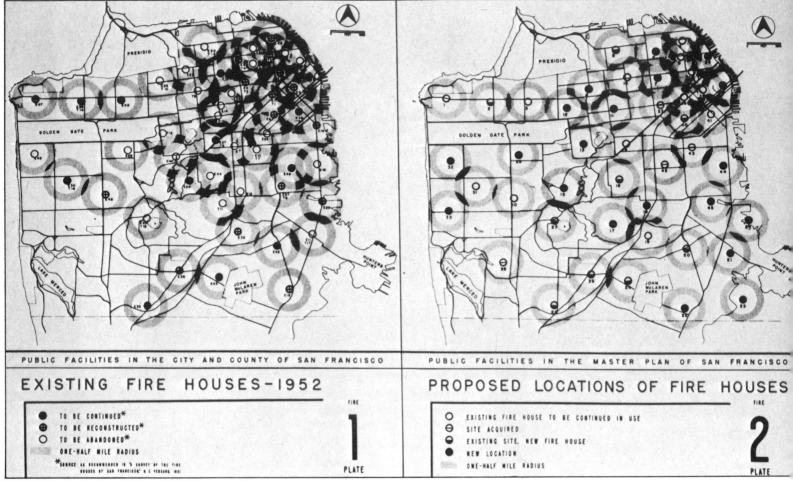

PUBLIC FACILITIES IN THE CITY AND COUNTY OF SAN FRANCISCO

EXISTING FIRE HOUSES–1952

FIRE

1

PLATE

- ● TO BE CONTINUED*
- ⊕ TO BE RECONSTRUCTED*
- ○ TO BE ABANDONED*
- ▓ ONE-HALF MILE RADIUS

*SOURCE AS RECOMMENDED IN 'A SURVEY OF THE FIRE
HOUSES OF SAN FRANCISCO' R C VERSACE 1951

PUBLIC FACILITIES IN THE MASTER PLAN OF SAN FRANCISCO

PROPOSED LOCATIONS OF FIRE HOUSES

FIRE

2

PLATE

- ○ EXISTING FIRE HOUSE TO BE CONTINUED IN USE
- ⊖ SITE ACQUIRED
- ◒ EXISTING SITE, NEW FIRE HOUSE
- ● NEW LOCATION
- ▓ ONE-HALF MILE RADIUS

196

turers relocated to industrial parks and encouraged workers to move away from the city. Old downtown areas were abandoned and new sections planned that were farther apart and less densely built than urban neighborhoods had been. The old arrangement of fire stations, with many clustered in downtown districts and others built one at a time in response to requests from new sections of town, simply could not serve the new kind of city.

For the first time, fire department officials considered fire protection as a unified system and planned for its orderly growth. Following the tactics of city planners and zoning officials, they tried to predict the path of future expansion, then purchased sites, and sometimes erected fire stations in sections that, although not yet built up, would be within the next five or ten years. At the same time, they tried to predict the rate at which downtowns would decay and older fire stations be abandoned. The plans took into account not only combin-

ing several older stations into one but also reducing the number of personnel. As a report prepared by the city planning board of St. Paul explained in 1961, "The purpose of this study is to find a way to provide complete fire station coverage of all parts of the City with a minimum number of stations, and to make it possible for the appropriate authorities to schedule abandonments and capital improvement projects so that each stage of the long-range program will bring improved fire protection throughout the entire City." Commissioners in Wichita, Kansas, hoped that a comprehensive plan would bring them not only better fire protection and reduced insurance rates but also reduce the cost of firefighting by eliminating superfluous engine companies.

The methods used to put together a master plan were based on those of urban planners. The first step was to determine where the areas of greatest fire risk were. Planners would then make an inventory of existing fire stations and plot their locations on a map, while noting at the same time which buildings needed repair or were no longer large enough to accommodate the companies and apparatus assigned to them. Next would come calculations to determine how long it took a company to get from the fire station to a fire at any given location, taking into account unique features, such as the city's terrain and traffic patterns. Then the chief would decide how long it ought to take to get water onto a fire, and how long to allow for additional equipment to respond to second and third alarms. At this point many planners turned to the publications of the National Board of Fire Underwriters, a private organization that set the rates for fire insurance and sponsored research in fire protection. According to the Underwriters' report of 1959, no point in a commercial or industrial district should be more than three-quarters of a mile from an engine company and one-and-a-half miles from a ladder company; the distance could expand to one-and-a-half miles for pumpers in residential sections and three miles in areas of "scattered development," At the same time, the Underwriters recommended a maximum response time of two to three minutes for the first alarm, meaning that in cities like San Francisco, where hills and narrow streets slow the response of fire engines, stations should be located closer together.

With the figures arrived at from their earlier calculations as a guide, the fire department would then prepare two maps. The first would show all existing fire stations in the city,

with a ring drawn around each building to indicate the area its equipment could reach within the recommended response time. Any space outside the rings probably needed a new fire station; any space covered by overlapping rings probably had too many. The second map would show the city divided into zones according to fire risk, with a set of rings drawn over it edge to edge, allowing for some overlap in high-value districts. The ideal locations for fire stations would be in the middle of each of those rings. Using these maps and the results of their surveys, fire chiefs could assess the power of the equipment they already had and see where more was needed.

Soon their calculations took on greater sophistication. Planners in Spokane combined the study of fire department locations with an analysis of the city's pattern of growth and annexation to put together a timetable for improvements that projected fifty years into the future. Other fire departments undertook a program of "pre-fire planning": in-depth studies of selected high-risk buildings, with maps of their sprinkler systems, extinguishers, and exits, to determine in advance the best attack to follow if a fire ever should break out. In recent years the Rand Corporation and other commercial firms have put together computer programs that can be used by any city to prepare detailed analyses of fire needs (taking into account factors from the rate of obsolescence of equipment to the location of fire hydrants) and to choose between several alternative plans, complete with a cost-benefit analysis for each. Using similar technology and

196

197. *Floor plan from* Fire Engineering, *June 1945. The drive-through floor plan was an important innovation in the postwar period. It allowed access to the apparatus floor from every room in the building, and did away with the need to back apparatus in through the front door.*

information, the "Starfire" computer dispatch system recently unveiled in New York City can now, on receipt of an alarm, instantly decide which companies should respond and which should fill in for them, provide the drivers with maps showing the best route to the fire, and even send out floor plans of the burning building with location of the fire and exits marked.

Even without the elaborate statistics of a computer report, the planning studies conducted in the 1950s and '60s contained enough information for fire departments all over the country to undertake massive reorganizations of their fire stations. For example, San Francisco's report recommended that the city abandon twenty-nine fire stations, keep or expand twenty-two existing buildings, and buy lots for twenty-four new ones. As a result of maps with overlapping circles, many fire stations that had served adequately since the days of the volunteer fire companies, especially in older sections of cities, met their end in the 1950s. They either were altered beyond recognition with new wings, new facades, and wider doors, or more often sold off or demolished. The city of Providence, Rhode Island, put fifteen old fire stations up for auction or lease between 1951 and 1957; by 1960 only two stations originally built for horse-drawn equipment remained in service. Beginning in 1960, the Underwriters suggested, "It is generally preferable to locate on the edge of, rather than within, a congested or hazardous district." Many chiefs followed their advice by moving fire stations out of downtown districts altogether; with faster,

more powerful equipment they could group several companies in new large buildings beyond the city core. Except in large cities like New York and Chicago, or in cities that did not expand significantly, the urban fire station was becoming a thing of the past.

Whether to fill a gap in a projected plan or to replace an older firehouse, a fire chief who decided to build a new station in the late 1950s could turn to a number of sources for advice. Publications by the National Board of Fire Underwriters, the National Fire Protection Association, and the American Society of Planning Officials, as well as articles in trade journals and (to a lesser extent) the Circul-air corporation's publication *Fire Station Design*, encouraged fire departments and their architects to carry the new attitude of strategic planning over into the design of individual buildings. For the last fifteen years the state of New York has had its own in-house "fire protection specialist," who gives advice to cities and towns considering building a fire station. Recently the United States Department of Commerce also began to publish suggestions for fire station design.

The Underwriters' recommendations began with the choice of the lot: it should be on a wide side street with easy access to a main road (one way streets should be avoided since they do not permit engines to "zigzag" through traffic lights). According to the Society of Planning Officials, the recommended lot size in 1957 was 125 by 140 feet for a two-company house, with space provided on site for a yard and parking lot. The building should be set

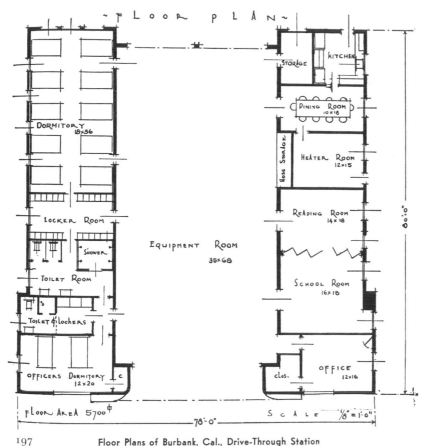

~ FLOOR PLAN ~

DORMITORY
18x36

LOCKER ROOM

SHOWER

TOILET ROOM

TOILET & LOCKERS

OFFICERS DORMITORY
12x20

FLOOR AREA 5700

EQUIPMENT ROOM
35x68

STORAGE   KITCHEN

DINING ROOM
10x18

HEATER ROOM
12x15

HOSE STORAGE

READING ROOM
14x18

SCHOOL ROOM
16x18

OFFICE
12x16

clos.

60'-0"

78'-0"   SCALE ⅛"=1'-0"

197   Floor Plans of Burbank, Cal., Drive-Through Station

back at least 30 feet from the street to permit engines to be pulled out all the way into the front driveway or "apron" for cleaning. Not many downtown lots could meet all of these requirements—further reason to relocate companies to the outskirts of town.

All sources recommended a one-story layout; however, in buildings whose restricted sites demanded a two-story design, wide stairs were suggested instead of poles. The floor plans proposed were different from those of a bungalow fire station of 1910. As discussed in Chapter Six, the first priority for architects who designed bungalow stations usually had been to make the building look smaller; designers arranged the rooms to fit the functions of a normal fire station into a building with a lower profile. Now fire chiefs and architects tried to design their one-story stations from the inside out, and to arrange the rooms to provide the greatest efficiency of action. They prepared their plans along the lines of a flow chart, analyzing the movements of men within the building as a planner would analyze the re-

sponse patterns of apparatus within a city. The ideal fire station would enable firemen to reach the apparatus quickly from any room in the building and would reduce the amount of time and work necessary to get the engine back into the station, unloaded, cleaned, and ready to go again. In the interest of efficiency most experts now recommended some sort of drive-through arrangement, as had architect George 197 Ernest Robinson in the 1920s (see Chapter Seven). Circul-air and *Fire Engineering* both discussed the need for a separate watch room, "the focal point and nerve center of every fire station," where all the communications and alarm equipment could be isolated behind a glass barrier in a spot that gave the watchman full view of all entrances.

Design of Fire Stations, a book published by the standards committee of the State of Washington fire chiefs in 1963, was even more specific in its recommendations for floor plans. Its authors advocated a U-shaped "wrap- 198 around" plan, like that of the 1941 Columbus, Indiana, headquarters, with one drive-through

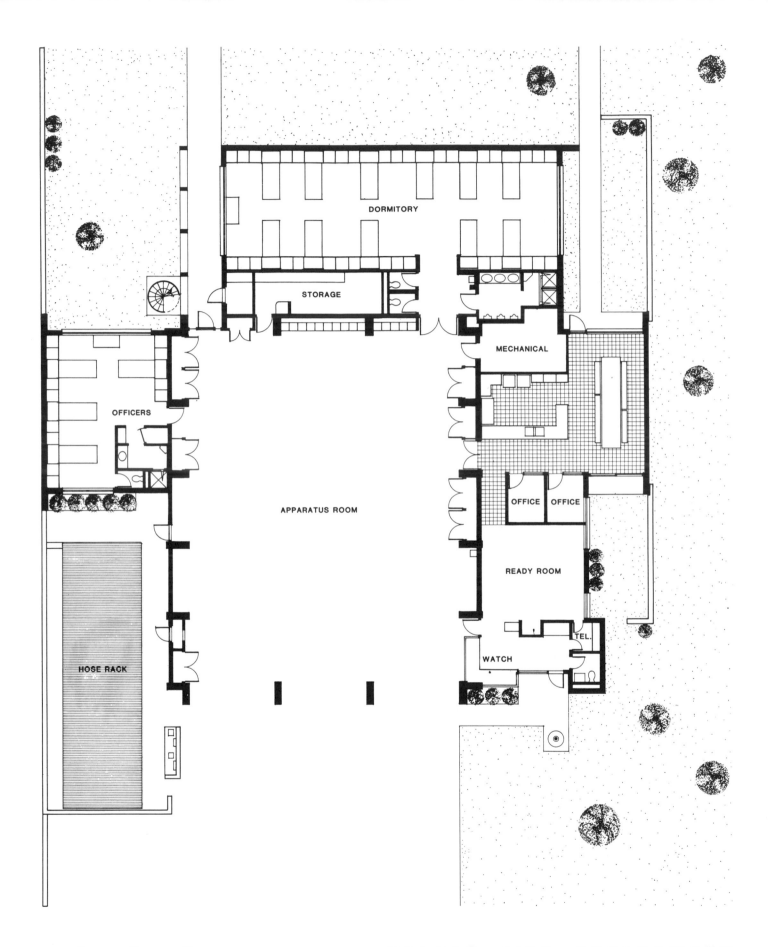

DORMITORY

STORAGE

MECHANICAL

OFFICERS

OFFICE OFFICE

APPARATUS ROOM

READY ROOM

HOSE RACK

TEL.

WATCH

WILLIAM H. HIDELL · ARCHITECTS
INCORPORATED

DALLAS FIRE DEPARTMENT
FIRE STATION NO. 1

apparatus door and a hose tower or drying machines at the back of the apparatus floor, where hose could be unloaded directly from the back of the truck (they did not prefer Circul-air). Rooms were to be arranged so as to eliminate the need for corridors or hallways, while providing maximum privacy for living areas and dormitories.

That basic plan has been popular ever since—Austin Siegfried's residential fire stations in Denver and William Hidell's Engine 1 in Dallas are among the recent fire stations that use it. A variation employed increasingly in recent years is a three-part layout that groups all the rooms in wings on either side of the apparatus floor and leaves the engine room completely open in front and back. This layout can in turn be modified for two-story stations by stacking one wing on top of the other so that the dormitory, offices, and locker room are directly over the downstairs kitchen and lounge, in a wing on one side of the apparatus floor. In the last few years the Chicago Fire Department has experimented with a "tri-level" arrangement, which has one wing off to the side of the engine room, with dormitory and locker room up one half-flight of stairs from the apparatus floor and kitchen and lounge underneath, half a flight down.

All in all, the changes made possible by new technology and recommendations from specialists have made the modern fire station quite different from one of 1920. Instead of being a tall, narrow building or a small house with one wing to the side, it is usually a long, horizontal block, one story in height. Instead of arched swing-out doors or an opening disguised as a porch, it will have a row of glass roll-up doors across the front, giving a view of the engines inside, and there will be at least one apparatus door in back to allow for a drive-through floor plan. Inside, the apparatus room is often large enough for four to eight pieces of equipment. Instead of a gong and a ticker-tape at a rolltop desk, the watch area usually occupies a glassed-in module filled with radio communications equipment. At the back of the engine room, helmets and turn-out coats will still hang along one wall, with racks of rolled hose nearby. Instead of a door leading to the tower, there is often a metal hose-drying cabinet. Wood floors, tongue-and-groove paneling or plaster walls, and stamped-tin ceiling, have given way to cement, cinderblock, or glazed brick, and exposed metal trusses that all can be hosed down.

A one-story fire station has no poles or stairs. The apparatus room no longer fills the entire front of the building, and the kitchen, dining area, and dayroom are often combined in a long room on one side, which may have access through sliding glass doors to a yard or patio. The kitchen, at the back of this space, will have appliances unheard of in 1920, and may have locks on some of the cupboards. The billiard tables, spittoons, and rockers or Windsor chairs found in an old recreation room will have been replaced by a television set, ashtrays, and upholstered chairs or vinyl-covered couches. There is no fireplace, and there probably are no radiators; the rooms usually have baseboard heat and air conditioning.

208

199–201

205, 206

199

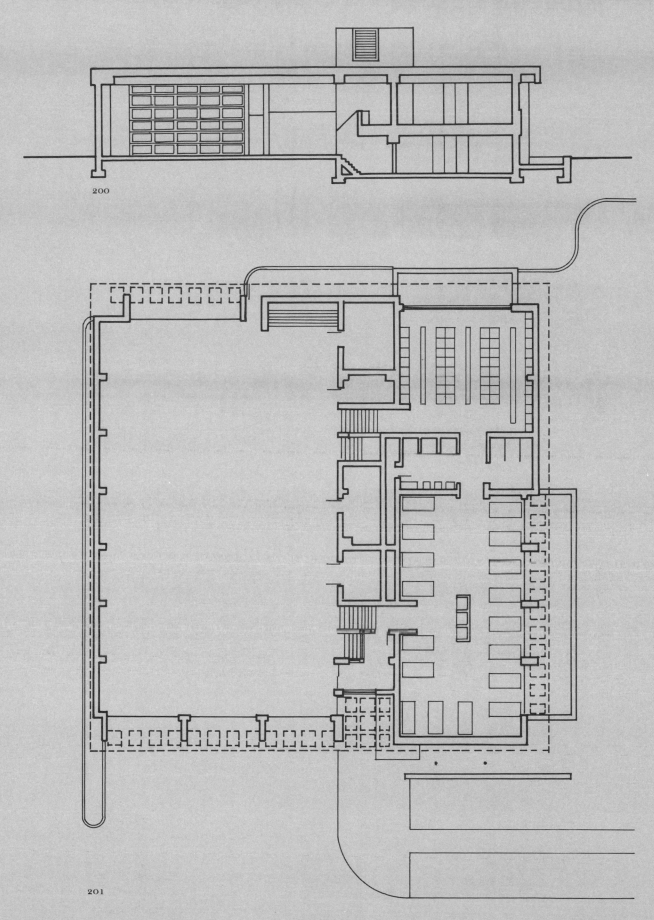

200

201

202. *Locker room, Fire Station 24, Kansas City, Missouri, 1979. Ridgeley, Shaughnessy, Hinkle and Scott, architects.* 203. *Dormitory, Fire Station 27, Hollywood, California, 1929, P. K. Schabarum, architect (see figs. 138, 139).* 204. *Dormitory, Fire Station 1, Dallas, Texas. Modern living quarters use plastic, vinyl, and other washable materials—a far cry from the wood and brass fittings of earlier buildings. Murphy beds allow the bunkroom at Fire Station 1 to double as a classroom during the day.*

The dormitory, bathroom, locker room, and offices (which used to be located on the second floor or in one wing of a bungalow) now take up the side of the building opposite the kitchen/living area, and may extend across the back. They are all much larger than they were in 1920, because they are likely to accommodate from eight to fifteen men. In the dormitory, the iron bedsteads have been replaced by Murphy beds that fold up to allow the room to double as a classroom or study during the day. The bathroom will have a row of showers instead of a tub, with plastic laminate, vinyl, aluminum, and chrome where the old bathrooms had marble, tile, and brass. Off of the bathroom, a separate locker room with metal, not wooden, lockers is probably better ventilated than it would have been in 1920. Offices, closets, and storage areas probably have not changed significantly. The modern fire station has no coal bin, and probably no basement.

While specialists in the last thirty years have published a wide range of ingenious and sensible suggestions for improving the layout and interior features of the fire station, they seem suddenly to run out of good ideas when it comes to questions of architecture. Circulair's prediction that the drying machine would usher in an age of "limitless possibilities" in fire station design has not been borne out in the buildings illustrated in the company's publications or in general articles on "planning the functional fire station." The only point about design that every writer has been sure to make is that whatever you do, you have to please the neighbors: "When it is necessary to locate a fire station in a residential part of a city, it will usually be necessary to overcome some resistance on the part of some residents. Such resistance can be overcome by a competent architect designing a building with a residential character, and also by the use of screening and landscaping. Extra expense for this purpose is justified in this case. Early salesmanship establishing good public relations with pre-planning and public meetings is necessary." As more people moved to the suburbs and zoning laws became stricter, incidents like those that gave birth to the bungalow fire station in Portland and Denver (see Chapter Six) have happened more and more often. Residents of luxury neighborhoods in southern California seem to have been especially vocal in their protests against new fire stations; it took nine years and a serious fire for the Laurel Canyon section of Los Angeles to consent to construction of a fire station. An article from *Fire Engineering* describing Engine 71 on Sunset Boulevard in 1954 has a familiar ring to it: "Engine 71 has been awarded first prize in the fire station division of the Los Angeles Chamber of Commerce. This $119,000 station, believed to be the most expensive single engine house west of Chicago, is located in the heart of the residential area of Hollywood's film colony. Some of moviedom's top names are frequent visitors at the station." It also shows how times had changed. While Engine 23 in Los Angeles, described in 1910 as "the most elaborate and richest engine house west of New York" (see Chapter Five), had been built at the whim of a

203

204

205. *Kitchen at Dixwell Fire Station, New Haven, Connecticut, 1974. Venturi and Rauch, architects.* 206. *Kitchen at Fire Station 2, Dallas, Texas, 1978. Forrest Upshaw, architect. Kitchens in recent fire stations range from the compact to the palatial, depending on the request of the fire chief, the habits of the men, and the architect's own idea of the fireman's routine.*

207. *Glen Echo Volunteer Fire Department, Glen Echo, Maryland, 1954. Edward T. Dunlap, architect. While technology for firefighting grew by leaps and bounds in the 1950s, the architecture of fire stations stagnated. "Phoney Colonial" remained the norm in the suburbs.*

205

206

fire chief, now local residents had the final say about where the money would be spent.

Most suburban dwellers did not get such extravagant results. Other than emphasizing the need to make fire stations "blend," the trade magazines offered no suggestions on how to improve residential fire stations. The illustrations they published were by and large terrible: clumsy versions of overgrown ranch houses or "colonial" types that only would need an orange roof to be dead ringers for a Howard Johnson's motel. As for designing fire stations in nonresidential districts (the ones that pre-

207

sumably did not require a "competent architect" or any special treatment), the experts presented no ideas at all. Thomas Schaardt, an architect and volunteer fireman who carried on the tradition of George Ernest Robinson by specializing in fire station design, told a meeting of the International Association of Fire Chiefs in 1957: "I feel that a new fire station should be of contemporary design, since it will stand up for many years as an example of the intelligence and progress of our age, just as the temples and churches of the Greek and Gothic periods were monuments of their

times." The editors of trade journals were not so sure; the 1949 edition of *Fire Station Design* described one volunteer station as "Modernistic in design, but held well within the bounds of good taste."

The examples they illustrated, and most of Schaardt's own buildings, all followed one architectural model. Whatever the layout, the rooms were large and open, with cinderblock walls (or washable glazed brick in the apparatus room), metal fixtures, and fluorescent lights. Whether built on a steel frame or with traditional load-bearing walls, the buildings all looked like long, horizontal boxes with a few rectangular windows and the big, square doors in front. The usual suburban station took the same box and put a slanted roof on it.

These were the types of designs that appeared most often in both firefighting and architectural magazines in the 1950s, ones that Circul-air was especially anxious to promote (no "unsightly tower" to break up the boxy lines). Ugly to look at, efficient but depressing

193

to work in, and quite often cheaply built, these buildings were a long way from the fire stations of earlier generations, when the buildings' unique requirements had inspired such a variety of good architecture.

Appearances notwithstanding, the editors of professional journals had not succumbed to a sudden rash of bad taste in 1950; the buildings they chose to publish represented the state of fire station architecture at the time. In the past, most of the stations featured in *Fire Engineering* and *Fireman's Journal*, while less elegant than ones written up in *Architectural Forum*, had at least been well-proportioned, fairly imaginative, and generally handsome—some had been much more. Beginning in the fifties, even the buildings presented as examples of "excellence in design" or "functional beauty" were the same ugly boxes, over and over again. The boxes all had architects, professionals who had won their commissions because somebody with authority had liked their work. Though few of the architects responsible for fire stations in the 1950s and '60s were leaders in their profession—as Wheelwright, Bebb, Freeman, LeBrun, and Harry Hake had been at the turn of the century—they were certainly no worse trained and no less prominent locally than the architects who had designed Kansas City's Engine 26, Engine 1 in Los Angeles, or any of the other modest older buildings illustrated so far. Some of the entries published in *Fire Station Design* came from city architects' offices, which in the past had been the source of some excellent designs. But now even the best efforts were seldom anywhere near as competent as the average fire station built before 1935. The reasons for this decline in the overall distinction of fire station architecture are complicated but worth looking into. They have to do with the lack of quality prevailing in most public buildings today.

The most obvious explanation is the changing shape of the building. The horizontal, one-story plan of the modern fire station gives architects less to work with; without a tower it is hard to make a long, low box look like a fire station, or even to make it look very important. George Stewart had recognized this problem of design in 1931 when he added a false stepped front to Fire Station 6 in Seattle. Robert Venturi would choose a similar solution in 1967 for Fire Station 4 in Columbus, Indiana. But these designs are exceptional—few architects in recent years have been able to equal them. The problem goes beyond the floor plan to the process of design and the way the architects are chosen.

One reason that the design of fire stations has suffered since the 1950s is that the people who devote most attention to their study are not primarily interested in architecture. Just as the equipment inside the red brick fire station of the 1880s was usually more remarkable than the building itself, the modern fire station is distinguished more by its interior than its exterior. Experts in the 1950s turned their attention and skill to re-thinking the equipment, functions, and floor plan of fire stations; they encouraged architects to plan a building from the inside out. The changes they recommended went far beyond the surface "modernization" of the 1930s toward improving the actual workings of the fire department. Many of the fire stations of the 1960s that were architecturally imaginative but not functionally innovative never appeared in firemen's journals.

Today when George Proper (New York State's fire station specialist) analyzes or rates a fire station, he looks first for fireproof construction, then for efficiency of layout. Easy entrance, exit, and unobstructed views for drivers are of special concern; for this reason Proper considers staggered apparatus doors and "tunnel doorways" generally to be a bad idea. He then asks whether the building wastes energy, disapproving of stations he calls "greenhouses," like Engine 30 in Kansas City, that use glass walls to "showcase" the fire trucks. Proper is not an architect, and does not consider it his job to make aesthetic judgments. With these priorities, most questions of visual effect become excess window dressing—nice if you happen to get it, but not an integral part of the plan. Some of the fire stations that Proper

234

224, 225

208

likes best are the ones he calls "Plain Janes," the prefabricated metal buildings favored by small volunteer fire departments.

The box form achieved some of its popularity in the 1950s simply because it was considered modern. At that time the phenomenon that the historian Daniel Boorstin describes as "the search for novelty" extended to popular taste in architecture; the mixed feelings that people had expressed about modern design in the 1930s gave way to a full-fledged enthusiasm for buildings that looked new. Attitudes toward the architecture of the past changed, as Americans set about "modernizing" their environment. This was the period when thousands of shopkeepers covered over old-fashioned storefronts with new paneling, and homeowners stripped the trim from their Victorian houses. It was also the time of the first urban renewal programs that wiped out entire sections of older cities to replace them with modern highways, shopping malls, highrise office buildings, and housing projects. The split-level ranch brought modern design into the suburbs, and even traditional "Colonial Revival" design was modified, stripped down, and given a newer look.

The Circul-air publications give some idea of how the new attitude affected the design of fire stations. No one ever had thought that hose towers were "unsightly" before—in fact, as we have seen, architects often had emphasized them as decorative elements that distinguished the fire station from other types of buildings (even for streamlined buildings like the Central Station at Columbus, Indiana). But now Circul-air claimed that buildings with towers *looked* out-of-date. In the 1950s, that argument was enough to convince many readers.

Even some architecture that had been considered "modern" in the past looked old-fashioned by 1950. The streamlined and modernistic styles with their metal ornament and curving walls died out after World War II, and with them went most of the futuristic fantasy that had been connected with machine imagery. Like the 1930s gas stations discussed in Chapter Seven, most modern architecture of the 1950s was closer to European models, which always had been simpler, more restrained, and less decorative. It was a German architect who had popularized the phrase, "less is more." Unlike American stripped classicism, the European Bauhaus or "International Style" architecture was based on the thin walls and large, ribbon windows characteristic of curtain-frame construction. As a result, American buildings of the 1950s, from houses to factories to the United Nations headquarters, followed the form of a glass box. Architects of fire stations sought to embody that light, boxy look even in buildings with traditional load-bearing walls.

Developments in the building industry helped the European ideal of "less is more" take hold. The cost of architectural detail was going up, along with the cost of labor. Stonecutters and carpenters now considered themselves skilled workers and demanded higher wages; bricklayers no longer could be expected to create ornamental patterns. At the same time, the cheap molded terra-cotta, pressed brick, and stamped metal decoration that nineteenth-century architects had ordered from catalogs was no longer available—changing taste and production costs had driven it off the market. While in the 1880s Napoleon LeBrun had been able to design quite ornate —and dirt cheap (under $16,000)—buildings such as Engine 54 using no fancier materials than brick and pre-cast metal, by 1959 even some simple wooden trim required custom millwork. Part of the reason for the passing of streamlined design was that its rounded shapes, and especially the curved glass, were difficult to mass produce. It was much easier for manufacturers to prefabricate panels and windows in standard rectangular forms and for builders to assemble them into right-angled buildings. "Less is more" cost less.

Concern for economy was an important factor in the popularity of the box-type fire station. A 1954 article on architectural trends in *Fire Engineering* noted: "Never before have fire department budgets and costs been subject to such scrutiny and the paring knife. Costs of municipal government, fire protection included, have continued to mount while, proportionately, revenue has failed to keep pace. The result is that the rule of economy is applied wherever and whenever possible." Also contributing to the rising costs was the fact that, following the recommendations of comprehensive planning reports, fire chiefs in the 1950s usually tried to build several stations at a time. For example, as part of its reorganization plan in the late fifties Boston built four fire stations at a total cost of $1,299,465. This

figure came under attack from the city's municipal research bureau, which claimed that the city should have been able to build at least five fire stations with the money they already had spent.

Analysis of the four stations shows that Boston has gone overboard in fire station construction . . . costs of over $20 per square foot are a luxury. . . . Among the unnecessary features are full basements, wide-span roofs, lavish finish materials plus lavish use of finish materials, fancy window grilles, glazed tile in the hose drying room, acoustic ceiling on top of plaster, and snow-melting equipment under aprons. . . .

Fire Department officials must set standards for less expensive stations if the city is to proceed with future stations.

The bureau advised the city to save architects' fees by choosing standard designs for two- and three-bay stations at the cost of $18 per square foot, and recommended: "The fire station should be purely functional . . . the apparatus room should be a king-sized garage. The City should consider building the apparatus room as inexpensively as a warehouse or commercial garage . . . [and planning living quarters] almost as a separate building."

Many other cities used standardized plans in the 1950s, though as seen in Chapters Three, Four, and Five, this was hardly a new idea. What was new was the use of prefabricated parts. After analyzing changing growth pat-

210

209

terns, some cities decided that new fire stations could be expected only to serve for a limited time, and accordingly erected portable or temporary buildings. In 1978 the Montgomery, Alabama, fire department put together a mobile home and a pre-engineered metal garage over a cement slab foundation for a $25,000 engine house.

"Less is more" was originally an aesthetic judgment: it was meant to apply to luxury apartment buildings as well as to factories. But when used with two other slogans quoted by modern architects at the time—"form follows function" and "ornament is a crime"—it had an especially serious effect on low-budget buildings such as fire stations. Though the architects who coined these phrases probably would have deplored the results, their ideas in combination with the changes taking place in the building industry caused city building departments to discourage any architectural features that could not be proved "functional." We can see that attitude at work in the Boston Municipal Research Bureau's advice that "the fire station should be purely functional" and in this 1957 memo on fire station design from consulting engineer Horatio Bond to the National Fire Protection Association: "In constructing modern fire stations, useless attic spaces, Mansard roofs and dormer windows should be eliminated as they are examples of useless fire hazards . . . where hose towers are still employed, they should not be made too tall and ornamental as they have on occasion been cited as examples of wasted public expenditure." This kind of thinking in turn gave rise to the perverse idea that to pay attention to aesthetics at all was to waste the taxpayers' money. An official in the building department in Kansas City, Missouri, summed it up a few years ago: "There are basically two kinds of buildings, your functional and your aesthetic. We can't afford your aesthetic-type buildings."

By the time the box-type fire station took hold, fire chiefs were especially sensitive to charges of wasting public funds. The specter of the pinochle-playing fireman haunted them even more than it had in the 1930s. Articles in fire journals suggested that if fire departments could improve their image they might get as big a share of the municipal budget as police did. As a result, many fire departments appointed full-time public relations officers in the early 1960s and trained some of their men in public speaking.

More efforts were made to dispel the idea that firemen spend most of their time at leisure: part of the reason that pre-fire planning called for entire companies to conduct on-site inspections of buildings was simply to get the men out of the fire station and into the street, where the public could see them busy at work between fires. Similarly, New York and other cities made attendance at fire college mandatory in the 1950s, not only to improve the firemen's skills but also to keep them occupied. Back at the fire station, men were instructed to stay away from the front of the building and the apparatus floor unless they were working. Architects designing new fire stations were advised to put lounges and din-

211

ing rooms at the back of the building, out of public view, and to expand the watch desk area. Visitors entering the stations would now be met by a watchman as soon as they walked through the door instead of being allowed to wander through the building on their own.

As in the 1930s, the concern with projecting a hard-working image carried over into the use of modern styles for fire stations. But now the motivation was a little more complicated. Pressed by budget considerations and trying to avoid accusations that the fireman's job was too easy, the fire chief of the fifties wanted buildings that not only were cheap but looked cheap. The International Style box, with its no-frills message, fit the bill.

Even within the tight parameters of budget and the rigors of the modern style, there was still room for better buildings than the typical fire station of 1960. Except for headquarters buildings and the "castles and palaces" of the turn of the century, municipally funded fire stations usually have been relatively low-cost buildings. However, most of the time the low budgets have not excluded distinguished design. Since 1950 two new factors have brought about a turn for the worse. One is the idea discussed above that there is a difference between functional buildings and aesthetic ones, with the implication being that aesthetic buildings are uselessly expensive, and functional buildings are ugly. The other is that firemen do not need or deserve aesthetic buildings. These ideas are nebulous and nearly impossible to prove, but they have been deciding factors in the downward trend of fire station architecture in the last thirty years.

Since the days of the volunteers, the design of fire stations has been characterized by an unusual combination of features: their role as public buildings, their program that calls for both a garage and living quarters, their peculiar size and shape, and the fact that they are associated with the fire service and whatever it stands for. Because fire stations have been linked with the popular image of firemen and fire engines, they often have had an extra element of humor or fantasy—you might even call it affection—that sets them apart from other buildings. The expensive fire stations of the turn of the century were built at a time when firemen enjoyed great popularity. Part of the reason that boss mayors attended the opening ceremonies was to identify themselves to the public as a friend of the fireman. Bungalow stations of the 1910s and '20s, though considerably less grand than earlier buildings, still provided the "good neighbor" fireman with very comfortable quarters. Even the streamlined fire stations built before World War II, while more businesslike and less luxurious than other stations had been, were not scanty; they still tried to be impressive, even monumental, in their own way. Responding to the idea that the fireman should be considered a skilled worker, architects had tried to ensure that he would be amply provided with all the facilities and equipment needed to do his job.

The budget-cutting approach that has determined fire station design in the last thirty years comes in response to a new public mandate. In a way, it goes back to the sentiment that prevailed at the time the first paid fire departments were established in the 1860s. At no other time have taxpayers been so wary of spending money on buildings for firemen; modern fire stations have a good deal in common with the storefront stations with hidden towers. Since the 1950s, popular ideas about the fireman's job have been changing. People think of firemen less often as self-sacrificing or heroic and more often as ordinary blue-collar workers. The acceptance of the three-platoon system after the war and subsequent modifications have brought the fireman's work week closer to the average forty hours. In recent years firemen have shown us they are as concerned about fair wages and benefits as any other municipal employees, and that they will go out on strike (albeit reluctantly) to get them. With these trends in mind, a 1970 article in *Fire Command* on "Fire Stations of the Future" advised: "The old role of the fire station should be changing from 'a home away from home.' . . . With the short work weeks the quarters need not be in the nature of the Grand Hotel; as long as they are comfortable and convenient, most fire fighters would rather have the money invested in shorter hours, good pay, and fringe benefits." Moreover, firemen themselves now think differently of their work. Though they are still performing services that most people would never do for love *or* money, more and more of them will tell you, "it's just a job." Consequently the modern fire station is often designed as "just a place to work."

Now that firemen no longer have quite the same role as folk heroes that they used to, fire stations have been losing that element of fantasy or affection that distinguished them in the past. Whether they realize it or not, the changing conception of the fireman probably has influenced the thinking of everyone who has a say in the design process: architects, building officials, the writers of articles in fire journals, citizens' committees, and firemen themselves. At the same time, authorities no longer see the need to emphasize the fire department's role in city government by making fire stations look more important than other types of buildings. Since architects are being urged to think of the fire station as a "king-sized garage" or warehouse, many now design fire stations that could be confused with gas stations.

The result of this change in image is that since 1950 the fire station has lost the symbolic importance it once had. Magazines no longer describe fire stations as assets to the neighborhood or causes for civic pride. No one predicts, as one writer once did of Engine 31 in New York, that a fire station will "give so high a tone to the new buildings that are to postdate it." (See Chapter Five.) Instead, the trade publications urge architects to design unobtrusive buildings, for fear of offending the people who notice them. *Fire Command* has questioned, ". . . whether it makes much sense to build fire stations as though their purpose was to be enduring monuments to Boss Tweed, Boss Hague, or Boss Crump, or even Mayor Joe Doakes. Some elaborate fire stations involve lucrative contracts and substantial architectural fees (for designers favored by the administration)." They also discourage the idea of building fire stations as monuments to firemen or to the fire department. Instead of paying for architectural symbols, "the money saved from needless ornament should be put into better fire protection equipment."

Two instances where strong mayors tried to influence the design of fire stations show just how low these buildings had sunk in public esteem by the 1960s. In the tradition of Nathan Matthews, Mayor Richard C. Lee of New Haven, Connecticut, prided himself on changing the face of the city (though many historians now say the change was for the worse). Lee gained national prominence for being among the first mayors to take advantage of Federal funds for highways and urban renewal.

One of the first projects Lee's administration undertook was a redevelopment plan for an old Italian neighborhood that included relocation of the city's fire department headquarters. Responding to Lee's request for a "monumental" fire station that would serve as a "gateway" to the neighborhood, architects Carlin, Millard and Pozzi chose to reject the standard brick and glass box format and designed a concrete fortress marked by towers at each of its corners. Carlin actually asked the fire department's permission to include a hose tower (instead of the basement drying racks normally used in New Haven) in order to provide "a strong vertical emphasis" that would make the building stand out from those around it while visually linking it to the office buildings downtown (it also enabled him to build the fire station without a basement). In 1960 the architects received an award for their "highly imaginative and forceful scheme" in the annual competition sponsored by *Progressive Architecture* magazine. But the project provoked the wrath of the award jury's chairman, Dean Charles Colbert of Princeton University, who insisted on publishing a dissenting opinion. Dean Colbert's complaint was not with the building's design but with the fact that it was a fire station in the first place:

I don't feel that a fire house is, or should be, "foreground" architecture. One essentially inconsequential function has been developed

214

far beyond its purposeful use by the community. This man has an idea; he has something to say, but doesn't have the medium to say it with.

I think it's capricious and preconceived disorder trying to achieve some form of plastic statement at the expense of the public good. I think it's inappropriate; I think it's a tour de force; I think it refutes the industrial process that architecture has tried to become part of. . . . It is too bad that a man with this much ability has to limit it to a fire station. He should have a greater opportunity.

Colbert's statement seemed intended to tell the architectural establishment to treat the fire station as a gas station—to stuff the design back into a 1950s box.

Whereas Mayor Lee was attacked for commissioning a "foreground" fire station, when Richard Daley of Chicago tried to build a fire station that would be a political symbol, all he could get was a definitely "background" building. Just before the Democratic Convention of 1968 he opened a $700,000, eight-company station said to be "the largest working neighborhood firehouse in the nation." It included central air conditioning, marble-lined shower stalls, and "sleeping quarters good enough for Army officers." Daley staged a dedication ceremony that would have impressed Boss Martin Behrman of New Orleans:

Mayor Richard J. Daley and the Fire Department band helped dedicate the building with rousing oratory and the peppy tune "Chicago." Daley reminisced that he used to visit his neighborhood firehouse, to admire firemen and horses alike, as a boy.

"We hope and pray," he said, "this will not be just a house, because there are too many houses in America . . . but a home."

[Fire] Commissioner Quinn got up and practically nominated Daley for President with:

"Mister Mayor, you've got a great week coming up. . . . I sincerely hope you're the man they come up with. . . . I think you're the man to save our country and bring it back in the right direction."

Daley smiled and shook his head.

Despite its title as "the city's newest, largest and most modern fire station," from the outside "Daley's Pride" looked like an overgrown mobile home—a stone-clad carton on stilts. All the mayor's power could not command a building with authority or a distinctive identity.

Daley's predicament, which stems from the fire station's loss of importance as an architectural symbol in the last thirty years, was also part of a larger architectural trend. A recent study of courthouses notes that since World War II those buildings have been characterized by "anonymity, a lack of originality, and designs which give no indication of the building's public function." The same critique could apply equally well to schools, libraries, city halls, Federal buildings, and even to some houses of worship. Public buildings just do not have the importance and power as symbols that they

233

used to. Since they all tend to look alike, it is no longer possible to associate a particular kind of building with a particular architectural form: libraries look like supermarkets, museums look like shopping malls, courthouses look like office buildings, and office buildings look like glass castles. Small wonder, then, that some fire stations look like gas stations. Non-architects have compared recent examples to boats, hamburger stands, and Lutheran churches.

At the same time, downtown buildings, especially governmental ones, no longer play as important a role as they used to in most people's lives. Just as citizens' groups have organized to protest fire stations only in their own neighborhood, now that people spend most of their time in the suburbs (where even commercial buildings look like houses), the question of what an urban building ought to stand for no longer "hits them where they live." "Civic pride" applies more to baseball teams than to municipal architecture. The buildings that Americans think about most are the ones they see most: houses, shopping centers, entertainment complexes, and corporate office buildings. Some architectural historians actually have proposed the freeway as one of the most important architectural forms for the future.

While people no longer pay as much attention to public architecture as they used to, architects have been struggling to design governmental buildings that command attention and respect. F. A. Gutheim's observation that "public architecture cannot rise higher than the unfortunate state of the art itself" is as true now as it was in 1933. In the last forty years public buildings have suffered from the problems architects have had trying to use modern styles for buildings that are supposed to look important. "Functionalist" modern architecture, with its basis in the lightweight construction techniques originally used for factory buildings, makes little provision for abstract ideas like civic pride. As early as 1938, the critic Lewis Mumford had noticed the paradox: "The notion of a modern monument is a contradiction in terms; if it is a monument it is not modern, and if it is modern, it cannot be a monument." The problem came to a head with the competition for a memorial to Franklin Delano Roosevelt in 1959. When the winning design was rejected by an act of Congress, architects began to wonder if today's culture "is indeed able to create a monument to which a majority of us can emotionally respond."

Since that time, architects searching for alternatives to the International Style have branched out in so many directions at once that a 1961 article in *Progressive Architecture* termed the dominant movement "chaoticism." The debate over an appropriate form for important modern buildings is still going on, and probably will continue for a long time to come. Until the question is solved, modern architecture will continue in an unprecedented state of freedom and confusion. Having no accepted rules to follow anymore, architects have had the chance to offer a wealth of innovative solutions, with some fine results. But for too many, the new freedom has been more than they know what to do with; "chaoticism"

215

continues as their failed attempts clutter our skyline.

In the meantime, the current state of confusion also has had unfortunate effects on smaller, nonmonumental buildings such as fire stations. For architects who cannot or do not want to propose a new interpretation of modern architecture with every building they design, the absence of a standard vocabulary and the rules to use it with can be unwelcome. In the past, even an uninspired architect could come up with pleasing designs just by copying features from pattern books and from other buildings, combining them according to established, traditional formulas. Now that all options are open, we can no longer count on the same minimum level of decent design. "Average" buildings are not as good as they were.

Confusion about modern architecture has extended to the public, who no longer have a sure set of standards by which to judge the buildings around them. Faced with a welter of competing ideas about design, people are beginning to suspect that architects may not know what they are doing anymore—especially as some of the more spectacular "aesthetic-type" buildings of recent years have collapsed from flaws in engineering. As a result, we tend to believe the false economy of municipal building departments. Instead of questioning the quality of public buildings, we chalk up the bad construction to "politics," and accept the designs as the best we are likely to get. Maybe the combination of functional and aesthetic really was too much to ask for. In the end, "less is more" has led us to settle for less.

216

CHAPTER NINE

Recent Alternatives
to the Box

1960–

Happily, the mediocrity that has ruled most public architecture in the last twenty years has admitted a few exceptions, including some first-rate fire stations. During the judging of the *Progressive Architecture* competition in 1960, architect Cloethiel Woodward Smith spoke up in defense of the Central Fire Station in New Haven: "There is a drama in fighting fires which everyone loves; I think fire houses should be played up." All along there have been a few architects and administrators who have agreed with her, who have attempted to capture the fire station's traditional symbolism and re-introduce that element of fantasy lacking in the standard box-type building. As in the eclectic 1890s, the general confusion over appropriate styles for public buildings has permitted these architects the freedom to explore kinds of design they might not have used for a more "serious" type of building. And, as in earlier generations, the fire station's combination of small scale and unusual function has

216. *Fire Station 4, Columbus, Indiana, 1967–68. Venturi and Rauch, architects (photograph by Theresa Beyer).* **217.** *Fire Station 2, Dallas, Texas, 1978. Forrest Upshaw, architect. Two ways to fit a modern firehouse into an urban setting: Upshaw camouflaged the building, Venturi turned it into a billboard.*

inspired some fine results that give these buildings a power beyond their size.

For the first time, fire stations are winning architectural awards and turning up in histories of American architecture as some of the best illustrations of current architectural theory. But quality is hard to measure in a time of architectural experiment, and the buildings most praised by critics are often least liked by the people who use them. The response of firemen to some of these buildings shows an unfortunate state of misunderstanding between architects and clients, reflecting a broader alienation of modern architecture from modern life.

In most cases these out-of-the-ordinary fire stations have been designed in response to unusual requests from outside parties. We already have seen how some strong mayors have continued to take a special interest in city buildings; it is only necessary to add here that despite the furor over the New Haven headquarters building, Mayor Richard C. Lee went on to commission two more fire stations that were even more distinctive than the first. Pressure from residents of exclusive neighborhoods has remained the strongest influence on fire station design. Fire Station 2 in Dallas, Texas, is an extreme example of a "camouflaged"

217

218

building; the architect Forrest Upshaw moved the apparatus doors around to the side of the building so that none of the fire station's functions would be visible from the street.

In the case of Station 4 in Berkeley, California, residents of the surrounding area were so set against a fire station in their neighborhood that they appealed to the state supreme court. After seven years of argument the fire department agreed to locate the building in a city-owned park, to commission Professor Robert W. Ratcliff, of the University of California school of architecture, to design it, and to require him to work with a committee of local residents in drawing up his plans. Ratcliff's solution was not to disguise the building but to make it a positive addition to the park. The result is a series of round, tentlike pavilions of glass, cement, and redwood that fit in quite easily among the trees and are hardly visible from the street. The circular format allowed the building to accommodate all the necessary functions while leaving the greatest number of trees intact.

218–220

218, 219, 220. *Fire Station 4, Berkeley, California, 1960. Robert W. Ratcliff, architect. Neighbors protested plans to build a fire station until the fire department proposed this tent-like building to be constructed in a city park. The circular floor plan permitted the architect to leave most of the trees on the site. But the attracive and unusual design has its drawbacks—the living quarters are awkward and uncomfortably cramped.*

219

220

221

221, 222, 223. *Whitney Avenue Fire Station, New Haven, Connecticut, 1962. Carlin, Millard and Pozzi, architects. Like Upshaw and Ratcliff, Carlin was asked to design a fire station to please the neighbors. Instead of disguising the building he chose heavy-duty industrial materials, then scaled the details to complement the other houses on the street (photographs by Robert Perron).*

222

221–223 Vocal neighbors also had a hand in the plans for the Whitney Avenue Fire Station in New Haven, which, like the earlier headquarters building there, was designed by Carlin, Millard and Pozzi. Here the problem was to fit the building in among a neighborhood of large old houses that all front onto a wide main street. Instead of trying to make the building look like another house, Carlin sensitively combined domestic-scale details with industrial materials; the concrete was cast in forms lined with clapboards, and the metal windows and apparatus doors were carefully scaled to match the proportions of nearby buildings. A series of walls, chimneys, and setbacks cleverly mask the stairwells and the company parking lot. The firemen who work there are pleased that the architects chose heavy-duty brick, cement, and terrazzo for the interiors, for they have held up much better over the last twenty years than the cozier redwood paneling at Station 4 in Berkeley.

Sometimes a city will get an innovative design for a fire station entirely by accident, as

223

224, 225 at Kansas City's Fire Station 30, which won an award from the American Institute of Architects shortly after it opened in 1968. The site was out in the middle of an undeveloped area with nothing nearby but an amusement park, and the city had no special interest in making the building any kind of showpiece. Left to their own devices, the architects Seligson-Eggens took advantage of the lack of restrictions to design a fire station that looks like a giant mechanical toy, with the engines put on display behind glass walls. According to the members of the company, the building is still as sunny, pleasant, and cheerful to work in as it was when it opened; the glass presents no particular maintenance problems.

It is not surprising that the fire station best known to students of architecture around the world is in the small town of Columbus, Indiana; nearly every public building there is a modern landmark. Since 1957, the Cummins Engine Company (mentioned in Chapter Eight in connection with diesel fire trucks) has had a standing agreement with the local government 216, 226

224

to pay the architects' fees for any public building erected in Columbus, provided that the architects are chosen from a list of young, nationally known firms drawn up by the American Institute of Architects. The town must choose a different architect for each project; however, some of the firms have since been asked back to design buildings for private businesses. Columbus prides itself on having more noteworthy architecture per square mile than any other place in America, and the public schools, the library, the post office, and even the local telephone plant stand as models of their types.

Although the firm of Venturi and Rauch had not yet achieved its current prominence when it received the commission for Fire Station 4 in 1967, Robert Venturi already was considered one of America's most important and radical architectural theorists. Venturi was among the first to condemn the "functionalist" ideal of modern architecture for its anonymity and lack of meaning. Instead of "less is more," he claimed "less is a bore" and argued for a return to symbolism and ornament in architecture. At the same time, he urged modern architects to stop trying to redesign the world from scratch, to start paying more attention to the "ordinary" commercial and suburban buildings around them. These ideas put Venturi in a unique position to solve the problem of the modern fire station: how to combine civic symbol and utilitarian function in a building that no longer occupies a central place in the city, or in the minds of the public. No other architect has understood the fire station's com-

plex symbolic function quite so well. Venturi and Rauch rank their designs for fire stations at Columbus and New Haven, Connecticut, among the firm's proudest achievements.

In Columbus, Venturi's approach impressed the local building committee, whose members had feared that an outside architect would insist on designing a "high style" building at their expense. The chief had not been pleased with the town's last fire station, a building designed by local architects in 1963 that had a decorative butterfly roof that leaked. Venturi's simple design stayed within a low $100,000 budget precisely because he made a point of using "ordinary" construction techniques and materials that came out of the standard builders' catalogs.

The site of Fire Station 4, located on a highway in an area to be developed for tract housing, presented a particular challenge for the architects. It called for a building that was less elaborate than a castle, less informal than a ranch house, more than merely a garage. Drawing on the tradition of roadside architecture, Venturi made the back of the building as simple as possible and treated the front as a sign. The tower and decoration are designed to make the building seem taller than it really is (the architects call it "a little building with a big scale") and to identify it as a fire station. The arrangement of doors and windows symbolizes the building's double function. On one side, a "domestic, human scale" window, crossed like one from a child's drawing of a house, marks the living quarters; on the other side, the "engine scale" apparatus door is set

216

225

back for emphasis. Venturi's studied think-ing-out of what a fire station stands for makes this building look important without being pre-tentious. His accomplishment becomes clear 192, 209 as soon as you compare Fire Station 4 with a building like Engine 112 in Chicago or Station 21 in Denver. Whatever its other flaws—and there are many (see below)—it has the distinc-tion of being one of the only modern fire sta-tions that looks like a fire station.

Venturi and Rauch had another chance to tackle these questions when Mayor Lee asked the firm to design the Dixwell Fire Station in 226-228, 230, 231, 205 New Haven in 1972. Here the problem was slightly different from that in Columbus, since the surrounding area already was filled with an assortment of other buildings. The fire sta-tion is sited with its main visitors' entrance on a corner, in order to allow maximum access and visibility for the engines. One side of the lot marks the beginning of a housing project, and a row of run-down garages, car dealers, and

226, 227, 228. *Dixwell Fire Station, New Haven, Connecticut, 1974. Robert Venturi, architect.* **229.** *Floor plan. Fire Station 4, Columbus, Indiana (see fig. 216). Rather than hide the Dixwell Station or make it stand out (like his Fire Station 4), Venturi based his design on the ordinary structures around it, but with a difference. The red brick—a slightly deeper color than usual—blends with the older buildings across the street but also identifies the fire station. Venturi paid attention to proportion, and thought about the best way to balance doors and windows, and to make the building make sense from close up or from far away. The curving panel that wraps around the corner helps both sides of the building to read as one long wall. Inside, the emphasis was on high-quality materials—genuine brass poles, and glazed brick instead of cinderblock for the walls.*

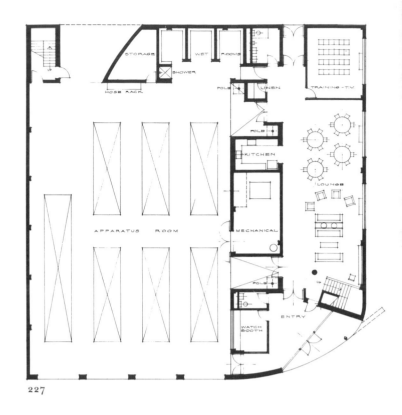

227

226

228

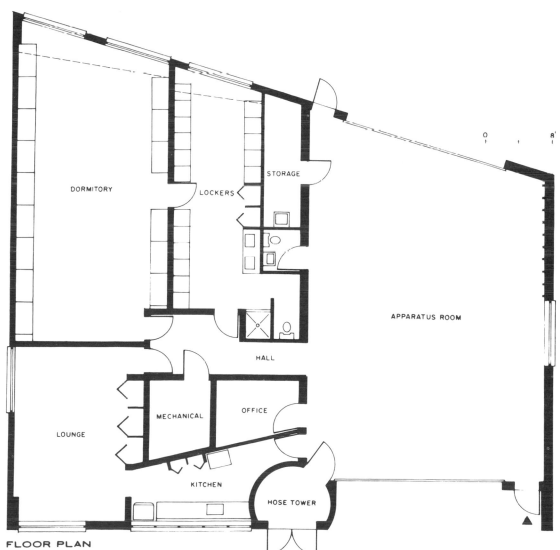

229

FLOOR PLAN

DORMITORY

LOCKERS

STORAGE

APPARATUS ROOM

HALL

LOUNGE

MECHANICAL

OFFICE

KITCHEN

HOSE TOWER

230

other commercial buildings runs along the other two sides. There is an old red brick church directly across the street.

Although this neighborhood is not a high-class suburb, and no citizens' group demanded that the fire station "blend," Venturi wanted to design a building that respected the surrounding architecture yet stood apart from it. He aimed for what he calls a "second-glance building"—at first it looks like all the others around it, but closer inspection shows that the treatment of "ordinary" materials is extraordinarily fine. "Let's face it," Venturi has said of this project, "buildings like this are not a tea party. In the old days you could do a marvelous fire station with arched doors, fancy brickwork, and a bell tower. Now all you can afford is the simplest building, well thought-out, with just the right amount of ornament." The fire station resembles some of the commercial garages nearby, but with a difference. There is nothing accidental about the style of lettering that wraps around the front of the building, or the way the entrance is set in from the rounded corner and marked with a marble panel, or the arrangement of windows along the Goffe Street side. Every detail has been carefully planned with respect to the other parts of the building, to the engines visible from outside, and to the surrounding area. The result is a fire station that conveys great dignity without imitating a grander type of building.

That thinking carries over into the interior, which takes all of the elements you would expect to find in a typical fire station of the 1930s and '40s and treats them all with new

respect. There is nothing elaborate, nothing to wear out, just high quality materials used thoughtfully. The spacious drive-through apparatus room holds two engines, a ladder truck, and a rescue van with enough room for additional equipment. The walls are glazed brick (not cinderblock), the poles are genuine brass, and the metal doors with porthole windows could have come out of the 1941 streamlined station in Columbus, Indiana.

228

The long room that contains both lounge and dining area is big enough to comfortably hold all seventeen men who work there at a time. Following the idea of the "second glance," Venturi used checkerboard linoleum and dark rubber moldings, materials usually found in old institutional buildings, but he made them look almost luxurious. Combined with ample windows and a giant mural painted by one of the firemen who serve there, they make a very pleasant space that is easy to keep clean. The upstairs living quarters, similar to those at the Whitney Avenue Fire Station, are in a more contemporary style, with carpeting to add warmth and cut down noise. Beds are arranged on both sides of a low brick partition that gives the men more privacy.

231

230

Not only are these interiors comfortable, they also show a subtle understanding of the blend of domestic and institutional that characterizes a fire station. This comes in contrast to the recent trend among architects to treat firehouse interiors as if they were going to be written up in *House and Garden*. Instead of providing a trash compactor and natural oak paneling, Venturi put his money into better

206, 210

231

construction. He never lost sight of the fact that a fire station is a place where people work.

The men who work in the Dixwell station give it mixed reviews. On the whole they like the building—most sense that it is a cut above average. They appreciate the spacious rooms, the comfortable sleeping quarters, and the high-quality materials. The building is easy to maintain, and for the most part the layout makes sense. But officers point out that because of the location of the poles it takes longer than it should, when an alarm sounds, to get from the rooms at the back of the building down to the apparatus floor, to run up and check with the watch desk, and then to run back to the equipment. Everyone complains about the poor ventilation in the locker room—it has no air-conditioning and the window does not open; and with no provision for sound insulation, noise bounces off all the hard surfaces in the living/dining area, making it difficult to carry on a conversation at one end of the room if the television set is on at the other.

None of these problems is a major flaw in design; they all could have been avoided with a little extra thought. They are not likely to change the opinion of architectural critics, who rightly consider the Dixwell fire station an outstanding piece of work. But flaws like these detract from the building in small ways, by making the firemen's work just a little more difficult, and suggest that the architect did not think things out quite as well as he should have. They are especially serious in Venturi's case because he aims so high. How can we evaluate his understanding of the symbolism of the fire station without taking into account how well he understands the way the building works?

Similar flaws mark nearly every other firehouse built in the last twenty years, and not only those that depart from standard models. All across the country, the men serving in newer buildings find fault with their design; of the buildings discussed in this chapter so far, only the Whitney Avenue station and Station 2 in Dallas seem to be entirely satisfactory from the firemen's point of view. Firemen in other buildings complain about everything from leaking roofs to inadequate electrical outlets, and blame it all on the architects. Despite the myriad functional improvements and creature comforts built into modern fire stations, many men express nostalgia for the older buildings they used to serve in. Sitting in their C-shaped dayroom at Station 4 in Berkeley, with the skylights papered over to keep out the burning sun, firemen look back to the old "barns" with affection. They may not have been as pretty, but the rooms were big enough and the windows opened. And even though the typical nineteenth-century fire station interior described in Chapter Four was hardly luxurious, the men who still work in the older buildings seldom have many complaints about their design. Some prefer the drafty, high-ceilinged rooms and the old-fashioned kitchens to newer buildings with less "atmosphere."

The firemen's comments have to be taken with a grain of salt. Firefighting is one of the most exacting of occupations but it also can be one of the most boring, and when men spend a

232

long time sitting around between fires they tend to gripe. Firemen do not always realize the financial constraints an architect works under, or the limits other considerations can put on a design—for instance, that the main reasons the quarters are so cramped at Station 4 in Columbus, Indiana, is that the site is small and the building's dimensions were decided in advance by the fire chief. Firemen also blame architects for construction problems that usually can be traced to negligence on the part of contractors and building inspectors. But most

of the problems they point to are real ones, and worth thinking about.

Some of these problems stem from architects' not being familiar enough with the way equipment works, as at Columbus, where the shape of the building and the placement of the driveway make it nearly impossible to maneuver a truck around the back and through the drive-through door (the men back their engines in from the front, instead). Other complaints show that some architects do not appreciate the importance of adequate living

229

232, 233. *Fire Station 1, Dallas, Texas, 1978. William H. Hidell, architect. One of the first solar-powered fire stations in America, this building gets most of its power for heat, hot water, and part for air-conditioning from a set of panels on the roof. Firemen climb up to hose off the panels every few weeks.*

233

quarters. Firemen are known for their cooking, yet kitchens in fire stations are often meager, designed as if for an apartment instead of for a building where five or ten men work twenty-four hours a day. At Station 30 in Kansas City, Missouri, a built-in slate dining counter and stools go unused; the firemen bought their own plastic table and chairs because they wanted to eat facing each other. Sitting rooms are sometimes unnecessarily cramped or unpleasant (even after the firemen in Columbus painted over the walls of their lounge and added curtains, the room remains cold and uglier than "ordinary"). The living area at Fire Station 1 in Dallas only could hold the entire staff of twelve men if they sat in rows of folding chairs. The architect explains, "firemen spend too much of their time watching TV, anyway." Considered one at a time these complaints may seem minor, or even selfish. But taken together, they show a marked insensitivity on the part of architects to the way firemen live.

Firemen everywhere offer the same explanation for what they see as the problem with modern fire station design: "If the architect had spent any time in a firehouse he would have known better. If he'd asked us, we could have told him a thing or two." Architects in return always offer the same response, "I didn't have to talk with firemen. The chief told me what he wanted and checked my plans over every step of the way." They go on to say that since the fire chief has the final say over the design of the building, any problems—especially ones pertaining to operations, such as

the placement of the poles at the Dixwell Fire station—are really his fault. To which firemen often reply, "Maybe the chief should spend some more time in a firehouse himself."

In a way both sides are right, and it may be that the fire chiefs in some cities either do not know how to read architectural plans or are out of touch with their men. Certainly the chief is to blame when a building becomes too small as soon as new equipment is bought. On the other hand, sometimes the chief's opinions can be so influential that the fire department deserves more credit than the architects do for successful designs, as in the case of Station 21 in Denver. This is one of the few buildings that firemen not only do not criticize but actually go out of their way to praise. One fireman even told me that he looks forward to coming to work there. The architect Austin Siegfried never talked with firemen but simply followed the instructions of Secretary of Fire John Frasco, who handles all architectural matters for the Denver Fire Department. Most of the architectural features the firemen single out for praise—the materials, the hose tower, and the small bedrooms—were Frasco's ideas.

But when things do not go as well as they did at Denver, the firemen are always the losers—which strengthens their argument that, even if not required to, architects should spend more time in fire stations. In addition to meeting with neighbors, Forrest Upshaw visited several fire stations and talked with firemen before designing Station 2 in Dallas, and it shows. The building works well and is liked by everyone who uses it. If architects did more

209, 210

234

homework (surprisingly few of them say they even look at other fire stations, much less study floor plans or read special publications on fire station design), they probably could avoid some of the more obvious mistakes in layout. More important, if they took the time to talk with firemen they would have a better idea of the day-to-day routine that goes on inside the building.

The frequency and bitterness with which firemen complain about new stations points to deeper problems. They resent being left out of the design process by both architects and fire chiefs. Their resentment is a matter of wounded pride but also a matter of principle: they feel that architects should be willing to put some extra effort into finding out what makes a fire station work. They are right to complain. The best architecture always has shown an acute sensitivity to and an awareness and understanding of the nature and needs of its users. Firemen deserve no less.

Similar problems lie behind the firemen's second most frequent comment, "modern architects just want to build monuments to themselves, anyway." This remark comes up most often in reference to buildings such as Station 4 in Berkeley, where the usual ar-

rangement of the firehouse obviously was altered for architectural effect. Firemen also intend it as a general observation, and considering the current state of confusion in public architecture (see Chapter Eight) they may have a point. Their complaint takes on added meaning when firemen speak from their own experience with the buildings they work in and know best. Having sat by while fire stations were designed without any apparent concern for their ideas—then having to live with the results—firemen too often conclude that architects care more about getting their buildings into magazines than about serving their clients. They are not altogether right: it takes time to appreciate how buildings like the Dixwell Fire Station make a city a richer place to live in, and most people find it easier to point out a misplaced pipe than to think about what a building ought to mean. But until firemen and architects both understand each others' work a little better, no modern fire station will be a complete success.

A quick review of recent fire station designs shows a few new trends at work. Most important is a concern for energy efficiency. In the future we may see more solar-powered firehouses like Station 1 in Dallas, which gets most of its heat, hot water, and air conditioning from a range of collectors on the roof. Even more conventional fire stations probably will have better insulation, and living quarters that can be sealed off entirely from the apparatus floor to conserve heat. As fire departments try to cut back their use of electricity, hose drying machines have been losing their popularity. In climates that do not permit the use of outdoor hose racks, more fire stations are being built with towers like the ones in Boston and Denver, which have heaters, fans, and automatic hoists inside. Denver's Fire Secretary Frasco now advises architects to copy the design of a 1912 bungalow's "sunken" hose tower for new stations built in residential neighborhoods.

Other trends in fire station design reflect changing department policy. More buildings are being designed with separate bunks and washrooms for female firefighters, or with offices and studies that could be made over into extra bedrooms. Future fire stations may house fewer personnel, if financially strapped cities continue to cut the size of the average company back from five or six firefighters to three. Kansas City's new fire stations have no bedrooms, since under the contract ratified in 1979, all firefighters now work an eight-hour day.

To compensate for the decrease in manpower, new fire equipment is bigger and more powerful than ever. But it may be getting smaller in the future, as more cities supplement their larger equipment with lightweight "squirts" or "mini-pumpers." These small trucks can carry enough water, chemical additives, two-inch hose, supply line, and short ladders to handle the average neighborhood fire, and require a crew of only three men to function efficiently. Their short wheelbase makes them easy to maneuver on city streets. As companies and equipment shrink, there could be a return to smaller downtown and neighborhood fire stations.

Or there may be no fire stations at all. One article in *Fire Command* has predicted that fire departments soon will rent garage space in high-rise buildings for their downtown companies, and rely on roving patrol units for neighborhood fire protection:

> With firefighters' salaries approaching the $1,000 a month range for a short work week, it is doubtful if in years to come they will spend much of their on-duty time in quarters. Gradually it will dawn on fire administrators that particular home quarters for fire companies are relatively unimportant (this is a hold over from hand engines and horse-drawn engines and the days when the individual "company" was more important than the fire department). . . . Neighborhood fire stations will be only a base of operations and a place to get out of a storm. . . . Exit the old neighborhood firehouses where men waited long hours for alarms.

But that day is still a long way off. Not everyone is ready to see the old type of fire stations disappear. In the face of proposed cutbacks, neighborhood groups in Boston have

234

251

235

235, 236. *Central Fire Station, Cortland, New York, 1914–15. Sacket and Park, architects. Renovation 1977-79, Werner Seligman, engineer. City planners in Cortland found that they could build a badly needed new fire station by revamping the one they already had. The project qualified for funds from both preservation and fire protection agencies.*

been organizing to stop plans to close their local fire stations, arguing that whatever the computer studies say they still prefer to have protection nearby. Cities that cannot afford new construction are taking a closer look at their existing fire stations, and they are finding that some of the old buildings still provide adequate space and the best locations for protecting the surrounding areas.

235, 236   The city of Cortland, New York, was able to build a suitable new central fire station by revamping the one it already had. The transition worked because Cortland's population (20,000) and city limits have remained fairly stable since this station was built in 1914. When firemen and voters protested poor conditions in the dilapidated building, city officials had two choices: either tear down the old station to build a new one on its site or refurbish the existing structure. There was no question of restoring the station for some other use. The building was too big for a private residence, Cortland already had one firehouse restaurant, and there was little need for a shopping mall or community center. Besides, the location was perfect—the city had grown up around a downtown core that is still central. Though one preliminary engineering study recommended building a new station, the city decided to renovate rather than demolish.

They were helped by the fact that the old central fire station happens to be an architectural prize—a prominent building in Cortland and one of the finest remaining examples of the pseudo-Dutch style so popular in upstate New York at the turn of the century. With

support from the State Historic Preservation Office the building qualified for Federal community development funds earmarked for preservation projects as well as for monies from the Department of the Interior allocated for fire protection. Now Cortland's central station is one of two in the country to be listed on the National Register and still function as an active firehouse. (The Washington Company in Conshohocken, Pennsylvania, is the other.)

The engineer Werner Seligman was able to make major structural changes without substantially altering the original design. To prop up a floor that was never meant to hold modern apparatus, he installed a grid of tiles underneath with steel beams running under the path of the trucks' wheels. The old roof was lifted up to blow in insulation, and replaced with new tiles from the original manufacturer (found to be still in business after 60 years). With the addition of interior renovation and modern mechanical systems the building is now as handsome as it was on the day it opened, and should continue to be serviceable for some time.

There are some complaints, however, mainly from the firemen who wish that their living quarters were not so historically accurate. The uncarpeted rooms are bare and noisy, drafty in winter and not air-conditioned in summer. City officials disagree. "It's attractive, it still serves an appropriate function, and the quarters are adequate, if not palatial," argues Glenn Goldwyn, the Director of Community Development. A preservationist for the city adds, "the firemen would rather have a plastic

237

bowling alley with handball courts." The size of the building presents more serious problems, since the low doorways and apparatus room ceilings barely accommodate modern fire engines. Plans for extensively resurfacing the floor had to be scrapped when engineers realized that raising the floor level by more than one-sixteenth of an inch would make a dangerously tight squeeze. Some wonder what will happen if the city ever replaces its current equipment with larger trucks.

But even with these flaws, most people in Cortland are pleased with the renovation—not least because the fire station retains its architectural place as a city landmark. Underneath all the eclectic ornament, this building's form was designed to suit its function; thanks to the renovation it continues to do so.

The fire chief in Scranton, Pennsylvania, chose a simpler plan for refurbishing Fire Station 15 in 1980: he kept the turn-of-the-century frame structure intact, but spent $162,000 to renovate the living quarters, lengthen the engine room, and put a new front on the building. Because Scranton has suffered a depression ever since the mining industry left forty years ago, all new construction has to be on a modest scale. Keeping the restrictions of setting and budget in mind, the local architects Leung, Hemmler, Camayd approached the problem carefully. Before they prepared their plans, they consulted with the fire chief, neighbors, and several firemen—since David Hemmler was once a volunteer fireman himself, he appreciated the men's requests for more lockers, sturdier furniture, enclosed

showers, and a kitchen big enough to eat in. Then, realizing that local residents would suspect an overly glamorous design of being "effete," the architects took a lesson from Venturi and based the fire station's new front on the old wooden buildings around it. "Most of the modern fire stations we looked at don't mean a thing to their community," Alex Camayd explains. "They're overgrown garages. We wanted to design a building with a readily visible public character, that would still be sympathetic to the surrounding neighborhood." Both the firemen and the neighbors consider the design "a 100 percent improvement."

Fire Station 15's false clapboard front is similar to the stores and houses nearby, but all its details—doors, window, number, flag—are larger than life. Almost a cartoon of what a fire station used to look like, it sums up a long tradition: the oversized sign harks back to the flamboyant buildings of the early volunteer companies; the facade is based on a nineteenth-century storefront; the flag and number remind passers-by that this is a municipal building. The red paint stands for red brick, red shirts, and red fire engines and recalls how much tradition still lingers in the modern fire service. This good-humored little building makes a happy ending to a history of fire station architecture. It suggests that as long as we have a few more like it, as long as firemen march in parades, as long as some chiefs insist on painting fire engines red, and as long as books like *Report from Engine Company 82* stay on the best-seller list, the fire station will remain an American institution.

237

238

239

Appendix

Recycling Vintage Fire Stations

Situations like those in Cortland and Scranton, where old fire stations have been revamped and brought up to date, are the exception rather than the rule. More often fire departments are choosing to abandon or replace the buildings that no longer meet their needs. Even the most diehard traditionalist would have to agree that in some cases it just does not make sense to keep using an old building—forms must change as functions change. The fire station's design always has been determined by the functions it performs; now that equipment and techniques are different from what they used to be, the designs of the nineteenth century are not always the right ones for a twentieth-century job. Some of the older buildings, especially the bungalow stations designed to look like cottages in the 1920s, are now too small to hold modern equipment. Others are so big that the spaces intended for hanging harnesses have proven wasteful to heat and cool. Firemen today demand more from a fire station than they did a hundred years ago. They expect a modern workplace to be safe, easy to keep clean, to have an ample kitchen, locker room, and washroom, and to be fireproof—and not every older building measures up. Moreover, cities that undertake the kind of systematic planning studies described in Chapter Eight are discovering that even if their old fire stations are still operational, there may be too many of them. As a result, many cities are putting old fire stations on the market, and the question of finding new functions for these sturdy buildings is going to come up more and more often.

The buildings left behind, while no longer suited for their original use, still have many features that make them worth preserving. Because they were designed to house heavy equipment and to stand up to round-the-clock use by firemen, fire stations are more solidly built than other structures of comparable size. Fire stations have an architectural presence that is hard to find on any scale these days. Whether it is the smallest building on a downtown block or the largest one in a residential neighborhood, an old fire station tends to stand out from the newer buildings around it. This combination of unusual functional requirements and distinctive character that made the

238. *Shohet House (former Fire Station 31), San Francisco, California, 1908. Newton Tharp, architect. Renovated 1978.* **239.** *Ortiz House (former Fire Station 12), San Diego, California, 1912. Renovated 1964–79 (photograph by Theresa Beyer). Both apartment houses once were fire stations, but as Number 12's owner/architect explains, "I'm a Capricorn. I collect things."*

240

fire station unique when it was built now presents interesting challenges for adaptive re-use. Fire stations are fairly small buildings, yet of a different scale from houses. Their interiors combine conventional-size offices with garages, locker rooms, and dormitories—the kinds of open space usually found in a factory or loft. The fire station's two most noticeable elements are also its least adaptable ones: not many other small buildings need oversized garage doors in front or twenty-five-foot-high towers in back. But for architects who are willing to take on the challenge, these unusual characteristics can be turned to their advantage. Old fire stations can be given a new life, with the right combination of imagination and flexibility. The examples that follow show a few of the innovative ways in which old fire stations have been put to use in the last fifteen years.

Studios and workshops

For artists who can buy a surplus building from the city at a low price and do their own restoration work, a fire station makes an ideal live-in studio. Instead of having to rent a loft in a commercial building or an abandoned factory, the artist can use the old apparatus floor and dormitory as work spaces and convert the smaller rooms upstairs into a private apartment. In Los Angeles, the sculptor Jim Croak has been renting former Engine 23 from the city in exchange for doing restoration work on the building. Without changing any of the fire station's original architecture, he

has turned the entire ground floor into a workshop, which provides plenty of room for constructing large wooden sculptures, and he uses the second floor for storage and an office. Over the last four years Croak gradually has been restoring the luxurious third-floor officers quarters that caused such a furor when the building opened in 1913 (see Chapter Five), and he now enjoys a mahogany-paneled living room and marble-lined bath that are quite different from the usual accommodations of a "starving artist."

The photographer Ray Metzker needed less open space than a sculptor does, but because he makes prints that are four feet square he wanted a darkroom with extra-high ceilings to house his oversized equipment. A small storefront fire station met his needs, "but not excessively." The building is only fifteen feet wide, but the ceilings are twelve feet high, and when Metzker bought it each floor was one open room. Because the fire station was wedged between the other buildings on the block, the first three floors had no side windows and easily could be sealed off from light. The building's four stories permitted him to separate "clean operations" from dirty ones. He used the ground floor as a carpentry shop for building picture frames; the second floor has a conventional darkroom at the back and an open area in front that serves as storage, studio, and a place to work with giant enlargers. The top two floors form a handsome apartment. Since there were no interior walls when he moved in, Metzker had free rein in planning the arrangement of his rooms. He

settled on a plan that is "open, like a cabin." Having grown up in the Midwest, he felt cramped in the narrow spaces of a typical townhouse and opened up the ceiling over the third-floor living room to form a sleeping loft upstairs. Extra windows added along the north and east walls fill these rooms with natural light, which a photographer always appreciates.

The old Niagara Fire Station in Providence, Rhode Island, is not strictly a studio, since the ground floor has been renovated as commercial rental space. The rest of the building now serves as headquarters for a collection of designers and architects who call themselves the Niagara Group, after the fire company that served here when the building opened in 1866. The group's founder, Morris Nathanson, had looked for a centrally located space to rent but

could not afford a conventional office big enough to hold his studio. Though the fire station was not very prepossessing when he bought it in 1970 (sold by the city in the 1950s, it had been used as a fish market, then boarded up), the designer realized that it could provide all the room he needed, with an unusual architectural charm that would impress potential clients. The problem would be to restore as much as possible of the building's original detail while renovating it for a new use—without trying to hide the fact that the structure had been altered over the years. For example, the original arched apparatus opening had been widened, then filled in, with aluminum doors added, and a steel beam had been run across the front wall. Instead of trying to recreate the original stone arch (which would have been structurally impossible to do) or cover-

243, 244. *Niagara Group Offices (former Niagara Engine 2), Providence, Rhode Island, 1866. Renovated 1974, Morris Nathanson, designer. The former Niagara Fire station is now the headquarters for a group of designers. An open plan upstairs allows all of them to share space without getting in each other's way.*

245. *Brandywine's restaurant (former Ladder 2), Providence, Rhode Island, 1892. Renovated 1975, Morris Nathanson, designer.* **246.** *Engine House 5 Restaurant, Columbus, Ohio, 1891–92. John Flynn, architect. Renovated 1975, Roger Sherman, architect (see fig. 67 and frontispiece). Nathanson constructed new interiors using industrial materials. The front windows were once apparatus doors. On the other hand, Sherman had spacious rooms to work with, and filled them with memorabilia collected by the owner's friends.*

243

244

ing over the entrance with a false "period" balcony, Nathanson put a piece of wood (an "architectural Band-Aid" stained to match the brownstone trim) over the steel beam, and he redesigned the doors in a scale and color that complemented the rest of the structure. A thorough cleaning revealed the top part of the arch intact, so now the original keystone, with its carved fire helmet and inscription, serves as a logo for the new owners.

Inside there was no question of restoration; the interiors had been completely stripped by previous tenants. Nathanson cleaned up the ground floor but left it as one open room —to make a flexible space that he could rent out (first to a florist shop and now to a beauty salon). The upper two floors were divided into a variety of offices, conference rooms, and work space for the designers and architects of the Niagara Group. The entire front end of the building forms an open studio, two stories high, where draftsmen and designers can work side by side. Even the old hose tower, usually a wasted space in converted fire stations, has been put to use: Nathanson clustered all the building's wiring and mechanical systems inside, thus making them accessible for repairs while freeing the basement for storage. The arrangement has been adaptable enough to accommodate all the different kinds of projects that the office has brought in, while allowing the individual partners room to work without getting in each other's way. Now that the surrounding neighborhood is starting to revive as a commercial district, the old Niagara fire station, with its tower based on a medieval Italian prototype, once again provides a focus for nearby architecture.

245

246

Commercial buildings and restaurants

Throughout the country you can find former fire stations being used as stores and warehouses without having undergone any renovation at all. Merchants looking for cheap storage and garage space, centrally located, find that a fire station serves well enough.

Since most of the businesses that move into old fire stations do not require distinctive architectural settings, the buildings rarely receive special treatment. The exceptions are usually more fashionable shops in prominent locations, such as the Outdoor Traders boutique on the green in Litchfield, Connecticut. All the picturesque details of the exterior have been carefully preserved, and visitors still can admire the original volunteer company's fireplace and bowling alley inside. A ballet teacher rents out the meeting room upstairs to use as a dance studio. In Kansas City, Missouri, the Tudor-style fire station built as part of the swank Brookside neighborhood in 1914 (see Chapter Six) has found an eminently logical new use: threatened with demolition a few years ago by neighbors who considered the abandoned building undesirable, it now serves as a very elegant showroom for a foreign car dealer.

Unlike many merchants, restaurant owners go out of their way to provide "atmosphere" for their clients and seek out old fire stations precisely because they look different from other kinds of buildings. Unfortunately, the

247

standard type of converted firehouse interior, involving exposed bricks, lots of red and black decor, and too many old prints of firemen on the walls, is quickly becoming a cliché. Some establishments take the "nostalgia" theme so far that they add stained glass and "old-fashioned" light fixtures where none existed before. If the management really gets carried away, waitresses will slide down the brass pole to deliver birthday cakes. But firehouse restaurants can range from the ridiculous to the delightful, including some very creative remodeling schemes. The secret seems to be to take advantage of the open space on the ground floor to keep the building from getting too cluttered, and to treat the interior as a public lobby rather than a private living room. Engine Company 5, a restaurant in Columbus, Ohio, holds enough memorabilia to fill three engine houses, but the arrangement inside the high-ceilinged rooms is strikingly elegant. At Brandywine's Pub, formerly Engine 2, in Providence, the designer Morris Nathanson of the Niagara Group has once again shown his knack for blending modern design and historic detail in a charming, good-humored way. Since a prior tenant had gutted the building, plastered over the walls, and installed hung ceilings, all the "atmosphere" had to be imported. Rather than fill the building with artifacts, the designer chose a combination of natural wood and industrial-type metal railings and light fixtures that complement the building's factory-like exterior, while making it a very pleasant place.

248

249

Houses

Converting a fire station into a private residence usually requires some structural alteration. Domestic-scaled bungalow firehouses like the former Station 33 in Seattle can be adapted fairly easily, but in most cases new owners must decide whether to keep the large spaces or break them up into smaller rooms. Family-sized kitchens and bathrooms with modern fixtures usually have to be added. Since not many people want twelve-foot-high doors in their living rooms, the owners of fire stations either have to use the ground floor as a private garage, block off the old apparatus doors entirely, or replace them with a smaller entrance. But for people with imagination and a taste for unusual architecture, living in a former fire station can be worth all the work of restoration. Because of the way the buildings were sited in the nineteenth and early twentieth centuries, old fire stations can be found in residential neighborhoods as well as in the downtown locations that artists prefer for their studios. The sturdy construction, the open spaces, and the distinctive architecture of these buildings endear them to their owners—how many other houses can boast their own bell towers? In New York City and San Francisco, where urban housing of any size is scarce and architects are increasingly willing to improvise, old fire stations are actually becoming fashionable. Stylish renovation schemes are published in decorators' magazines, and the cities' building departments have to maintain waiting lists every time another fire station goes up

for auction. In other cities, ambitious buyers who are willing to put in some time still can find fire stations at prices much lower than those for houses of comparable size in the same neighborhood. What the new owners make of the spaces inside depends on their budget, the way they live, and their attitudes toward the building.

The station built for Chemical Engine 12 in New Orleans in 1895 was a shambles when John and Lynn Schackai bought it. Over the years the fire department had removed a tower and gables from the roof, altered windows and doors, and nearly gutted the interior. What remained inside under the sheetrock and linoleum was an open space much larger than the building's compact facade suggests, with sixteen feet from floor to roofline and another nine feet of clear space under the roof (the windows are each ten feet tall). Working from a set of original plans they unearthed at City Hall, the Schackais uncovered some original millwork and hardwood floors inside, and recreated the original arrangement of doors and windows. A self-trained architect, John Schackai approached the restoration intuitively: "the fire department had pretty much corrupted the building. I tried to look at it as if I was an 1890s architect. I wouldn't have wanted to try to make it appear anything else but a fire station."

Inside, restoration stopped and renovation began. By adding ceilings and a cantilevered staircase, Schackai squeezed two interlocking apartments into three floors while keeping the full-length windows and high ceil-

250, 251. *Ground floor, Johnson/Dermenjian House, Newton, Massachusetts. An oversized window knocked into the rear (south) wall was the only major architectural change needed to convert the building to solar power. It draws in sunlight that is stored in the brick wall separating the two apartments. Shiny white partitions serve to "bounce" light into the storage wall. Johnson made one "reference" to the building's former function—he bought a new brass pole and designed a staircase around it.*

250

ings in his living room. An old office became an oversized kitchen for the owners, who are both avid cooks. With the addition of skylights, the area under the roof was opened up to form a third floor for bedrooms, with an extra play nook for the Schackais' daughter. As they have gotten more involved in the project, they have been considering hiring an artist to paint a trompe-l'oeil view of a nineteenth-century firehouse over the boarded-in apparatus doors. It certainly would amuse the crew of firemen who drive up in their engine from time to time to see how work is coming along. In the meantime, the house has inspired its owner to study for a professional degree in architecture—"I guess you could say it drove me crazy and it drove me to school."

A turn-of-the-century brick firehouse in Newton, Massachusetts, is undergoing an even more ingenious renovation. Its new owners— Charles Dermenjian, an engineer, and Timothy Johnson, a professor of architecture at M.I.T.—were interested in heating the building with alternate sources of energy. The town of Newton's real estate board wanted to preserve the character of the surrounding residential area. Although the fire station had undergone some renovation when it was made into a public library in 1923 and the apparatus doors no longer functioned, most of its architectural details remained intact. Johnson's design took advantage of the building's orientation and the trees around it to test out a special insulating glass that he had developed earlier for passive solar heating. By replacing all the windows with "heat mirrors," adding

insulation, and opening up a section of the rear (south) wall, the fire station could be retrofitted to get a large portion of its heat from the sun, without the need for complicated mechanisms and without substantially altering the original architecture. The reflective glass draws the sun's light into the building and keeps heat from escaping; since each silver-blue window is twice as effective as conventional thermal-pane glass, the fire station's windows take in twice as much heat and light as would an ordinary opening of twice the size. Any other solar energy system would have required mounting panels on the roof, adding a greenhouse at the back of the building, enlarging the existing windows, installing shutters, or knocking new windows into the walls of the building.

The interiors have been redesigned to take advantage of the sun. A sixteen-inch-thick brick wall added across the back of the old apparatus area divides the building into two condominium units and serves to absorb and hold heat. The remaining walls have been insulated, covered with sheet rock, and painted white, "so that the light coming in can bounce around and find its way into the storage wall," which in turn releases heat back into the building. Johnson's unit, at the back of the building, is the more drastically remodeled of the two; rather than attempt to recreate the look of a turn-of-the-century firehouse (since this area orginally housed stalls and a hayloft it never had much atmosphere), he gutted the walls and built new rooms in an open plan that allows light to flow through the space. With

251

bags of chemicals to store extra heat under the second floor, and a set of radiant electric panels mounted in the ceiling as a back-up, Johnson expects to get between one-half and two-thirds of his heat from the sun. Historical references are confined to a few details that Johnson calls "iconic gestures," like the spiral staircase built around a new brass pole.

Dermenjian's apartment looks more like a fire station. He has retained the original layout and restored most of the woodwork (his living room floor still shows the marks of horses' hooves). Since he wanted an area big enough to accommodate his jazz band's jam sessions, Dermenjian left the apparatus floor as one open room and will add some kitchen equipment behind the sealed-off doors at the front. Upstairs the hallway and smaller rooms off it will remain just as they were; the meeting room at the front of the building is now the master bedroom. Because these traditional rooms may be difficult to heat, Dermenjian will supplement the heat from the sun with a coal stove and a heat-pump furnace.

Except for the large window at the back, Hose Company 6's exterior gives no hint of the changes made inside. Relying on old photographs and the memories of their neighbors, Johnson and Dermenjian have replicated the original apparatus doors and will soon commission a new sign.

Community Centers

Before a city puts a surplus building up for auction, it usually offers the property to other municipal departments. Many old fire stations are re-used as municipal warehouses and garages without receiving any special architectural treatment. With the addition of a few temporary walls and some linoleum, other fire stations have been converted into branch libraries or recreation centers (see, for example, Chapter Six: Fire Station 20 in Portland, Oregon, is now used as a boys' club). The city of Butte, Montana, has turned its old fire department headquarters into a public archives, where local residents can research genealogy and history. Its simple renovation was designed and carried out by volunteers.

Now and then a city will undertake a more ambitious renovation. In recent years, several of the most innovative and successful rehabilitations of fire stations have been for city-sponsored community centers. In many ways, the transition is a natural one. Large apparatus and dormitory areas easily become all-purpose performing and assembly space, small rooms are made over into offices and classrooms, and oversized, institutional kitchens and bathrooms can be kept for their original use. The well-constructed buildings usually can stand up to a good deal of wear. More important,

252

these renovations permit the fire station to continue its symbolic role as a public building. Designed to be a landmark in the neighborhood, the fire station is already a community center before the community center moves in.

A Tudor-style fire station in Portland, Oregon, is now a community music center offering lessons and performances to local residents. The city rents the building to the private, nonprofit organization for a dollar a year. The handsome renovation is the work of Robert Oringdulph, a longtime supporter of the music center, who donated his services for the project. In an effort to "maintain the building's original attitude" while making it "warm, comfortable and inviting," Oringdulph restored the exterior masonry but stripped away original woodwork inside to expose the brick walls. He then added sound insulation wherever he could. He divided the officers quarters, locker room, and dormitory into classrooms, and installed prefabricated practice rooms in the basement. The tower houses the main staircase; bathrooms went into the former hayloft. The apparatus room is now (in the words of the music center's director) "*the* nicest small concert hall in the city." On a typical weekday afternoon, all these rooms will be in use at once. As a tribute to its popularity, after nearly fifteen years of constant use the building remains unvandalized—local school-

children have confined their graffiti to lettering slogans such as "ATONAL IS ASEXUAL" on the blackboards.

The architect William Burks used a more preservation-oriented approach in renovating the fire department headquarters in Baton Rouge as a fire museum and new quarters for the city's Arts and Humanities Council. He took great pains in restoring the delicate 1920s Gothic facade which had been brutally "modernized" in the 1950s. Underneath a false aluminum front, Burks found enough of the pink and green terra-cotta ornament to recreate the design using replacement parts ordered from the original manufacturer. With plate glass where the apparatus doors used to be, the front of the building now provides display windows for the museum. Inside a new paint scheme and carpeting have turned the fire station's interiors into quite elegant rooms. The ground floor is one open gallery; the area that once housed the locker room and chief's quarters on the second floor has been made into a suite of offices for the Arts and Humanities Council. The old dormitory, the only room that still retained its hardwood floor, now serves as a multipurpose performance space, classroom, and exhibition hall. By preserving as much as possible of the building's ornament and maintaining a similar scale and style for the new carpentry work, Burks struck a pleas-

253

254

ing balance between traditional and contemporary that still looks like a fire station.

The story behind the renovation of Fire Station 9 in a working-class neighborhood of Kansas City, Kansas, is a particularly happy one because it shows how a number of official preservation programs could be used exactly as they were supposed to be. Preservationists, city officials, and a grass roots organization worked together to everyone's advantage.

The Prescott Neighborhood Association was formed in 1975 in response to an announcement that Kansas City's Community Development Agency had received Federal money to distribute to locally initiated groups for neighborhood improvement. Its leaders, Jo Ann Elliott and Rosemary Andriesevic, saw the association as a means of "creating an identity" for the neighborhood and bringing old and young people together. They worked by rounding

267

255

256

up local support for their ideas, writing convincing grant proposals, persistently nagging city officials, and, as a last resort, plying people in power with Rosemary's home-made strudel. After their initial attempt to get the condemned Prescott school building for a headquarters failed, they saw an article describing the abandoned fire station and the city's newly formed preservation program (also administered by the Community Development Agency) and set out to get that building for the group. Their proposal impressed the agency's officials, who had been looking for a tenant that would put the building to active use (the city did not want to see it become a fire museum).

Under the terms established by the Community Development program, the city supervised and paid for the renovation of the building and remains its legal owner. Funds for restoration came from both Federal and local agencies with a good deal of clean-up work done by neighborhood volunteers. So far the total cost of the project has been $73,680. This low budget has covered an extremely well-researched and historically accurate rehabilitation, thanks largely to the efforts of Larry Hancks, a meticulous preservationist who is director of preservation for the Community Development Agency. After choosing the architectural firm of Solomon, Claybaugh, Young, he worked closely with them to ensure that each step of the rehabilitation would meet with the approval of the State Historic Preservation Office. Most of this detailed work required an extra amount of time but no

additional expense. Working from old photographs, Hancks had the architects design new rear and side doors "with the same sort of visual effect" as the originals—unfortunately funds ran out before he could reconstruct the front apparatus doors. Exterior woodwork was scraped down to determine its color in 1910, then repainted in the same green. The rest of the exterior restoration consisted of standard repointing, structural strengthening, and repairs to the roof.

Inside, too, the emphasis was on restoration—cleaning, strengthening, refurbishing—rather than renovation. The third floor room was refinished in its original colors, but otherwise historic accuracy was achieved by omission rather than commission. The budget prohibited any major changes and, as Claybaugh noted, "the building didn't need changing one way or the other to function as a community center." With the approval of the community group and Mr. Hancks, the architects chose an interior color scheme of cream-colored walls and gold trim, "a palette of colors that would work with the building and be pleasant." The bathroom needed considerable improvement, and a few light fixtures elsewhere were replaced. But basically the architects altered the interior as little as possible. Workers from the neighborhood center accumulated the collection of furniture by buying surplus from the city and persuading neighbors and local businesses to donate the rest.

Though this was a simple renovation, involving no demolition or new construction, it has proven very versatile. Part of the versatil-

257

255, 256, 257. *Prescott Neighborhood Center (former Fire Station 9), Kansas City, Kansas, 1910. William E. Harris, architect. Renovated 1977, Solomon, Claybaugh, Young, architects. A low-budget renovation that remains true to the building's original character. The exterior has been restored to its authentic colors (funds ran out before the front doors could be replaced), while the interiors remain functional, flexible rooms with a minimum of decoration (old photograph, c1920, courtesy of Kansas City Community Development Office).*

ity may come from the Prescott Association's requirements, which were more flexible than those in Portland and Baton Rouge. Since the directors are constantly coming up with new ideas for classes and projects, the center's programs have expanded to fit the building. The fire station's first floor, still one open room, has been used as a community lounge, a food co-op, and a classroom; when a set of auditorium seating (bought from the city) is pulled into the center of the room it becomes a meeting hall. The large front doors still operate and usually are left open. The kitchen and large bathroom upstairs still perform their original functions. With the addition of benches and a row of make-up mirrors the former locker room adjoining the bathroom has become a changing room. The old dayroom next to the kitchen is still used as a lounge, now furnished with overstuffed chairs. Teen groups hold their meetings here at night; during the day it is a quiet place to read. The large dormitory at the front of the building, lit by windows on three sides, is a kindergarten classroom during the day and used for crafts instruction after school and at night. The entire third floor originally was a gym. By adding bars to the windows and installing mirrors and a ballet bar along the walls the architects have converted the room into a dance studio, also used by exercise classes and a pre-school play group. Even the basement recently has been put to use as a ceramics studio. There are plans to turn the former coal bin into a darkroom as soon as Jo Ann can find funding for equipment and a teacher. At this rate, the fire

station should continue to be able to accommodate almost any activity the Prescott Neighborhood Association can dream up.

In addition to preservation of architectural details, this rehabilitation achieves great historic accuracy in remaining true to the building's original atmosphere. Old fire stations did not have wall-to-wall carpeting or track lighting. They were, and usually still are, furnished with odds and ends brought in by the men or thrown out by neighbors. The Prescott Center is one of the few renovated fire stations that retains the front apparatus doors; they come in handy for hauling equipment into the front room. A more stylish and elaborate renovation would not have suited the clients nearly so well. The delight of this building is that the preservationists' accuracy has proven so easy to live with.

Projects like the Prescott Center offer an important lesson to preservationists and administrators, especially now that most of the Federal programs that made this renovation possible are due to be cut back. Despite its low budget, this was a very careful renovation, and the local residents—some of whom have since organized walking tours of architecture in the neighborhood—appreciate the thought that went into it. Not only does the building provide some needed facilities, it also has helped to foster the kind of community pride that the Prescott Neighborhood Association was formed to achieve. In its new role as a community center, the former fire station should continue to be a focus for the neighborhood for a long time to come.

Notes
&
Annotated Bibliography

ABBREVIATIONS FOR FREQUENTLY CITED SOURCES:

AABN   *The American Architect and Building News*

Boorstin,   Daniel Boorstin. *The Americans; The Dem-*
Democratic   *ocratic Experience.* New York: Random
Experience   House, 1973.

Boorstin,   Daniel Boorstin. *The Americans; The Na-*
National   *tional Experience.* New York: Random
Experience   House, 1965.

Brickbuilder   *The Brickbuilder*

Ditzel   Paul Ditzel. *Fire Engines, Fire Fighters.*
     New York: Crown, 1976.

FC   *Fire Command!*

FE   *Fire Engineering*

FS   *Fire Service*

FH   *Fireman's Herald*

FJ   *Firemen's Journal*

Forum   *Architectural Forum*

Jordy, Vol. III   William H. Jordy. *American Buildings and*
     Their Architects; Progressive and Academic
     Ideals at the Turn of the Twentieth Century.

     New York: Doubleday, 1972.

Jordy, Vol. IV   William H. Jordy. *American Buildings and*
     Their Architects; The Impact of European
     Modernism in the Mid-Twentieth Century.
     New York: Doubleday, 1972.

Lyons   Paul Lyons. *Fire in America!* Boston: Na-
     tional Fire Protection Association, 1976.

NFPA   National Fire Protection Association

PA   *Progressive Architecture*

Pierson   William Pierson. *American Buildings and*
     Their Architects; The Colonial and Neoclas-
     sical Styles. New York: Doubleday, 1970.

Record   *Architectural Record*

Tunnard and   Christopher Tunnard and Henry Hope
Reed   Reed. *American Skyline.* New York: New
     American Library, 1956.

Warner   Sam Bass Warner. *The Urban Wilderness.*
     New York: Harper and Row, 1972.

CHAPTER ONE

For general background on life and government in early American cities see Carl Bridenbaugh, *Cities in the Wilderness; The First Century of Urban Life in America* (New York: The Ronald Press, 1938) and *Cities in Revolt; Urban Life in America, 1743–1776* (New York: Knopf, 1955). Kenneth Holcombe Dunshee, *As You Pass By* (New York: Hastings House, 1952) is a lively history of New York and its fire department.

Boston's building code: Lyons, p.7, and Bridenbaugh, *Wilderness*, p. 56. **Mount Holly:** Herman Burri, *Souvenir Program and History of the Relief Fire Engine Company Number 1* (privately printed, 1977) and "America's Oldest Fire Company," *FH* XLIV:6 (August 7, 1902), pp. 94–95. **Firefighting a shared responsibility:** Bridenbaugh, *Wilderness*, pp. 63–65, 210. **"Smoking out of dores," curfew:** Bridenbaugh, *Wilderness*, p. 209. **Chimney inspection, chimney sweeps:** Bridenbaugh, *Wilderness*, pp. 56–57. 208. **Early techniques:** Dunshee, *As You Pass By*, p. 32, Ditzel, pp. 18–20. **Water supplies:** Bri-

denbaugh, *Wilderness*, pp. 61–63, 213–15, 372–74. **"An ounce of prevention . . .":** "Protection of Towns from Fire," Pennsylvania Gazette (February 4, 1735) reprinted in Albert Henry (ed.), *The Writings of Benjamin Franklin* (Vol. II) (New York: Macmillan, 1905), p. 205. **"A pole . . . ridg of the house":** Bridenbaugh, *Wilderness*, p. 58. **Buckets required in New York:** Ditzel, p. 20. **Cincinnati:** Fireman's Protective Association of the Cincinnati Fire Department, *History of the Cincinnati Fire Department* (Cincinnati: Robert Clarke Company, 1895). **"A shed to keep the ladders under":** Bridenbaugh, *Wilderness*, p. 60. **Allentown:** Ronald P. Ruddell and Lee Walck, *The History of the Allentown Fire Department* (privately printed, 1975), p. 1. **Boston's fire engine:** Bridenbaugh, *Wilderness*, pp. 58–59, Ditzel, pp. 11, 21–22. **Newsham's engines:** Lyons, p. 13 and center spread. **Value of £70:** Bridenbaugh, *Wilderness*, pp. 409–13. **Somerville:** H. H. Easterbrook, *History of the Somerville Fire Department from 1842 to 1892* (Boston: Robinson Company, 1893). **Savannah:** John E. Maguire, *Historical Souvenir, Savannah Fire Department* (Savannah: Fireman's Relief Fund Association, 1906) p. 7. **"Proper**

men: St. Louis Fire Department, *Justifiably Proud* (Marcelline: Walsworth Printing Company, 1977), p. 47; Charles Mackay, *Life and Liberty in America* (New York: Harper and Brothers, 1859), p. 37. **Providence finances:** Stokes, *Finances of Providence*, pp. 191–92. Quotation is from the Providence *Journal*, February 7, 1854. **Cincinnati political funeral:** Kathleen J. Kiefer, *A History of the Cincinnati Fire Department in the Nineteenth Century* (unpublished M.A. thesis, University of Cincinnati, 1967), p. 50. **"No citizen should have any pride . . .":** Baltimore *Sun* quoted in William A. Murray, *The Unheralded Heroes of Baltimore's Big Blazes* (Baltimore: E. John Schmitz and Sons, 1969), p. 4. **Cincinnati:** See Ditzel, Chapter 12, and Kiefer, *History of the Cincinnati Fire Department*. Also articles on the fire department in the Cincinnati *Daily Commercial* for January 5, 1853; March 1, 1853; March 15, 1853; and Miles Greenwood, *Report of the Chief Engineer of the Cincinnati Fire Department* (1853). **"In a dense population . . . condition":** Committee on the Reorganization of the Fire Department, *Report on the Re-Organization of the Fire Department* (Cincinnati, 1853), p. 5. **"Increase of ruffianism":** Cincinnati *Daily Commercial*, February 28, 1853. **"It is enough . . . civil restraint":** Cincinnati *Daily Enquirer*, March 18, 1853. **"It never gets drunk . . .":** Clyde William Park, *The Cincinnati Equitable Insurance Company, Oldest Fire Insurance Company West of the Alleghenies* (Cincinnati: Equitable Insurance Company, 1954), p. 105. **Other cities institute paid departments:** Stokes, *Finances of Providence*, p. 193. Members of the Liberty Engine Company 6 set fire to their station rather than cede it to the city; see *Justifiably Proud*, p. 56. **Steam fire engines:** William T. King, *History of the American Steam Fire Engine* (Boston: William King, 1896), pp. 34–52. **"Do you think, sir . . .":** Quincy, *Municipal History*, p. 156. **"Love, benevolence . . . he is paid":** *Historical Sketches of the Formation and Founders of the Philadelphia Hose Company . . .* (Philadelphia: by order of the Company, 1854), p. 55. **Policemen protest uniforms:** Lane, *Policing the City*, p. 105; Richardson, *Urban Police*, p. 28. **Sanitary commission:** George M. Frederickson, *The Inner Civil War; Northern Intellectuals and the Crisis of the Union* (New York: Harper and Row, 1965), pp. 107–9. **"Our former course . . . Line":** Thomas O'Connor, *History of the Fire Department of New Orleans* (New Orleans, 1896), pp. 163–64. **Professionalism:** Despite the new technology, old attitudes lingered. In 1873 a critic complained, "As the American engine company was a political power, it was necessary to give it a large share in the new organization, and, as a consequence, the traditions of the old system govern the new. There is much display, noise, and enthusiasm, but very little training or discipline." M. Bugbee, "Fires and Fire Departments," *North American Review* CLXV (July 1873), p. 142. **St. Louis smokestacks:** St. Louis, *Justifiably Proud*, pp. 80–81. **1871 inventory:** Cincinnati *Chief Engineer's Report* for 1871, p. 75. **Families in fire stations:** Boston *Post*, March 10, 1875. **Uniform stations in Brooklyn:** See report prepared by Christopher Gray for the Landmarks Conservancy of New York on New York fire stations in 1979. **Hannaford, Anderson, Bevis:** Cincinnati, *Annual Report of the City Auditor* for 1872, pp. 158, 384. **Hannaford's obituary:** Cincinnati *Enquirer*, January 9, 1911. **Harrod:** "Major B. M. Harrod Called by Death," New Orleans *Daily Picayune*, September 8, 1912.

CHAPTER FOUR

The best source for information on the activities of fire departments is in the trade journals *Fireman's Herald*, *Firemen's Journal*, and *Fire and Water*, all of which began publishing in the last quarter of the nineteenth century; see Boorstin, *Democratic Experience*. For city planning see Warner and Tunnard and Reed. William H. Pierson, *American Buildings and Their Architects; Technology and the Picturesque, the Corporate and Early Gothic Styles* (Garden City: Doubleday, 1978) treats some of the architecture of the period, but the best information on individual buildings can be found in the inventory forms and National Register nominations prepared by local state Historic Preservation offices. See also the fire stations and other public buildings illustrated in *The American Architect and Building News*, which began publication in 1876.

Spread of midwestern cities: Warner, pp. 68–73. **Wards in Columbus, Ohio:** "Columbus (O.) Fire Department," *Fire and Water* XIII:3 (January 21, 1893), p. 25. Also U.S. Census Office, *Census Reports; Eleventh Census* (1890) and *Twelfth Census* (1900) (Washington: Government Printing Office, 1892–1902). Between 2,000 and 7,000 people lived in each ward. **Ann Arbor:** Kingsbury Marzolf and Wystan Stevens, "Ann Arbor's Historic Firehouse," Ann Arbor Historical Commission Leaflet Series, #1 (unpaged). **Fort Wayne:** George Bradley, *Fort Wayne's Fire Department 1839–1964* (Fort Wayne: Allen County–Fort Wayne Historical Society, 1964), p. 36. **"Of enduring brick . . . compare at all":** The Fireman's Pension Fund and the Police Benefit Association, *A Review of the Department of Public Safety of Columbus, Ohio* (Columbus: Hann and Adair, 1894). p. 54. **Monumental Building, Sidney, Ohio:** "Monumental Building. A Complete and Impartial History of the Structure," *Sidney Journal* (May 19, 1900). **Ward meeting rooms:** See account of similar rooms in Newport, Rhode Island, stations in "Newport Enterprise," Providence *Sunday Journal*, December 11, 1887. **Ann Arbor temperance meetings:** Marzolf and Stevens, "Historic Firehouse." **New York—"rearrange all houses":** *AABN* XX:558 (September 4, 1886), p. 105. **"Rapidly becoming central":** New York Fire Department. *Annual Report of the Chief Engineer* (1886), pp. 109–11. **Headquarters, New York:** Augustine Costello, *Our Firemen, A History of the New York Fire Department* (New York: A. E. Costello, 1887), pp. 1043–44. **Boston Engine 33 and Ladder 15:** As late as 1878 this site was marshland. The city purchased the lot in 1881. See Savit Bhotiwihdk, Michael Finkowski, and David Moulton, "A Documented Report on Engine 33, Ladder 15" (unpublished paper, Department of Visual and Environmental Studies, Harvard University, 1969). **"They were all that was claimed for them . . .":** "Columbus Fire Department," *Fire and Water*, p. 25. **Providence, Engine 17's stables:** City Council Resolution 162, May 2, 1881. **"The house of Hook and Ladder company one . . .":** "Random Sparks," *FJ* IV (July 19, 1879), p. 50. **Rolling pen, New Orleans:** New Orleans City Surveyor's Office. *Specification Book #8* (January 1885–April 1888). p. 177. Original copy in Louisiana Division, New Orleans Public Library. **"Severe attacks . . . conflagrations":** William H. Rideing, "The Life of a New York City Fireman," *Harper's New Monthly Magazine* LV: 329 (October 1877), pp. 659–72. **Poles:** Ditzel, p. 128. **Drop harness:** Ditzel, pp. 127–28. **Fire alarm:** Ditzel, p. 96, and "The New Headquarters of the Fire Department of the City of New York," *Scientific American* LVII:5, n.s. (July 30, 1887), p. 68. **Little Joker:** "Electrical Devices in Fire Engine House," *AABN* IX: 282 (May 21, 1881), p. 250. **Hale horse cover:** George C. Hale (comp.), *Souvenir of Kansas City and her Fire Department to the Grand International Fire Congress and Exposition . . .* (Kansas City: Tiernan Havens, 1893), p. 52. **"Model Engine House":** "The New York Fire Department," *Scientific American* LI:6, n.s. (August 9, 1884), cover and p. 89. **Steamer poem:** *FH* (March 9, 1882). **Self-propelling engine:** *Report of the Commissioners of the Great Fire in Boston* (Boston: Rockwell and Churchill, 1873), pp. 652–53. Ditzel (p. 127, 155) notes that self-propelled engines never became very popular, perhaps because of their high cost and cumbersome steering mechanism. **Early Hook and Ladder, aerial trucks:** Ditzel, pp. 156–58. **Chemical Engine:** Harold S. Walker, "The Little Giant," *Firemen* (January 1964), p. 11. **"Seeing the engines . . .":** Letter from Sidney Fisher, 1980. **Red brick:** Bainbridge Bunting, *Houses of Boston's Back Bay* (Cambridge, Massachusetts: Harvard University Press, 1967), p. 195. **"Bright new edifice . . .":** Samuel Clemens (Mark Twain), *Life on The Mississippi* (1883), Chapter

25. **Factory design:** Pierson, *Technology and the Picturesque*, Chapter 2. **Black mortar:** "Mortar Black," *AABN* IX:273 (March 19, 1881), p. 141. **"Imposing and complete . . .":** "Columbus Fire Department," *Fire and Water*, p. 25. **Albany, Steamer 1:** Warren Abriel, *The History of the Paid Albany Fire Department* (Albany: Argus-Greenwood, 1967), p. 45.

CHAPTER FIVE

For information on firefighting in this period see the books and magazines already cited and Elmer L. Smith, *Fire Fighting at the Turn of the Century* (Lebanon, Pennsylvania: Applied Arts, Inc., 1971). An article in the New York *Tribune*, "The Fireman's Day" (May 17, 1903), gives a general idea of fire department operations at the turn of the century. For city planning see Tunnard and Reed, parts V and VI, and the catalog of *The American Renaissance; 1876–1917* (Brooklyn: The Brooklyn Museum, 1979). *AABN*, *Brickbuilder*, and *Forum* all published many pictures of fire stations; see also the *Pacific Coast Architect*, published in Portland, Oregon, and San Francisco after 1910. The best article is Halsey Wainwright Parker, "Fire Department Buildings," *Brickbuilder* XIX:5 (May 1910), pp. 116–27. See also these studies of fire stations in individual cities: Jim Stevenson, *Seattle Firehouses of the Horse-Drawn and Early Motor Era* (privately printed, 1972); "San Francisco Municipal Buildings," *Architect and Engineer* (October 1910), pp. 81–89; Clarence R. Ward, "The Housing of a Fire Department," *Architect and Engineer* (July 1917), pp. 51–62; "Engine Houses for San Francisco, California, Fire Department," *AABN* CXIV: 2243 (December 18, 1918), plates 187–92.

"He jumps at the flames . . . torrents of water": Augustine Costello, *History of the Fire and Police Departments of Minneapolis* (Minneapolis: Relief Association, 1890), p. 4. **"And the fireman!":** Costello, *Minneapolis*, p. 5. **"It must be remembered . . . tiresome.":** Tudor Jenks, *The Fireman* (What Shall I Be? series) (Chicago: A. C. McClurg & Co., 1911, p. 13). **"He is naturally brave . . . too highly prized":** Charles E. White, *The Providence Fireman* (Providence: E. L. Freeman, 1887), p. 298. **"Give to the firemen . . .":** White, *Providence Fireman*, p. 4. **Brooklyn Fire Commissioner:** *Annual Report of the Commissioner of the Department of Fire of the City of Brooklyn, New York* (1894), pp. 16–17. **"The best place for the formation . . . useful life":** "Comfort of Men in Quarters," *FH* XLVIII:98 (November 19, 1904), p. 385. For an alternate view see "Easy Fireman's Life Ruins his Efficiency," *FN* LV:16 (April 18 1908), pp. 303–4. **Engine 31 in New York:** Clarence E. Meek, "Finest Firehouse in the World," *W.N.Y.F.* XX:1 (January 1959), pp. 4–5. **"A palace of stone . . .":** "A Fine New Fire House," *New York Sun* (November 10, 1895), p. 7. **Vanderbilt mansion:** illustrated in *The American Renaissance*, pp. 35–36, 66, 67. **Stanford White:** Meek, "Finest Fire House." **Interior fittings:** "A Fine Fire House," *FH* XXX:22 (November 28, 1895), unpaged. *AABN:* LIV (November 7, 1896), p. 46 and plates. **Brooklyn headquarters:** *Our Firemen: The Official History of the Brooklyn Fire Department* (Brooklyn: privately printed, 1892), pp. 100–103; "In the New Building," *FH* XXVII:13 (March 29, 1894), unpaged; Moses King, *King's Views of Brooklyn* (New York: Lawyer's Title Insurance Company, 1904), p. 11; Cervin Robinson, "Bravura in Brooklyn," *Forum* CXXXI:4 (November 1969), pp. 42–47. **"Hard Times Disappearing":** *AABN* XLVII:994 (January 12, 1895), p. 22. **The '90s:** Howard Mumford Jones, *The Age of Energy; Varieties of American Experience, 1865–1915* (New York: Viking, 1971), pp. 106–20 and *passim*. **Public service:** Ernest S. Griffith, *A History of American City Government. Volume 3: The Conspicuous Failure, 1870–1900* (New York: Praeger, 1974), p. 161. **City beautiful:** Richard Guy Wilson, "Expressions of Identity" and "Architecture, Landscape and City Planning" in *The American Renaissance*. **Kansas City headquarters:** "The Old Fire Headquarters," *FH* LXXVII:24

(June 14, 1919), p. 498; *Kansas City Star* (April 29, 1906), p. 8. **Little Rock headquarters:** "A Handsome New Central Station," *FH* LXXX:2 (July 10, 1915), p. 25. **San Francisco:** See articles cited at beginning of notes and "City Architect Tharp Dies Suddenly," San Francisco *Municipal Record* (May 13, 1909), p. 183. Also *Souvenir; Public Works of San Francisco since 1906* (Supplement to San Francisco *Municipal Reports* for 1908–09). **New building materials:** "Color in Brick and Terra Cotta Architecture," *Brickbuilder* IV:4 (April 1895), pp. 81–82. **Italian Villa:** "The Renaissance Villa of Italy Developed into a Complete Residential Type for Use in America," *Record* XXXI (March 1912), p. 201. **Inappropriate Boston comfort station:** Douglass Shand Tucci, *Built in Boston* (Boston: New York Graphic Society, 1978), p. 200. **Pittsburgh No. 25:** Pittsburgh Department of Public Safety, *Annual Reports of the Bureau of Fire . . . 1896* (Pittsburgh: Herald Print and Publishing Company, 1897). **Chemical 5, Buffalo:** Ulysses G. Orr, "Interesting Brickwork in Buffalo," *Brickbuilder* XI:10 (October 1902), pp. 210–14 **Engine 31, New York:** *AABN* LXX (November 24, 1900), p. 64, plate 1300. **Engine 21, Washington, D.C.:** *Brickbuilder* XIX:5 (May 1910), p. 125. **Bebb, Flagg, Reynolds:** see entries in Henry F. and Elsie Rathbone Withey, *A Biographical Dictionary of American Architects, Deceased* (1957). **Harry Hake:** Obituary in *Cincinnati Enquirer* (September 17, 1955). **Albany:** "Fire House, Albany, New York," *Brickbuilder* XXII:8 (August 1913), plate 123. **Gargoyles in San Francisco:** Engine 15, designed by P. J. O'Brien, was built in 1886. See the measured drawings made by the Historic American Buildings Survey, Nos. 31–73 and Albert Shumate (ed.), *Early California Firehouses and Equipment* (San Francisco: The Book Club of California, 1961), unpaged. **Growth of residential districts:** Warner, pp. 81–84, 101–02, 107–12. **Russian Hill, San Francisco:** Judith Waldhorn, *Vintage San Francisco Firehouses* (San Francisco: Saint Francis Hook and Ladder Society, 1978), p. 20; *Municipal Record* I:9 (December 3, 1908). **Newport, R. I.:** "Newport Enterprise," *Providence Sunday Journal* (December 11, 1887). **Lake Forest:** "Town Hall and Fire Station, Lake Forest, Illinois," *Brickbuilder* XII:9 (September 1903), plates 68–69. **South Orange:** "The Building of the Village Hall, South Orange, New Jersey" (unpublished paper at the South Orange Public Library); *New York Times* (October 14, 1894), p. 24. **Expensive houses in New York:** Herbert Croly, "The Contemporary New York Residence," *Record* XII:7 (December 1902), p. 705. For other luxurious fire stations in New York see Engine 124 in Brooklyn, *Brickbuilder* XIII:12 (December 1904), p. 261; "A New Type of Fire House," *AABN* XCIV: 1702 (August 5, 1908), p. 47, and the engine houses listed in Norval White and Elliot Wilensky, *The AIA Guide to New York City* (2nd edition) (New York: American Institute of Architects, 1978). **Cleveland's engine 1:** "A Model Fire House," *FH* LII:22 (December 1, 1906), p. 445. **Washington's best company:** *FH* LII:22 (December 1, 1906), p. 445. **Brooklyn:** "Five New Engine Houses," *Brooklyn Eagle* (August 19, 1894), p. 24. **Chief Manley:** "Volunteer Fire Departments," *FH* L:14 (September 30, 1905), p. 295. **Libraries:** In Atlanta, where the public library supplied the books for firehouses, a librarian recorded that men in stations on the outskirts of the city asked for books about farming, poultry, dogs, and gardening, while urban firemen preferred "adventure, excitement, and the strenuous life—it cannot be said, however, that these books are of a trashy kind." "What Firemen Read," *FH* L: 4 (January 23, 1909), p. 65. **Boston's engine 22:** "Boston's Model Station," *FH* XLII:18 (October 31, 1901), p. 369. Illustration is from *Brickbuilder*. XIX:5 (May 1910), plate 62. **Talbot, civil service in Denver:** "Only Fire Department Gymnasium," *Denver Sunday Times* (July 31, 1898). **Atlanta gym:** "The Fire Department Gymnasium," *FH* (September 6, 1900), p. 1. **Boston, spending:** Nathan Matthews, *The City Government of Boston; A Valedictory Address to the Members of the City Council, January 5, 1895* (Boston: Rockwell and Churchill, 1895), pp. 75–81. **"When Matthews took office . . . public** architecture": Francis W. Chandler, *Municipal Architecture in Boston from Designs by Edmund M. Wheelwright, City Architect, from 1891 to 1895* (Boston: Bates and Guild, 1898), pp. 1–2; also Tucci, *Built in Boston*. **Wheelwright biography:** see Withey, *Biographical Dictionary*. **Headquarters:** An Imposing Structure," *FH* XXVII:9 (March 1894), unpaged; "Recent Brickwork in Boston," *Brickbuilder* I:10 (October 1892), p. 75; Chandler, *Municipal Architecture*, vol. 2, pp. 35–37. **Martin Behrman:** John R. Kemp (ed.), *Martin Behrman of New Orleans; Memoirs of a City Boss* (Baton Rouge: Louisiana State University Press, 1977), p. xxiii. **E. A. Christy:** obituary, New Orleans *Times Picayune* (August 5, 1959), p. 5. **"Examples of Old English timber work":** *Architectural Art and its Allies* IV:12 (June 1902), p. 19; see also illustration of J. K. Newman Residence, October 1909. **"Every piece of timber . . .":** W. R. Burk, "Public Buildings," *Architectural Art and its Allies* VI:9 (March 1911), p. 21. **"Elegant tiled bathrooms . . .":** Model Fire House Scene of Celebration," New Orleans *Daily Picayune* (April 1, 1910), p. 6. **Exercise machines:** "New Engine House," New Orleans *Daily Picayune* (December 3, 1911), p. 7. **"Both a comfortable home . . .":** Burk, "Public Buildings," pp. 21–22. **National Board of Fire Underwriters:** Committee on Fire Prevention, *Report on the City of New Orleans*, Louisiana (New York: National Board of Fire Underwriters, 1909), pp. 23, 25. **Opening ceremonies:** "Model Fire House Scene of Celebration," *op. cit.* **Los Angeles:** "the most elaborate . . . banquet hall": *Sybaritical Effort, This,*" *Los Angeles Times* (September 29, 1910), part 2, p. 1. **"The $53,000 artistic spasm . . .":** "Will Dedicate No. 23, the $53,000 Engine House," Los Angeles *Call Record* (September 29, 1910). **"Another of those things . . .":** "Fire Chief Goes to New Quarters," unidentified clipping from scrapbooks at Old Plaza Firehouse Museum, Los Angeles, p. 149. **Good government mayor:** "Ask Public Inspection of Marble Fire House," *Los Angeles Herald* (September 30, 1910). **Lips resigns:** "Investigation of Fire Department to Follow Resignation of Lips," Los Angeles *Call Record* (March 25, 1910). **Uniform engine houses:** Uniformity in Style Saves, Says Mayor," *Los Angeles Express* (May 16, 1910). **Waukegan:** "Two Examples of Modern Fire Houses," *The American City* VI:2 (February 1912), pp. 519–21. **Engine 61, Pittsburgh:** *Pittsburgh's Professional Firefighters* (Pittsburgh: Fire Department, 1974). **Fire Station 14,** Kansas City: original blueprints are on file at the University of Missouri, Kansas City, library.

CHAPTER SIX

For background on suburbs in this period, skim the magazines *The American City* and *Architectural Forum*; see Tunnard and Reed, and Gwendolyn Wright, *Building the Dream; A Social History of Housing in America* (New York: Pantheon, 1981). On bungalow fire stations see "Firehouses Need Not Be Eyesores," *American City* (October 1927), pp. 437–41 and "Fire Protection in Small Cities," *American Architect—The Architectural Review* CXXVI:2431 (July 30, 1924), pp. 89–94. Randolph W. Sexton, *American Public Buildings of To-day* (New York: Architectural Book Publishing Company, 1931) includes many fire stations. The leading firemen's magazines of the period were *Fire Engineering* and *Fire Service*; *Fireman's Herald* also continued to publish.
Atlanta: Atlanta Firemen's Recreation Club, *Prompt to Action; Atlanta Fire Department 1860–1960* (privately printed, 1961); *Souvenir History of the Atlanta Fire Department* (Atlanta: Byrd Publishing Company, 1917). **Sacramento Chemical 4:** "Sacramento's Standard Fire Station," *FH* LXXII:16 (October 14, 1916), unpaged. **Fire Station 48, Cincinnati:** *Annual Report of the Cincinnati Fire Department for 1913*, pp. 229, 235. **Seattle:** Jim Stevenson, *Seattle Firehouses of the Horse-Drawn and Early Motor Era* (privately printed, 1972), unpaged. **Gasoline engines, New London:** Ditzel, p. 190. **Wayne, Pennsylvania:** Walter McCall, *American Fire Engines Since 1900* (Glen Ellyn,

Illinois: Crestline Publishing Company, 1976), p. 8. **"Progress of motorization":** "Fire Equipment Statistics," *FH* (March 1, 1919), pp. 163–98; "Gasoline vs. Oats," *FH* LXII:1 (July 1, 1911), p. 3. **Baltimore,** "FINAL RITES": William A. Murray, *The Unheralded Heroes of Baltimore's Big Blazes* (Baltimore: E. John Schmitz and Sons, 1969), p. 79. (Quote from Baltimore *Sun*, June 30, 1919). **Tractorized engines:** "Equipment for Small Cities," *FH* LXIII:4 (January 27, 1912), p. 63; McCall, *American Fire Engines*, p. 62. **Bungalow plan:** "Automobile Fire Stations," *FH* LXVIII:18 (October 31, 1914), pp. 388–90. **"The introduction of motor apparatus . . . the night":** "Automobile Fire Apparatus," *FH* LV:25 (June 20, 1908), pp. 483–85. **Single bedrooms for firemen:** "Dormitories or Separate Rooms?" *FH* LXX:3 (July 17, 1915), pp. 43–44. **"A menace to the health . . . to use":** "Sliding Poles or No Sliding Poles?" *FS* LXXXI:23 (November 14, 1928), p. 1061; "Two Central Fire Stations," *FS* LXXXVII:9 (March 1, 1924), p. 8. **Sliding chute in Seattle:** Stevenson, *Seattle Firehouses*, unpaged. **Two platoons:** "Two platoons at Kansas City," *FH* LXII:17 (October 21, 1911), p. 399; "Two Platoons in New York," *FH* LXII:21 (November 18, 1911), p. 483; "The Workings of Two-Platoon," *FH* LXIV:7 (August 17, 1912), pp. 139–40. **Kitchens—Champaign, Illinois:** "A Kitchen for Firemen," *FS* LXXXIII:3 (January 21, 1922), p. 5. **Chicopee, Massachusetts:** "Kitchenette in Fire Station," *FS* LXXXIV:19 (November 14, 1922), p. 8. **Boston, 1925:** "Firemen Cook Their Own," *FS* LXXXIX:19 (May 19, 1925), p. 5. **Worcester:** "Cooking at Headquarters," *FS* LXXXVIII:20 (November 15, 1924), p. 8. **"Stand out . . . sore thumb":** "Fire Station Architecture," *FH* (June 30, 1917), p. 542. **Brookside station, Kansas City:** *Kansas City Times* (July 17, 1917); see also report prepared by Kansas City Landmarks Commission in 1977. **Denver, 1912:** "Bungalow Fire Station of Artistic Design . . ." *Denver Municipal Facts* IV:14 (April 6, 1912), pp. 6–7; "New Fire Station for the City Park," Denver *Republican* (February 18, 1912); "At Work on Park Hill Bungalow Fire House," Denver *Republican* (April 6, 1912). The building was illustrated in *FH* LXIV:11 (September 14, 1912), p. 237. **Portland, Oregon, "beauty of the neighborhood marred":** "Fire House Unique," *The Oregonian* (March 23, 1913). **Lee Holden:** *Fire Protection Service* XCII:10 (October 1927), p. 15. **"Not only free from objection . . . pleased with it":** "A Bungalow Fire Station," *American City* XVI:2 (February 1917), pp. 191–92. **Shreveport, wealthy neighbors:** "A Model Fire Station," *FS* XXXIV:8 (August 19, 1922), p. 9. **"Average American fire station not a thing of beauty . . .":** "Fire Station Architecture," *FH* LXIII:16 (April 20, 1912), p. 340. **"The evidence accumulates . . . pain":** "Fire Station Architecture," *FH* (June 30, 1917), p. 542. **"Providing a building . . . purpose":** "Artistic Fire Stations," *FS* XC:12 (September 19, 1925), p. 10. **California Supreme Court Ruling:** Decision of the State Supreme Court of California in Miller vs. Board of Public Works (69 Cal. Dec. 215) reprinted as "A Supreme Court on the Civic and Social Values of Single-Family Residence Districts," *American City* XXXII:6 (June 1925), p. 683. **"Here, masked among trees . . . garages":** Sinclair Lewis, *Dodsworth* (New York: Harcourt Brace, 1929), Chapter 19. **Santa Barbara:** Herb Andree and Noel Young, *Santa Barbara Architecture; From Colonial to Modern* (Santa Barbara: Capra Press, 1975), pp. 105–6, 177–79; David Gebhard and Robert Winter, *A Guide to Architecture in Los Angeles and Southern California* (Santa Barbara: Peregrine Smith, 1977), pp. 521–23. **Stratford:** "New Station for Stratford," *FE* XCIII:10 (October 1940), p. 524. **Providence, R.I.:** "New Fire Station to Embody Beauty," *Providence Journal* (June 28, 1928). **Fire station 28, Oakland:** "Oakland Has Novel Fire Station," *FE* LXXX:22 (November 2, 1927), p. 1128 and "Fire Stations Need Not Be Eyesores," p. 440. See also "Cottage Type Suburban Fire Station, San Antonio, Texas," *Architecture* LIII:1 (January 1926), p. 30. **Los Angeles, "added element of interest":** "County's New Fire Houses Set a High Standard of Neighborhood Architecture," *American City* XLII:5 (May 1930), pp.

112–13. **"Knitting craze"**: "The Shawl Knitting Fad," *FH* LXIII:18 (May 4, 1912), p. 384. Firemen in Denver made stag-horn furniture—see *Denver Municipal Facts* I:45 (December 25, 1905), p. 5. **"The fireman is a good neighbor..."**: "In the New Homes of Denver Firemen," *Denver Municipal Facts* XII:12–13 (September/October 1929), p. 10. **Fire dogs left behind**: "No more 'mascots,'" *FS* LXXXII:27 (December 31, 1921). **"Cut out the checker game..."**: "Exit the Sliding Pole," *FS* LXXXVIII:17 (October 25, 1924), p. 4. **"There is nothing to it anymore..."**: Murray, *Unheralded Heroes*, p. 74.

CHAPTER SEVEN

For general background on city planning and government during this period see Tunnard and Reed, parts VII and VIII. For information on the American version of modern architecture, see Jordy, vol. IV, chapters one and two; Cervin Robinson and Rosemarie Haag Bletter, *Skyscraper Style; Art Deco New York* (New York: Oxford University Press, 1975); Rem Koolhaas, *Delirious New York* (New York: Oxford University Press, 1978); Forrest F. Lisle, Jr., "Chicago's Century of Progress Exposition; The Moderne as Popular Culture," *Journal of the Society of Architectural Historians* XXX:3 (October 1972), p. 230 and Jeffrey Meikle, *Twentieth Century Limited* (Philadelphia: Temple University Press, 1980).

"Democratic, responsive...": Charles M. Fassett, "Assets of the Ideal City," *American City* XXIV:4 (April 1921), pp. 343–47. Fassett was the former mayor of Spokane, Washington. This article was an excerpt from a book he published by the same title. **Denver county consolidation**: Leo H. Joachim, "Dollars Speak in City and County Consolidation," *American City* XXIV:1 (January 1921), p. 67. **"City useful... same and useful channels"**: Fassett, "Assets," p. 344. Also Nelson P. Lewis, *The Planning of the Modern City* (New York: Wiley, 1916), pp. 10–11. **691 municipalities**: "Is Your City in this List of Forward-Looking Municipalities Having Planning Commissions?" *American City* XLII:3 (March 1930), pp. 99–100. **Adams**: Thomas Adams, *The Design of Residential Areas* (Cambridge, Mass.: Harvard University Press, 1934). **Audubon, New York**: Newell I. Nussbaumer, "Audubon Village Adapts the Radburn Plan," *American City* XL:4 (April 1929), pp. 140–42. **Mutual aid**: DeWayne E. Nolting, "Cooperative Fire Fighting," *American City* LI:8 (August 1936), pp. 53–55. Also A. L. Kimball, "Three Fire Departments Join in Mutual Aid System," *American City* XXXVI:1 (January 1927), p. 96. **Baltimore fire of 1904**: Lyons, pp. 113–22. **New York Chief Dougherty**: Thomas F. Dougherty and Paul W. Kearney, *Fire* (New York: Putnam, 1931), pp. 154–58. **Fire colleges**: "A Fire College in Los Angeles," *American City* XLII:2 (February 1930), p. 21; "Extensive Fire Training Course for Oklahoma Cities," *American City* XLVIII:1 (January 1933), p. 19. **Fire College at Portland**: Edward L. Boatright, collection of mimeographed notes, lessons, and papers from the Portland Fire College, 1931–38, known as the "Boatright Bible" at the Portland Fire Headquarters. **New fire hazards**: Dougherty, *Fire*, p. 225. **Fire prevention**: "The Obligation of the City to its Citizens," *American City* XXIV:6 (June 1921), p. 603; William J. Leonard, "Fire Prevention Window Displays," *American City* XXIII:1 (July 1920); Percy Bugbee, "Getting Ready for a Local Observance of Fire Prevention Week," *American City* XXIX:3 (September 1923), p. 276. Statistics are from Percy Bugbee, "Municipal Fire Protection Proves its Value," *American City* XLII:5 (May 1930), pp. 87–88. **Allentown, Pennsylvania**: Ronald P. Ruddell and Lee Walck, *History of the Allentown Fire Department* (mimeographed pamphlet, 1975), p. 4. **Flying squadron**: Ditzel, p. 194. **Rescue squads**: Ditzel, p. 195. **New equipment in '20s**: Ditzel, pp. 195–97. **George Ernest Robinson**: "Fire Station Design" (address before the NFPA Firemen's Forum in Philadelphia, 1944) reprinted in *Volunteer Firemen*; Harry Belknap, "Architect Specializes in

Fire Station Designs," *FE* LXXIX:24 (December 25, 1926), pp. 1299–1300; George Ernest Robinson, "Fire Station Design as an Architect Sees It," *FE* LXXXIV:11 (May 27, 1931), pp. 381–82. **Arlington, Massachusetts, central station**: Harry Belknap, "Centralizing the Department in One Station," *FE* LXXIX:7 (April 10, 1926), pp. 339–40; "Arlington's New Fire Station Novel in its Main Features," *Arlington Advocate* (April 3, 1925), p. 6; "Arlington: A Town of Homes and Business Enterprise," supplement to *Arlington Advocate* (March 12, 1926); "Fire-Houses Need Not Be Eyesores," *American City* XXXVI:10 (October 1927), pp. 40–41; "On the Designing of Fire Houses," *Forum* XLVI:6 (June 1927), p. 586 and plate 123. **Engine Room at Gloucester**: Harry Belknap, "Central Fire Station Opened in Gloucester," *FE* LXXX:3 (February 9, 1927), pp. 121–22. **"Men are just as good firemen..."**: Fassett, "Assets," p. 346. **"Much of the discontent..."**: Belknap, "Architect Specializes," p. 1299. **Bowling alley**: "Boston to Build Largest Fire Station in Country," *American City* XL:4 (April 1929), p. 151. **Libraries**: "Libraries in City Fire Station," *American City* XXIII:1 (July 1920), p. 32. **Yonkers**: "New Yonkers Fire Headquarters to Cost Nearly Half Million," *FE* LXXX:1 (January 12, 1927), p. 18. The former fire stations at Albuquerque and Baton Rouge (see Appendix) still have drill towers in their back yards. **Beaux-Arts Institute of Design**: "Judgment of January 15, 1929; Class 'B' Project; 'A Fire House,'" *The Bulletin of the Beaux-Arts Institute of Design* V:4 (February 1929), pp. 4–5, 12–13. **Engine 6 in Seattle**: Jim Stevenson, *Seattle Firehouses of the Horse-Drawn and Early Motor Era* (privately printed, 1976). Stevenson coined the term "Flash Gordon Style." **Columbus, Indiana**: Melvin Lostutter, *City Fire Department of Columbus, Indiana, 1835–1941: Souvenir Booklet Issued for the Dedication of the New Central Fire Station* (no publisher listed, 1941). **Modern architecture**: David Gebhard, "The Moderne in the United States," *Architectural Association Quarterly* II:3 (July 1970), pp. 4–21. Streamline style is discussed in Meikle, *Twentieth Century Limited*. For more on industrial design and the idea of "modernizing," see Norman Bel Geddes, *Horizon* (Boston: Little Brown, 1932). Bel Geddes was one of the leading designers of the period. **Fire engines redesigned**: Walter P. McCall, *American Fire Engines Since 1900* (Sarasota: Crestline, 1976), pp. 109–54. **Big Bill Thompson**: Chicago Fire Department, "Achievement and Work of the Chicago Fire Department, 1928," pamphlet at the Municipal Reference Library, Chicago. "Chicago's Fire Department Modernization Program," *American City* XLII:6 (June 1930), p. 104. "New Station Planned for Chicago," *FE* LXXXI:7 (April 4, 1928), p. 290. **Jimmy Walker**: Robert A. Caro, *The Power Broker; Robert Moses and the Fall of New York* (New York: Vintage, 1975), p. 325; Lowell M. Limpus, *History of the New York Fire Department* (New York: Dutton, 1940), p. 325; Annual reports of the New York City fire department for 1929–33. **Technology in 1927**: Robert A. M. Stern, "Relevance of the Decade," *Journal of the Society of Architectural Historians* XXIV:1 (March 1965), pp. 6–10; "Even the lightest pleasure cars": "One-Half of Fire Apparatus Now in Use is Obsolete," *FE* LXXXIX:7 (July 1936), pp. 295–300. **Fire departments suspicious of new technology**: Ditzel, chapters 20–23. Two articles on fire departments that did use radios suggest how rare the idea was before 1940: "Fire Alarms Broadcast to Fire Houses," *American City* LIII:11 (November 1938), p. 15; H. R. Chase, "Fire Radio Saves Waste," *American City* LVI:11 (November 1941), pp. 69–70. **New York's standard plan**: "Fire Station Design," pamphlet issued by the publishers of *FE* (no date), p. 4, copy at the NFPA library. **Portland, Maine**: "Ideal Central Fire Stations," *FS* LXXXVI:6 (August 11, 1923), p. 4. **"Symbolize the rapid movement . . . the same thing!"**: Edith Elmer Wood, "Recent Housing in the Netherlands," *Forum* XXXVIII:4 (April 1923), p. 174. *Life* **magazine competition**: "Eight Houses for Modern Living," *Life* V:13 (September 26, 1938), pp. 45–67. Letters to the editor were published in the next four issues; the letter quoted is from H. A.

Warner of Seattle, Washington, and appeared in the October 17 issue. *Life* later commissioned furniture designers to furnish some of the model homes. Many of these designs actually were built. Readers could order plans and models from *Life*. The November, 1938, issue of *Forum* was devoted to the competition. **Hawaii's two styles at once:** "Beautification of Honolulu Fire Stations," *FE* LXXXIX:2 (February 1936), pp. 54–55. **L.A. Municipal Art Commission:** "Types of Architecture for Municipal Buildings Recently Erected in the City of Los Angeles," *Southwest Builder and Contractor* LXIV:12 (September 19, 1924), p. 46. **Engine 11 in Kansas City:** Kansas City *Star*, March 15, 1931. **"No-style":** See for example the headquarters at Haverhill, Massachusetts: "Haverhill Erects New Station," *FE* LXXX:23 (November 16, 1927), p. 1175; Headquarters at Milford, Connecticut: "Milford to Have New Central Fire Station," *FE* LXXXI:17 (August 22, 1928), p. 734; and the Webster Hose, Hook and Ladder Company at Ansonia, Connecticut, published in C. W. Short and R. Stanley-Brown, *Public Buildings; A Survey of Architecture of Projects Constructed by Federal and Other Governmental Agencies Between the Years 1933 and 1939* (Washington, D.C.: Government Printing Office, 1939), p. 77. Robinson's own headquarters for Plainfield, New Jersey, illustrated in Belknap, "Architect Specializes," is another example. **Federal building programs:** Most of the observations that follow are based on the buildings illustrated in Short and Stanley-Brown, *Survey*. See also *America Builds; The Record of the P.W.A.* (Washington, D.C.: Government Printing Office, 1939); United States Federal Works Agency, *Second Annual Report* (Washington, D.C.: Government Printing Office, 1941); *Report on Progress of the W.P.A. Program* (Washington, D.C.: Government Printing Office, 1940); *Inventory; An Appraisal of the Results of the Works Progress Administration* (Washington, D.C.: Government Printing Office, 1938). The long quotation about building policy is from the United States Works Progress Administration, *Final Report on the W.P.A. Program* (Washington, D.C.: Government Printing Office, 1943), p. 52. For examples of other fire stations built by the W.P.A. see "New Station for Albuquerque," *FE* LXXXIX:11 (November 1936), p. 540, and "New Station for Saginaw, Michigan," *FE* XCIII:1 (January 1940), p. 22. **"The Rock":** Stevenson, *Seattle Firehouses*. **Greenwich, Connecticut:** Short and Stanley-Brown, *Survey*. **Hartford, Connecticut:** "New Station Opened," *FE* XCIII:3 (March 1940), p. 120. **"The PWA does not . . . unsound":** Short and Stanley-Brown, *Survey*, Chapter 3. "Although some of the buildings . . . architectural standards": W.P.A. *Final Report*, p. 52. **Gutheim's critique:** F. A. Gutheim, "The Quality of Public Works," *The American Magazine of Art* XXVII:4 (April 1934), pp. 183–87. **East Orange:** "East Orange Has New Headquarters," *FE* LXXXVI:12 (December 1933), p. 397. **Gas stations:** Daniel I. Vieyra, *Fill 'Er Up; An Architectural History of America's Gas Stations* (New York: Macmillan, 1978).

CHAPTER EIGHT

For background on American culture, history, and technology after World War II see Boorstin, *Democratic Experience*. Information on apparatus comes from Ditzel, chapters 21–26. Other information on fire department procedure comes from general reading in trade magazines, including *Fire Engineering*, *Fire Command*, and *Firemen*.

For trade publications on fire stations, see *Fire Station Design*, published by the Circul-air Corporation. There have been eight volumes published since it first appeared in 1947. Other references are in the notes. The National Board of Fire Underwriters, now the American Insurance Association, has published a few pertinent Special Interest Bulletins, which it periodically updates. See No. 230: "Fire Stations" (1946), No. 175: "Fire Department Stations—Planning the Building" (1959), No. 176: "Fire Department Buildings—Planning the Location" (1959), No. 284: "Fire Station Hazards" (1949),

and subsequent revisions. The library at the NFPA in Quincy, Massachusetts, has much unpublished material on this subject. I am grateful to Mr. Howard Blythe of Greenwich, Connecticut, for calling my attention to many articles on fire station design that have appeared in trade magazines in the last twenty years.

For general background on American architecture in the 1950s, '60s, and '70s see Vincent Scully, *American Architecture and Urbanism* (New York: Praeger, 1969). Tunnard and Reed has some information on suburbs, as does Warner. The best source is the leading magazines, *Progressive Architecture* and *Architectural Record*. See especially, "The Sixties; A Symposium on the State of Architecture" which ran in *PA* in three parts. Part One, XLII:3 (March 1961); Part Two XLII:4 (April 1961); Part Three XLII:5 (March 1961).

Planning for fire service after the war: Fred Shepperd, "The Post-War Fireman" (Paper presented to the Fire Department Instructors' Conference, Memphis, January 9, 1945) *FE* XCVIII:1 (January 1945), pp. 25–27, 40–49; Sanford Dewey, "Fire Departments Urged to Modernize," *FE* XCVIII:3 (March 1945), p. 211; Percy Bugbee, "Postwar Planning for Fire Administration," *Public Management* XXVI:8 (August 1944), pp. 226–29. **Mearlfoam:** *FE* XCVIII:3 (March 1945), p. 201. **Navy training:** "Navy Firefighting Techniques to Benefit City Firefighters," *FE* XCVII:10 (October 1945), pp. 756–57; Harold J. Burke, "Impact of Wartime Defense Upon Peacetime Fire Fighting," *FE* XCVIII:11 (November 1945), pp. 828–31. **Radio:** Roi B. Woolley, "FCC Assigns Fire Service Radio Communication Channels," *FE* XCVIII:3 (February 1945), p. 102; Thomas Magner, "New Haven Installs Radio for Sole Use of Fire Department," *FE* XCVIII:3 (March 1945), p. 174. **Research and development, technology:** Boorstin, *Democratic Experience*, pp. 537–84. **Hose:** Dick Sylvia, "From Leather to Cotton to Synthetic," *FE* CXXX:8 (August 1978), pp. 148–53. **Diesel engines:** Hubert Walker, "Why a Diesel Engine?" *FC* XXXCIII:11 (November 1971), pp. 18–22. **"Automatic gadgets galore":** Roi B. Woolley, "Fire Station Design—Tomorrow," *FE* XCVIII:6 (June 1945), pp. 378–84. **Snorkel, super pumper:** Ditzel, pp. 220, 209–10. **Fire stations burn down:** "Fire Station Hazards," National Board of Fire Underwriters Special Interest Bulletin No. 284, 1949. Also, "Suggested Revisions for Pamphlet 192" (unpublished memo at NFPA Library, dated 1957). More recent examples: Jim Casey, "Fire Stations Need Protection Too," *FE* CXXI:3 (March 1968), p. 49; Thomas C. Disbrow, "Penn Yan, N.Y., Fire Dept. Rises from the Ashes," *FE* CXXII:9 (September 1969), p. 55. **Circul-air:** See introductory note. "With the thousands of dollars . . . functional design" from undated Circul-air pamphlet at NFPA Library. "Suggestions and ideas . . . engine house" from "Foreword," *Fire Station Design* I (1947). "No more unsightly towers . . ." from Roi B. Woolley, "Functional Fire Station Planning," *Fire Station Design* II (1949), p. 22. **Chiefs prefer towers or racks:** "What Chiefs Prefer in Fire Hose," *FE* CXI:8 (August 1958), p. 680. See Chapter Nine for further discussion of towers and drying machines. **Fire station planning:** Most of the information in this section comes from the collection of unpublished planning reports at the Frances Loeb Library, Harvard University. San Francisco Department of City Planning, "Report on a Plan for the Location of Firehouses in San Francisco" (1952); San Jose Planning Commission, "Planning San Jose; Fire Station Location Plan" (1953); Kansas City, Missouri, City Plan Commission, "Master Plan for the Location of Fire Stations" (1955); Wichita Master Plan, "Pattern for Fire Stations" (1956); City of Phoenix Planning Department, "Fire Station Plan for the City of Phoenix" (1961); City Planning Board of Saint Paul, "Plan for Fire Stations, Saint Paul, Minnesota" (1961); Spokane, Washington, Fire Department and City Plan Commission, "Fire Station Plan, Spokane, Washington" (1962). See also American Society of Planning Officials Advisory Service, "Information Report No. 98; Fire House Location Planning" (1957) and Jacob P. Damelle, "Relocating Peoria's Fire Stations," *American City* LXIX:5 (May 1954), pp. 138–39. **Rand corporation planning package:** James Thurmond, "Computer Helps Pick Station Site," *FE* CXXVIII:1 (November 1975), pp. 44–45. **"It is generally preferable . . . hazardous district":** National Board of Fire Underwriters Special Interest Bulletin No. 176. **Society of Planning Officials:** "Information Report No. 98" (unpaged). **Advice on fire station design:** Joshua Moldenhour, *Design of Fire Stations* (Seattle: Washington State Association of Fire Chiefs, 1965); William Allen, "Let's Build Better Fire Stations," *FE* (February 1961), pp. 116–18; Marion K. Varner, "How to Get the Most Fire Station for Your Money," *FE* (October 1964), pp. 853–55. **Laurel Canyon:** Cliff Dektar, "Los Angeles' Fire Station Builder," *FE* (August 1962), p. 637. **Thomas Schaardt, 1957:** "Fire Station Design," *Firemen* (January 1958); W. Thomas Schaardt, "Building a Fire Station Must be Done by Design," *FE* (October 1969), pp. 97–99. **Box-type designs:** See articles cited in "Advice" note above and "Some New Fire Stations Which Indicate Trends in Design," *FE* CVII:10 (October 1954), pp. 907–9; "Functional Beauty Marks New Fire Stations," *FE* CXIII:8 (August 1960), pp. 720–21; "Fire Department Construction Keeps Pace with Times," *FE* CXVI:10 (October 1963), pp. 838–39; "Excellence of Design Marks New Stations," *FE* CXVII:10 (October 1964), pp. 880–81; "New Trends in Station Design," *Firemen* XXXV:7 (July 1968), pp. 15–19; Paul R. Lyons, "Trends in Fire Stations," *Fire Command* XXXVIII:9 (September 1971), pp. 15–17. **George Proper:** conversation, November 1978. Proper is the principal author of the "Guide to Planning Fire Stations" issued by the New York State Division of Fire Prevention and Control. **Napoleon LeBrun in the 1880s:** See announcements in the "Building Intelligence" section of *AABN* for August 14, 1880; March 5, 1881; April 23, 1881. **Prefabricated parts:** Diana S. Waite (ed.), *Architectural Elements; The Technological Revolution* (Princeton: The Pyne Press, 1973). The standard source for building supplies since the 1920s has been the annual catalogues issued by the Sweet's Catalogue Service. **"Never before have . . . wherever possible":** "Some New Trends in Fire Stations," p. 907. **Boston Municipal Research Bureau attacks expense:** "Fire Stations Can Be Expensive," *Boston Municipal Research Bureau Blotter* II:11 (June 1960), pp. 1–4. **Montgomery mobile home:** G. E. Reeves, "Prefabs Used as Temporary Stations," *FE* CXXXI:4 (April 1978), pp. 30–31. **"In constructing modern stations . . . public expenditure":** Horatio H. Bond, "Memorandum on the Construction and Arrangement of Fire Stations," unpublished manuscript c1957 at the NFPA Library. **Improving image:** "There's a Better Alternative Than Striking," *FE* CXIX:11 (November 1966), p. 39 (recommends public relations department); John H. Polker, "The Image of the Firefighter; Is it Changing?" *FC* XXXVII:10 (October 1977), pp. 16–18. **More training:** Roi B. Woolley, "Museum Provides Background for New York City Fire College," *FE* CIII:3 (March 1950), pp. 184–89; "Education; Which Way for the Fire Service?" *Firemen* XXXIV:12 (December 1967), pp. 28–29. **Wasting public money:** See for example Varner, "How to Get the Most Fire Station," p. 854: "Nothing is harder to hide than a poorly designed, overly expensive, costly-to-maintain fire station. There isn't a civic rug big enough to sweep it under." **Firemen go on strike:** "There's a Better Alternative," also Thomas W. Dawson, "Collective Bargaining and Arbitration in the Fire Department," *FC* XXVII:6 (June 1980), pp. 18–19. **"Whether it makes much sense . . . administration":** Warren Y. Kimball, "Fire Stations of the Future," *FC* XXXVII:7 (July 1970), pp. 48–51. **New Haven Central Fire Station:** Mary Homann, *Wooster Square Design; A Report on the Background, Experience, and Design Procedures in Redevelopment and Rehabilitation in an Urban Renewal Project* (New Haven: New Haven Redevelopment Agency, 1965); "Eighth Annual Design Awards," *PA* XLII:1 (January 1961), entire issue. Colbert's statement appears on pp. 154–56; "P/A Design Award

Seminar, 1961," *PA* XLII:7 (July 1961), pp. 132–35; "Foreground Firehouse," *PA* XLIII:9 (September 1962), pp. 120–25. **"Daley's Pride":** Robert J. Herguth, "Plush New Firehouse Opens," *Chicago Daily News* (August 20, 1968). **Court houses:** See essay by Henry-Russell Hitchcock and William Seale in Richard Pare (ed), *Court House; A Photographic Document* (New York: Horizon, 1978), p. 248. **"The notion of a modern monument . . .":** Quoted in Wolf von Eckhardt, "Is a Modern Monument Possible?" *PA* XLIII:9 (September 1962), pp. 182–85. This article is a discussion of the competition for the F.D.R. memorial. **Confusion in architecture:** Tom Wolfe, *From Bauhaus to Our House* (New York: Farrar, Straus, Giroux), 1981.

CHAPTER NINE

Most of the material in this chapter is based on conversations with architects, firemen, and fire chiefs in 1978, 1979, and 1980. Specific references appear in the notes below. Three unusual fire stations not discussed in this chapter also raise interesting questions. See David Morton, "Olean Central Fire Station, Olean, New York; A Fitting Image?" *PA* LXI:7 (July 1980), pp. 66–69 for a sensitive discussion of a fire station, designed by Werner Seligman, that firemen dislike. The municipal fire station in Corning, New York, designed by Gunnar Birkerts and Associates in 1974, caused some disagreement among judges in the *Progressive Architecture* Annual Awards Program in 1974. See "Comment; The Machines," *PA* LV:1 (January 1974), p. 66; "Two Machines," *PA* LVIII:3 (March 1977), pp. 58–61; Charles F. Houper, "Fire Triangle Reflected in Corning, New York, Station," *FE* CXXIX:4 (April 1976), pp. 24–25. The Central Fire Station at Nanticoke, Pennsylvania, designed by Jon Michael Schwarting is discussed in David Morton, "Quiet" Dialogue," *PA* LVII:2 (February 1976), pp. 69–71.

Station 4, Berkeley: "Fire Station Number Four, Berkeley, California, U.S.A.," *Architectural Design* XXXII:2 (February 1962), pp. 88–91. The Berkeley Public Library has a clipping file documenting the protests by local citizens' groups about this building. Station 4 is also mentioned in David Gebhard's *Guide to Architecture in San Francisco and Northern California* (Santa Barbara: Peregrine Smith, 1974). **Whitney Avenue Fire Station, New Haven:** "The Firehouse Next Door," *PA* XLV:3 (March 1964), pp. 126–31. This fire station and the headquarters building in New Haven are also discussed in Vincent Scully, *American Architecture and Urbanism* (New York: Praeger, 1969); Robert A. M. Stern, *New Directions in American Architecture* (New York: Braziller, 1969); Don Metz, *New Architecture in New Haven* (Cambridge, Massachusetts: M.I.T. Press, 1966). **Fire Station 30, Kansas City:** "New Plan for Fire Station," *Kansas City Star* (June 1, 1969). The building received an Award of Excellence from the American Institute of Architects in Autumn, 1974. **Columbus, Indiana:** Columbus Area Chamber of Commerce, *Columbus Indiana; A Look at Architecture* (Columbus: Visitors Center, 1974); John Rutherford, "For City Fire Station; Use Ceco Architect Plan," *Columbus Republic* (June 8, 1966); "City Council OK's Fire Station Plan," *Republic* (September 7, 1966); "City to Go Ahead with Fire Station," *Republic* (April 18, 1967); "Two New Buildings by Venturi and Rauch," *PA* XLIX:11 (November 1968), pp. 118–25. This building is also discussed in the books by Scully and Stern cited above. Notice how similar it is to the earlier Central Fire Station in Columbus. For Venturi's theoretical writing see Robert Venturi, *Complexity and Contradiction in Architecture* (New York: Museum of Modern Art and Graham Foundation, 1966); Robert Venturi, Denise Scott Brown, and Steven Izenour, *Learning from Las Vegas* (Cambridge, Massachusetts: M.I.T. Press, 1972), later reissued as *Learning from Las Vegas; The Forgotten Symbolism of Architectural Form* in 1977. The first edition has a long discussion of Fire Station 4 on page 112. The second edition compares Fire Station 4 with the New Haven Central Fire Station, pp. 129–30. The second edition also has a complete bibliography of writings by and about Venturi, Rauch, and Scott Brown. Quotations are taken from a conversation with Venturi on July 20, 1979. **Dixwell Fire Station, New Haven:** In addition to material on Venturi cited above, see "New Haven Opens Four Bay Station," *FE* CXXVIII:5 (May 1975), p. 23; Robert E. Miller, "New Haven's Dixwell Fire Station," *Architectural Record* CLIX:6 (June 1976), pp. 111–16. **Denver:** This information is based on conversations with Austin Siegfried and Secretary of Fire John Frasco in April, 1979. Frasco has used Siegfried's basic design for three fire stations in Denver: Numbers 7, 13, and 21, all erected between 1977 and 1979. **Dallas, Number 2:** Conversations with architect Forrest Upshaw and Captain Darryl Stauffer of the Dallas Fire Department, January 1979. **Fire Station 1, Dallas:** R. L. Nailen, "Sun Helps Heat, Cool Dallas Station," *FE* CXXXI:3 (March 1978), pp. 26–27. Other information comes from a conversation with architect William Hidell, January 1979. For other solar-powered fire stations see Cliff Dektar, "L.A. City Continues Station Program," *FE* CXXXIII:4 (April 1980), p. 55. **Fewer men per company:** "Fire Department Efficiency," American Insurance Association (formerly National Board of Fire Underwriters), Special Interest Bulletin No. 131 (1975); Nancy Kelleher, "Fire Fighters vs. Chicago," *FC* XLVII:6 (June 1980), p. 16. **Equipment:** Warren Y. Kimball, "Future Fire Apparatus and Procedures," *FC* XXXVIII:11 (November 1971), pp. 16–17; "Trends in Fire Apparatus," *FC* XXXVIII:11 (November 1971), p. 23; Tony Marsalek, "Minipumper handles 90% of Alarms," *FE* CXXVIII:1 (January 1975), p. 48. **"With firefighters' salaries . . . for alarms":** Warren Y. Kimball, "Fire Stations of the Future," *FC* XXXVII:7 (July 1970), pp. 48–51, *passim*. **Scranton, Pennsylvania:** Douglas Brenner, "Masters of the Modest Proposal," *Architectural Record* CLXIX:8 (May 1981), pp. 75–81. Other information comes from a conversation with architect Alex Camayd, August 1981. **Red fire engines:** The question of a suitable color for fire engines goes back at least to the 1930s, when the Ward La France company began to advocate lime green, and several cities already were ordering white fire trucks. See Walter P. McCall, *American Fire Engines Since 1900* (Sarasota: Crestline, 1976), pp. 128–54. The Washington Fire Company of Conshohocken, Pennsylvania, claims the first mustard yellow equipment; when a green-painted wagon that was stored next to the stables developed a permanent yellow stain from the horses' urine, an irate chief decided, "if it wants to be yellow, let it stay yellow," and the company has been ordering custom-painted equipment ever since. Despite claims by experts that lime green or yellow is much more visible at night than red is, fire chiefs are reluctant to change. See "Chiefs Rate Apparatus Colors," *FE* CXXVI:2 (February 1973), p. 40. One chief's comment: "Our trucks have always been red and they're going to stay red. That's just the way it is." **Engine 82:** Dennis Smith, *Report from Engine Company 82* (New York: McCall, 1972).

APPENDIX

Several recent books on historic preservation include examples of firehouses converted to new uses. See Charles A. Fracchia and Jeremiah Bragstad, *Converted into Houses* (New York: Viking, 1976); Charles A. Fracchia, *So This is Where You Work!* (New York: Viking, 1979); Massachusetts Department of Community Affairs, *Built to Last; A Handbook on Recycling Old Buildings* (Washington: Preservation Press, 1977). Also these articles on individual buildings: "White Elegance in a Firehouse," *House and Garden* (June 1967), pp. 112–13; "The Renovation of an 1872 Firehouse," *New York Times* (December 13, 1979—note that the building actually dates from 1910); "For Puerto Rican Theater, Old Firehouse is New Home," *New York Times* (February 2, 1981); "Recycling; What to Do With an Old Boarding School or Firehouse," *Washington Post Magazine* (October 4, 1981), pp. 54–63.

Dermenjian/Johnson house: "Home, Where Fire Bells Once Clanged," *Boston Sunday Globe* (February 1, 1981), p. D17. **Engine 5, Columbus:** Robert H. Byler, Jr., "Restaurateur with a Taste for History," *Historic Preservation* XXXII:3 (May/June 1980), pp. 32–37. **Community centers:** Rebecca Zurier, "In Perspective; When They Grew Up," *PA* LX:11 (November 1979), pp. 49–57.

Index

258. *Fireman's Monument, Syracuse, New York. Over the years, the fireman has remained a hero in the eyes of the American public.*